More Praise for
Client at the Core

Bruce Marcus and August Aquila reward readers of *Client at the Core* with an imaginative map for the perilous journey through the twists and turns of marketing and managing today's professional services firm. It is creative, thorough and a catalyst for your further thought. Don't leave home without it.

—Gerry Riskin,
Partner, Edge International

In *Client at the Core*, the authors have captured the changing role of professional services marketing and firm management. There is valuable insight here, and a down-to-earth guide to competing successfully in the new environment.

—David Maister,
Author and Consultant

Finally, a practical book that focuses on what it means to put clients at the core! I was impressed with the practicality of the book from the standpoint of its common sense approach to keeping your professional services firm relevant in the 21st century's client driven economy. Aquila and Marcus have hit a home run with their insightful analysis and poignant prose. A must read for anyone that serves client from within a professional firm.

—Jeffrey S. Pawlow, Managing Shareholder,
The Growth Partnership, Inc.

At its heart, this book is *the* running shoe for law and accounting professionals who want to put the client first, not only because it the smartest thing to do, but because it is also the most profitable thing to do in an age of never ending competition. It says not only "just do it!" but here's how. Following the evolution of professional services marketing over the past 25 years, this is a must read for any professional services firm that wants to navigate and indeed lead in the turbulent and highly competitive waters ahead.

—Richard S. Levick, Esq.,
President of Levick Strategic Communications, LLC and
co-author of *Stop the Presses: The Litigation PR Desk Reference*

I'm overwhelmed! The book is a masterpiece! August J. Aquila and Bruce W. Marcus have produced THE essential guide for managing a professional services firm. It is as encyclopedic in its scope as it is timely as today's headlines. Aquila and Marcus have marshaled their considerable real-life experiences and far-reaching visions into a veritable operating manual for the successful firm. It is must-reading for any professional seeking to survive and thrive in today's markets and will remain a classic reference for years to come. Simply: This book is the last word on the subject.

—Rick Telberg, Editor/At Large
American Institute of Certified Public Accountants

This book hits the nail on the head in terms of the key issues of managing a professional services firm. It combines a unique blend of real world experience along with hard hitting, out of the box ideas for successful implementation. While both are noted authors and authorities on the topic of professional services firm management, this clearly is their best work to date. A definite must-read for anyone serious about professional services management.

—Allan D. Koltin, CPA, President & CEO,
PDI Global, Inc., Chicago, Illinois

In a world where performance is measured by what the accounting software is able to track, partners who carry the biggest sticks and who don't see themselves as requiring motivation or needing behavioral change, *Client at the Core* focuses on managing a firm from a refreshingly newer, perspective. Armed with a heavily marked up copy of the book as their guide to thoughtful planning and implementation, coupled with a strong focus toward the new way of managing in this complex, competitive industry of law, any management team will be racing down the course to win the gold. Stuck in old ways, other firms will be left at the starting line. The race is on and *Client at the Core* is an exemplary discourse on creating winning teams, strategies and client relationships. No firm should be without it as its management guide.

—Silvia L. Coulter
Chief Marketing and Business Development Officer
Dorsey & Whitney LLP

Excellent reading and a valuable reference material. *Client at the Core* is an appropriate title for a book that finally teaches us what our business is about... solving clients problems and providing services that they need and not what we want to sell. Superb discussion about how growth firms design their practices around their clients and stagnant firms are designed around themselves. I can't think of a better way to introduce younger staff to the substance of our profession than having them read *Client at the Core*. The book turns theoretical concepts into practical and useful tools.

—Barry W. Braun
Goldenberg Rosenthal LLP

August Aquila and Bruce Marcus are two of my favorite consultants, writers and thinkers in the professional services field. I was delighted they combined their towering wisdom and created *Client at the Core*, and you will be as well. Client selection and retention is one of the critical success factors for a professional service firm, and Aquila and Marcus do a masterful job at educating us on the necessary ingredients of each. But they don't stop there. I especially found the chapters on firm governance and paying for performance thought-provoking, and certainly challenging to the conventional wisdom. If you want a better understanding of marketing and leading a professional firm in these turbulent times, this book is an essential read.

—Ronald J. Baker, author,
Professional's Guide to Value Pricing and
The Firm of the Future

Client at the Core draws on the authors' extensive experience working with professional service firms to explain the changes in the practice environment, how to meet the needs of an ever more demanding and sophisticated clientele and the importance of building a marketing culture within a firm. The book provides a very contemporary and interesting look at world events and other factors that have changed the dynamics of professional practice. Aquila and Marcus write in plain terms their views of both the vital and the unnecessary steps needed to create a client-centric firm. With its practical tone and comprehensive content, *Client at the Core* will be instructive for anyone in professional services looking to upgrade the firm's marketing strategy.

—Sally J. Schmidt, President
Schmidt Marketing, Inc.

August and Bruce once again are blazing the trail for professional services marketing—creating a map for client-centric marketing performed by a firm with a client-centric structure and culture. They don't abandon the marketing lessons and disciplines learned in the past three decades, but show how to build on those lessons to attain the level of marketing sophistication necessary for the next decade. This book is sure to stay on the desk of any professional serious about getting and keeping clients!

—Martha H. Sawyer
Hudson Sawyer

Marcus and Aquila have important points to make, not trendy agendas to sell. They dramatize the challenges facing the professional services, and they do so without being preachy or tendentious. And, my goodness, a book about marketing that is actually well-written! There's no jargon here, just coherent strategies eloquently and forcefully prescribed. Books like *Client at the Core* imbue the business development process with dignity.

—Larry Smith, Director of Strategy,
Levick Strategic Communications, LLC
Author of *Inside/Outside–How Businesses Buy Legal Services* and
co-author of *Stop the Presses: The Litigation PR Desk Reference*

Meaty and rich with texture. The authors understand the *application* of marketing concepts to the CPA profession at a very deep level, and communicate clearly and concisely. Every page was another 'Yes!' when reading about the *application* of marketing principles to the CPA world. The authors nailed it.

—Gale Crosley, CPA
Crosley + Company

Aquila and Marcus have captured the scope of the significant changes evolving in professional service firms today. They have given us practical and useful ways to absorb these changes and to address the realities of today's professional firm management. I have one professional service firm management book that is on my desk constantly, dog-eared from use. I will now have two.

—Rita A. Keller, Director,
Brady, Ware & Schoenfeld, Inc.

Client at the Core gives readers real-world, contemporary advice on how to run a professional services firm. It's easily readable, and well organized with bullet points and options to choose from. I especially enjoyed the discussion of compensation, because as we know, what gets rewarded gets done. It is worth getting the book for the chapter on ROMI (return on marketing investment) alone. This book belongs on the desk of every professional who wants a satisfying and highly-paid practice.

—Larry Bodine,
Regional Director for North America, PM Forum, and
Executive Editor of *Professional Marketing* magazine

Client at the Core provides a blueprint for developing a client-focused approach to marketing and client service development. Follow what Aquila and Marcus recommend and you will be able to unlock the secrets to client-focused service development and marketing. A compulsory reading for anyone in a professional services firm.

—Mark Lloydbottom, FCA CPC CPEC
Managing Director
Practice WEB, United Kingdom

Readers of *Client at the Core* will benefit from the vast experience of my colleagues August Aquila and Bruce Marcus. It is critical to understand the nuances of marketing professional services. This book does just that, providing a roadmap that begins with how to take care of clients and how to obtain more quality clients and ends with how to provide services to clients profitably and with value—a huge undertaking done with their usual insight and style.

—Jean Marie Caragher
Capstone Marketing
www.capstonemarketing.com

CLIENT AT THE CORE

MARKETING AND MANAGING TODAY'S
PROFESSIONAL SERVICES FIRM

AUGUST J. AQUILA, PhD

BRUCE W. MARCUS

WILEY

JOHN WILEY & SONS, INC.

For general information on our other products and services, or technical support, please contact
our Customer Care Department within the United States at 800-762-2974, outside the United
States at 317-572-3993 or fax 317-572-4002.

Wiley also publishes its books in a variety of electronic formats. Some content that appears in
print may not be available in electronic books.

For more information about Wiley products, visit our web site at www. wiley.com.

Library of Congress Cataloging-in-Publication Data

Aquila, August J.
    Client at the core : marketing and managing today's professional services firm /
August J. Aquila, Bruce W. Marcus.
        p.   cm.
    Includes bibliographical references (p.) and index.
    ISBN 0-471-45313-7 (cloth)
    1. Accounting firms—Marketing.   2. Law firms—Marketing.   3. Accounting
firms—United States—Marketing.   4. Law firms—United States—Marketing.
I. Marcus, Bruce W., 1925–   II. Title.
    HF5628.5.A68 2004
    340'.068'8—dc22
                                                          2004003671

Printed in the United States of America
10 9 8 7 6 5 4 3 2 1

To my exceptionally strong and courageous daughter, Kate, who makes the world a better place to live

August J. Aquila

To my wife, Mana, who has sustained my spirit through many books, through many words, through life's assaults on reason—and who has sustained my life as joyful

Bruce W. Marcus

ABOUT THE AUTHORS

August J. Aquila

August J. Aquila is an internationally known consultant, speaker, and author. He has held leading positions in the accounting profession for more than 25 years—as the first regional marketing director for an international firm, as a partner in a top 50 accounting firm and as executive vice president of a marketing consulting firm, and in executive positions with American Express Tax & Business Services. He currently heads the Practice Management Consulting division for The Growth Partnership, Inc., a full service consulting firm to the accounting profession. As a consultant, he focuses on management implementation and specializes in CPA firm mergers & acquisitions, management and partnership issues, and facilitating firm retreats. He is the editor of *Partner Advantage Advisory*, a monthly newsletter, and has written and co-authored four other books.

Bruce W. Marcus

Bruce W. Marcus is a widely published author and consultant who has practiced marketing for professionals for almost half a century. As the author of hundreds of articles and more than a dozen books on marketing, marketing related subjects, and the capital markets, and as the editor of *The Marcus Letter on Professional Services Marketing*—one of the most widely read publications on the subject—he has been at the forefront of the changes and maturity of the art of marketing professional services, and he has brought innovative marketing programs to both large and small professional firms. He is the co-author, most recently, of *New Dimension in Investor Relations: Competing for Capital in the 21st Century* (Wiley).

CONTENTS

*In this world of change naught which comes stays and
naught which goes is lost.*

Factors causing economic change...Effect of competition on professional
firms...Adapting to competition...The multi-discipline practice...
Internal management problems.

*It seems so perfectly rational that if you don't offer what the client
wants and needs, then the client will go elsewhere.*

The difference between professional firms and manufacturing firms...The
boundaries between law and accounting firms...Globalization...What
today's client knows...The client's options...Being a professional as a
comfort factor...The new demands for new skills.

FOREWORD

by Patrick J. McKenna

In the world of professional services, a professional firm's approach to its clients has evolved through a number of distinct and identifiable phases over the years since the *Bates* decision. The result is that today, most sophisticated accounting, law, consulting, and other professional service providers approach marketing and their clients very differently than they did 20 or even 10 years ago.

In its first iteration, throughout the 1970s and into the early 1980s, a competent group of professionals needed only find ways to let prospective clients know of the availability of their firm. Back then we didn't call it marketing, nor did we dare to ever mention the term *sales*, lest someone think us overly commercial, rather than considering us as esteemed professionals. Indeed, we referred to what industry commonly called marketing as *practice development*, but only in hushed tones and never in front of the client.

In many cases, there was a great mystique attached to what a true professional actually did. A realization eventually dawned on some practitioners and firms that they needed to educate prospective clients on how and when to use their firm's services. In these early days, the emphasis was on gaining a competitive advantage by simply letting people know more about you and your firm. Not a bad argument, given that most professional firms had never even developed a brochure to outline for clients what services the firm provided.

Next came the *rainmaking* era. An increased comfort with commercialism and winning the argument for being a business rather than just a profession brought the advent of aggressive professional service firms advertising their wares through yellow page advertisements and even television infomercials. As increasing numbers of baby boomers graduated from professional schools, the expanded number of professionals entering the market introduced many to the concept of competition. This heralded the transition from lock-step systems that rewarded the lifetime contribution of a professional to his or her firm, to an internal system that rewarded those who were the best at bringing in new business. We spoke of developing personal marketing plans and our efforts to *target* prospective clients. We decided what to sell and to whom, and professional service firm marketing was something we *did* to people.

It was not until the mid-1990s that the view changed. Largely as a result of the Internet's making information easier to access and the concurrent demands of better educated and more sophisticated clients, the issue of client satisfaction became more germane. Increasingly, firms found that their best clients, those clients responsible for providing the greatest revenue stream to the firm, were corporations that had in-house departments retaining their services. Thus, a legal department selected the outside law firms, the financial control department chose the audit firm, and the advertising department coordinated the next round of creative pitches from various external vendors. And there was no air of mystique with these internal people. They pretty much knew exactly what they were looking for, had the necessary background to judge your firm's expertise, and knew when they were getting quality and service. The more enlightened professional firms started to pay a great deal more attention to the wishes and needs of these clients. The result was something of a sea change in how marketing was viewed—the beginning of a client-centric view that today dominates the field.

In my view, the most advanced firms have progressed through a further evolution as they moved beyond a client focus to becoming even more concerned with how they effectively develop relationships. Their concentration is not merely on the achievement of short-term or transactional satisfaction, but rather on the development of long-term solid relationships that will evidence clients seeing them as their preferred provider or strategic partner. Thus much of the marketing emphasis has now switched from merely getting good clients to also keeping them.

As I'm just old enough to have lived through and witnessed this evolution of marketing thinking over the past two decades, *Client at the Core* is an essential blueprint to helping us all take the next steps. The authors, battle-scarred by the evolution of professional firm management and marketing from then to now, have captured the changing needs of the firms in this turbulent new economic era. This is a well-written book that uses plain language to convey practical, well-thought-out ideas. It has been my rare gift to have known and collaborated with both of these authors over the years, and your gift is in having them come together to share their insights with you here.

So get your favorite colored highlighter, read this book with an eye toward learning from the masters, and you will see what I'm talking about.

Patrick J. McKenna is a leading consultant to professional service firms and co-author of the international business bestseller, *First Among Equals* (Free Press, 2002).

PREFACE

The professional world doesn't need another book on how to write a press release or write a brochure or run a seminar, so that's not what this book is about. The libraries of professional firms are replete with books and articles on the subject, and indeed we two have written a vast amount of it. We assume that any professional facing up to the realities of competition is inundated with this literature. The tools of marketing, we now know, are no more the essence of marketing than the fountain pen (or even the computer) are the essence of accounting and auditing.

What this book is about, then, is a new perspective on the crucial subject of how to keep your firm relevant to the needs of the marketplace you face in the coming decade. And while we do include some very cogent things we've learned about marketing practice and skills in the more than a quarter century that we've been doing this, and in fact go to great lengths to address some practices too often badly misused, we think you may find it more valuable to explore the profoundly changing environment for professional firms, and what the professional firm must do today to survive and thrive in the new marketing environment.

We address, then, the core subject of creating clients and building a marketing culture in the light of the current and distinctive business and regulatory environment; of making the professional services firm, no matter its size, relevant to the needs of the first decades of the twenty-first century. We address, as well, the need—and techniques—to build a marketing culture as an integral part of managing a firm, because we know now that nothing that happens in a law or accounting firm is unrelated to marketing.

We write this book knowing that conventional wisdom about marketing no longer applies as readily as it might have in the early days of professional services marketing. One has only to read the remarkable and authoritative book by Larry Smith on how in-house corporate counsel chooses outside counsel (*Inside/Outside*

—*How Businesses Buy Legal Services*) to recognize how utterly futile the traditional marketing techniques can often be in competing for clients. One need only read the works of the international consulting firm, Edge International, the work done by David Maister, the practical marketing musings of *The Marcus Letter*, and the astute observations of August Aquila in a broad spectrum of publications, including the newsletters *Partner Advantage Advisory* and its predecessor, *Partner to Partner Advisory*, to know that merely to reside in the mechanics and vehicles of marketing is no long sufficient.

We write, as well, about the differences between marketing a product and marketing a professional service, and why understanding these differences affects the professional services marketing process. These differences are significant. They render obsolete and make irrelevant so much of the traditional academic views of marketing, when those views are applied to professional services.

In the past 25 years since the *Bates* decision (*Bates v. State Bar of Arizona*, 1977) moved the professions of law and accounting into a new realm of competition—which is indeed what *Bates* did—the economic world has changed. It has moved the professional practice well beyond its hide-bound traditions and concepts of the anointed professional. The business environment we now face is driven more by the Peter Druckers of the world than by the arcane marketing practices of earlier times. Drucker, remember, propounded the first law of management, which is that the purpose of a company (or a firm) is to create a customer (or client). This principle, perhaps more than any other, drives us as marketing professionals.

Our intention is to convey, in the simplest, clearest terms, how the economic landscape for accountants and lawyers has changed, and what professionals must now understand and do to compete—to successfully and profitably traverse this new world. We mean to have you, the reader and professional, come to understand and to function effectively in this new context and competitive environment—to go beyond the mere practice of the mechanics of marketing to an understanding of how a new marketing culture works, and why it's imperative to have one. Marketing, we know now, is no longer an arbitrary activity. It's an integral part of law and accounting firm management. Those firms that understand this are the ones that thrive in a competitive environment. Our objective is to have you take that understanding and mold it to your own practice.

You'll find that we try to avoid the jargon and the clichés of marketing and management, simply because they communicate nothing but a knowledge of clichés and jargon. They are a wonderful way to avoid using insight to understand the marketing philosophy and process.

We don't talk of *vision* in its most frequent use, for example, because in the words of Patrick McKenna and David Maister in their wonderful book *First Among*

Equals, "Many management texts suggest that one key contribution of a leader is to create a 'vision.' We're skeptics. There may be those individuals who, through personal charisma or the painting of an irresistible future, can get large numbers of professionals to follow them. We just don't think many people can pull it off." We do, however, talk of vision in realistic—and valuable—terms. As is the case in so many terms used in marketing and management, it's not the concept that's bad—it's the misuse of it. We talk of vision as a clear view of opportunities, and the will and ability to seize them.

We don't talk of *mission* because a firm's mission is not the concern of clients, nor can it be creditably stated to affect a client's decisions, or to give comfort to clients and prospects. Mission, instead, is the dream of the firm managers. Beyond the firm, a mission is believable only in the performance, not in the statement or promise. And as anyone who has worked with a professional firm knows, mission is too often a myth perpetuated at the top and ignored or misunderstood farther down the line. "Don't speak of love," goes the old Rogers and Hammerstein song, "show me."

We speak instead of those measures that address the realities of firm management—understanding as best as possible the needs of the clientele and how to better serve those needs. How to convert knowledge into a management and marketing tool. How to communicate internally and effectively. How to build a marketing culture within a firm in professions that have no traditions of marketing. And finally, how to measure a firm's progress and results.

To some extent, the timing of this book is fortuitous. While we might well have written it from the standpoint of merely watching the hands of the clock move over 25 years, we are now jolted into reality by the current rash of scandals that have shaken the foundations, and questioned the integrity, of accounting and legal practice, of corporate governance, of investor and shareholder concern, of the real meaning to the business world of new technology, of the initial reactions (and overreactions) to the accounting and corporate scandals—of the maelstrom of economic and regulatory change.

It's easier to see in perspective the profound effects that Bates had on the professions since 1977, beyond simply freeing professionals from the strictures that prohibited frank marketing. New technology made a difference, as have the challenges to the profession precipitated by the massive failures in process and integrity of the first years of the twenty-first century.

But the most significant changes have been brought about by the ability of professional services firms to market and compete—processes that did not openly exist prior to *Bates* in 1977, nor for which there were traditions in any profession. These changes were precipitated less by the manifestations of the traditional marketing process than by the instinctive movement to compete by developing and offering clients new and innovative services. Few of today's accounting firms and law firms would have been recognizable in 1977 in their current configurations.

This change, in a dynamic world, continues today, and is indeed accelerating. Thus, the purpose of this book, which is to allow today's professional services firms to not only see themselves in the perspective of the past, present, and future, but to provide them with a blueprint of how to create a marketing structure, process, and culture. It is to allow the modern professional services firm, even in this maelstrom of economic and regulatory change, to prepare itself to serve its markets, to manage itself successfully, to compete effectively.

In the twenty-first century, it's virtually impossible to meet the marketing needs of a company without recognizing that the most significant part of marketing is the nature of the firm itself—how it is structured, how it is governed, how it is managed, and how it serves clients. And that, too, is what this book is about—managing a firm to serve the needs of the marketplace, and competing successfully in serving those needs. A firm first needs to be able to create clients before it can market to clients.

The configuration of the professions and the market they serve are changing, not as a manifestation of the accident of time—the new century—but rather as a function of events of the time and the evolution of the commercial and industrial world. Our objective is to help professional services firms and their advisors, no matter the size or the nature of the practice, become relevant to the needs of the next decade.

The ideas, suggestions, and orientations of this book, it should be noted, are not derived from abstract theory about a world that should be. They are based, rather, on the broad and extensive experience we both have had as practitioners of this arcane art—more than 50 years between us. Most of what we write about in this book, however old, however new and innovative, stems from our own experience and firsthand knowledge of what works. We offer no advice other than that which we know to be practical and viable, nor for which we have not had to take responsibility for results. We have drawn as well from comparable experience of others whom we know to be innovative and practical practitioners and sound advisors.

There is a mystery in marketing, and don't let anybody tell you otherwise. No matter how good we are, no matter how intensive our efforts or how broad our skills and experience, there is always too much we don't know.

We don't know all we need to know about the market for our services, nor exactly why people buy. We don't know as much as we think we do about how to inform and motivate our prospective clientele. We don't know a great deal, although we think we do, about how to motivate professionals to participate in the marketing process.

We do know that there is much more to learn about how to structure the contemporary law or accounting firm to meet the needs of the changing clientele. We know remarkably little about how to measure the effectiveness of our marketing efforts in professional services, when professionals must rely on circumstances beyond their control to bring the client through the door, rather than just in the efficacy of marketing efforts, nor do we know a great deal about how to distinguish one firm from another and project that distinction. In fact, we know very little about how to deal with change, and right now, there's a great deal of it. These are among the issues we explore here.

Too few professionals—and marketers—understand the profound differences between marketing a product and marketing a professional service, and why that difference matters. Product marketers have had more than 100 years to learn the basics of their craft, and they function in a context in which everyone in a company understands that marketing matters. They may not always remember it, nor function as if they ever knew it, but Peter Drucker put his finger on the awesome truth that the purpose of a company is to create a customer. Too many professionals still seem not to have learned that lesson, and think that the purpose of a professional firm is to practice the profession. But for whom? Would any accounting or law firm be able to bedazzle the world with brilliance if it had no clients, nor could get any? The problem is that there is no tradition of marketing in the professional practice, and a mere two or three decades are hardly enough time to establish one.

We know very little about productivity in marketing professional services, compared to what the product marketers know. After all, you can measure the efficacy of a product ad by counting the number of units you sell. Can you measure return on investment in marketing by the number of clients you get the day after your marketing program hits the street?

What do we know, then? We know, by now, the basic skills of marketing that take a stride toward establishing presence in a marketplace. We know enough of marketing skills to make some measure of difference. We know that when we realize that the client is at the core of the profession, it is the client's needs we must address, and not the litany of services we offer. Those services are smoke if they serve no client purpose or need.

We know that we must recognize what we don't know, and dedicate ourselves to learning what we don't know, and not reside in the small world of what we think we know.

Most important, we must recognize that whatever skills we bring to marketing, it is still ultimately an art form, and not quite the science we would like it to be. And so if you want to succeed in marketing, then, don't hire the scientist. Hire the artist.

There is hope. For those of us who were marketing professional services before *Bates*, or did it in those early days after *Bates*, we can say that marketing for professionals has come a great distance. More professionals now recognize the validity of marketing as an integral part of practice. More marketing professionals bring a sophistication to the process that we had not thought possible in 1977, the year of the *Bates* decision that made marketing for professionals a valid practice to address the hitherto unknown process of competition. When *Competing for Clients* (*Bruce W. Marcus*) came out in the early 1980s, it was called the first comprehensive manual on the subject. Today, the body of literature on the subject is extensive, and a lot of it is genuinely instructive and valuable. That's progress.

But marketing sophistication brings increased and effective competition, which then requires even more sophistication. And the profound changes in the business and regulatory environment we now see breed a need for greater knowledge, greater flexibility, and greater acuity.

There is indeed a mystery in marketing. The success of the marketer, then, depends upon the knowledge, the skill, the enthusiasm that so many of us have. But the secret ingredient that makes it work is the artfulness that's brought to the process. And the approach to artfulness is what this book is also about.

One last point. Every author hopes to write the last word on the subject, and we are no different. We do know, however, that there is no last word on the subject. Think of this as a process in motion, because even as we write, things change. We'll try to stay ahead.

August J. Aquila
Bruce W. Marcus

February 2004

ACKNOWLEDGMENTS

This book isn't finished yet. How can it be, when the economic world served by professionals addresses changes constantly?

In fact, a friend, a highly knowledgeable and respected professional, raised a question about our referring to "the next decade." "Will this book be obsolete after 10 years?" he asked.

Yes, it will be, because the world will have changed substantially. Some of it, anyway. And if what we say in this book is right, and helpful, that too might contribute to change.

Nevertheless, we could not have written this book without the help of a great many wise and competent people—all knowledgeable, experienced, and each outstanding in his or her field. Their contributions ranged from encouragement to shared experience, and always within the context of ideas contributed from the context of their own experience.

The list is long, and those not here are not here for lack of appreciation, but for lack of time and space. Among those who have influenced or informed us are Patrick McKenna and Gerry Riskin of Edge International, undoubtedly the leading law and professional firm marketing and consulting firm in the world; David Maister, who has turned professional firm management from a science to an art to a philosophy; Richard Levick and Larry Smith, of Levick Strategic Communications, LLC, the leading law firm public relations practitioners; Ronald J. Baker, whose thinking and writing on accounting firm management and especially on the concept of billable hours will undoubtedly change the nature of professional firm management; Silvia Coulter, who, as a leading professional marketer, knows more about selling professional services than anybody; Sally Schmidt, a pioneer who invented and codified much of what we do today in professional firm marketing; Ken Wright, who pioneered the best in international accounting firm marketing; Richard Weiner, who invented as much about public relations as any of the other pioneers; Jeff Pawlow, who is making business development a true science with his Disciplined Marketing™ approach; Leisa Gill, who as the past president of Association of Accounting Marketing (AAM) and marketing director of Lattimore Black Morgan & Cain continues to advance the role of accounting firm marketing professionals; Bill Carlino, the distinguished editor of *Accounting Today*, which has published so much of our material; Rick Telberg, who first raised trade publication editing to a world-class level; Jennifer Prosek, whose skill and intelligence moved a small public relations firm to a world-class one, by being smarter and more knowledgeable than most of her peers; Louise Rothery, who so ably and deftly edits more than one legal trade journal at a time; Gilbert Parker, who has changed the nature of firm proposals and presentations from traditional clunky to modern graceful; Larry Bodine, a leading force in law firm marketing; Kathryn Davis, who showed how deft, competent, and original a freelance writer can be; Richard Chaplin and Nadia Cristina, publisher and editor of the excellent publication *Professional Marketing*, who did for professional services marketing in England more than anybody else before or since; Chris Frederiksen, who has taught countless CPAs and CA in the United States and abroad how to build million dollar practices; and all the legal and accounting publications that have published our many, many articles over the years.

And finally and ultimately, our clients, who have taught us so much, perhaps without realizing that we are always learning even as we teach. We are, fortunately, informed by the very best, for which we are both awed and grateful.

Among the more substantial contributors to this effort were two wonderful, patient and supportive people—Emily Haliziw and Mana Marcus. We've often been told that writers' wives bear a far greater burden than the writers themselves. It's true, and we thank them. More than that, we appreciate them.

A vast measure of gratitude goes to the team at Wiley that's responsible for turning words into book. John DeRemigis, Judy Howarth, and Kerstin Nasdeo bring new luster to the definition of professionalism. Lucky the author to have this team to work with.

And by the way, readers of *The Marcus Letter* (www.marcusletter.com), that sometimes iconoclastic but always serious and often useful online journal, will recognize a substantial amount of the ideas in this book. So, too, will readers of the former *Partner-to-Partner Advisory*, now called *Partner Advantage Advisory*. Not that the book is a rehash of articles we wrote in those publications—it's just that sometimes, established ideas are a good foundation for new ideas, and that's what happened here.

August J. Aquila	Bruce W. Marcus
Minnetonka, MN	Easton, CT
	February 2, 2004

PART I

PROFESSIONS AND PROFESSIONALS IN TURMOIL

1

IF SOMETHING CAN CHANGE, IT WILL

Strategic Factors in a New Environment

In this world of change naught which comes stays and naught which goes is lost.

—Anne Sophie Swetchine, Russian author

To any accountant or lawyer who entered the twenty-first century with a few years of experience as a professional, the events of the first two years of the new century delivered profound shock. Even before the tragic events of September 11, 2001, the assault on the business world—the very source of professional practice—turned that world topsy-turvy. The universe in which the professional must practice today is markedly different from the traditional world in which the professions thrived for generations.

First came the failure of the dot-coms. A huge financial and stock market bubble that had grown at the speed of a malignancy finally burst, with failure and loss spewed all over the landscape. Then came the rash of frauds, defalcations, misuse of corporate funds—a kaleidoscope of events that virtually destroyed the stock market and investor confidence. Each day brought a new scandal. Many major accounting firms were shown to have departed from the traditions of probity, objectivity, and integrity. Law firms were devastated, with trust, integrity, and reputation eroded. Arthur Andersen, for generations one of the greatest accounting firms in the world, was totally destroyed as quickly as if it had been struck by lightning. And finally, the new administration in Washington, concentrating on the new war on terrorism, failed to stem what became a sharp downturn in the economy. Ultimately, recovery began to emerge, like crocuses bursting through the snow as a precursor of spring, but lacking the vigor and the heft of the earlier dot-com years.

3

As if these events were not enough to alter the nature of the economy, and most cogently, the practice of every professional, the outcry to stem the tide of disaster—to regulate the markets to forestall further disaster—created a helter-skelter regulatory rush that was at least as punitive as it was appropriate. It would seem that the regulatory garment was cut to fit all, when all don't wear the same size.

The result was to create an environment that called for a reexamination of traditional legal and accounting practices. New strategies and new approaches, fed by the changes in the business world, were dictated. What actually happened?

- The growing anxiety of a vast number of investors, both corporate and individual, and their skepticism about the information supplied by corporations and the accountants and lawyers became rampant. The value and integrity of brokers and analysts were sternly questioned. The financial markets were decimated. Regenerating lost trust and understanding in the legal, accounting, and financial professions now becomes a major concern and responsibility for corporations, for professionals, and for those responsible for marketing and communications.

- New regulations and law, promulgated by the Sarbanes-Oxley Act of 2002, the new regulatory structures of the Securities and Exchange Commission, and the stock exchanges, put greater controls on corporate governance, and on the independence of accountants and Wall Street researchers, and dictate strong civil and criminal punishments for violations. The decades-old battle to preserve self-regulation is lost. And although new regulators won't find it a cinch to control the professions, self-regulation is out. Oversight is in.

- Stronger controls on auditors, including separation of auditing and consulting practices, reexamining partnership structures, and new measures to detect corporate fraud, shift the burden of assuring integrity from within a firm's practice to outside bodies (although the responsibility to project integrity remains with the professionals and the corporations).

- Greater focus on the legal profession, and its responsibility in dealing with miscreant clients, pushes lawyers farther away from the comfortable residence of client-attorney privilege.

- Greater controls on corporate boards and audit committees are being put in force, altering the very nature of the corporation and its forms of governance. Gone are the days of the rubber-stamp board. And fading are the days of the despotic but charismatic leader.

- CEOs now have responsibility to sign off on financial statements, which puts a greater burden on CEOs whose specialties and experience, while appropriate to the needs of their companies, may be in nonfinancial areas, such as marketing or production.

- Potential reform of executive compensation structure is clearly in the works—a reaction to disproportionate executive compensation packages.

- Not exempt from this revolution are brokerage firms, security analysts, and sources of capital. Greater regulation, under a bright spotlight, substantially alters the structure and management of financial institutions. Wall Street and environs must now form a new accord with Main Street.

- The New York Stock Exchange, struck by exposure of the awesome compensation of its chief executive, and driven by the new U.S. Securities and Exchange commissioner William Donaldson (himself a former NYSE chairman), faced a massive structural reorganization.

As a counterpoint to these events, there is the role played by technology, which is no longer simply a phenomenon, but is now an integral part of business in all its aspects, and makes a significant difference.

- The increasing importance of the Internet in all aspects of communication—to shareholders, analysts, and other influentials in the investment community, and the business and financial press—redefines the access to information by investors and brings a new dimension to investment practice. This means new transparency for once-opaque professional firms and the companies they serve. The Internet also gives access to a new target audience for professionals and their marketers.

- Access to an overwhelming abundance of data and online databases, and problems in managing the data for value, effectiveness, and communication, gives investors more information than they ever had before—although still without meaningful interpretation, and now, with questionable accuracy and integrity.

- Consolidations of sources of data and external communications control the flow of information through new structures and alliances.

- More extensive business and financial news is available online, on radio and television, and in the press, putting a spotlight on events that may be more sensational than rational.

As if these events were not sufficient to distort the traditional universe in which the professional and financial world function, there is the economy itself...

- The 401(k) accounts, and the more than 50 million Americans who have them, are a powerful influence on the market. Account holders don't always bring sophistication to an orderly market. That's $1.9 trillion that, says Alicia Munnell, a former member of President Bill Clinton's Council of Economic

Advisors, is not always invested wisely. "People make mistakes at every step of the way," she says.

- The economic environment, at this writing, has been in decline and is only beginning to show faint signs of recovery. It may or may not be improving. If it improves, it may be two years before it is healthy again, by which time the landscape will have significantly changed.

- The rapid demise of the budget surplus, and the growing deficit, can feed economic downturn and ultimately, perhaps, inflation.

- The cost of the war on terrorism, and the invasion of Iraq, can substantially alter the economic landscape.

Concurrently, the growing recognition by professionals of the role of marketing in a professional practice has brought the marketing practice to a new maturity. Where once marketing was considered optional, that option became a mandate, as the battle to compete became more urgent. Today, the decision to market is no longer an option, but an integral part of accounting and law firm management. Which is not to say that acceptance of marketing is universal, but it's certainly farther along than it was just a few years ago.

These factors, separately and combined, dictate new strategies in informing and persuading investors, and those who advise them, of the values inherent in investing in a company's securities. These factors dictate, as well, a new relationship between the professional and the client, the professional and the investor.

The new regulatory environment has been a long time coming. The failure of self-regulation has contributed substantially to Congress's finally winning the decades-old regulatory battle between itself and the professions. The result is a new structure that will affect every accounting firm, including those that don't serve public companies.

New regulation brings a new perspective to a trend toward the multidiscipline practice—the MDP, which moves to blur the line between the accounting, legal, and consulting practices, even as it moves professionals into new practice definitions. In some cases, new rules indicate deceleration of the MDP process. The new regulations that attempt to separate auditing from consulting, for example, or that retard the movement of law firms into accounting practices and vice versa, cause a rethinking of the MDP process. But these events don't necessarily bring the process to a halt. There is a trend that once started is not easily reversed.

The root causes of the new regulatory regimen are complex, and for the professional to prevail in uncertain times, it may be useful to explore some of the events that generated this new regimen. The practices in the accounting and legal professions have emerged through decades of response to business needs and conditions of the time, and despite the best efforts of lawmakers and regulators, no simple stroke of the pen can erase those practices without ultimately causing damage. The regulatory threat is a high-speed train that can't be stopped on a dime.

It's not sloth and greed alone that created this accounting and legal morass, and to try to correct the situation that brought both law and accounting to this pass without understanding the recent history of professional practice will, more likely than not, burden the good accountant and lawyer as well as the bad.

There's no doubt that, in the current environment and with the anxiety about the integrity of financial statements, revenues of accounting firm SEC practices will increase in the short term. But ultimately, in the long term, the nature of the professions we know today will change. Business entities of all kinds react in their own way to changing environments, and it would be foolish to attempt to predict what the long-range effect of Sarbanes-Oxley and other regulatory initiatives will be. But things will indeed change.

Three economic phenomena, in addition to sloth and greed, brought us to this debacle—obsolescence in the methods to accurately account for the business and economic structures of the modern corporation; the need to find new ways for professional firms to compete; and internal communications structures that are not adequate to the needs of growing accounting and law firms.

The first derives from the fact that the business world changed profoundly in recent decades, and the accounting profession did not. In a *Business Week* interview in 2002, Barry Melancon of the American Institute of Certified Public Accountants said, "We need to move accounting from . . . an industrial age model to an information age model." In today's dynamic technological society, it's virtually impossible for a company or an investor to have a true and current picture of the company's financial condition using traditional static accounting techniques. Obviously, the profession's accounting methods must be made more relevant to modern business needs. It's extraordinarily difficult, as well, for the contemporary company to function in today's world without an array of expertise from many sources, which is the reality behind consulting. Most businesses need and benefit from the breadth of the accountant's expertise.

The second phenomenon began in 1977 with *Bates v. State Bar of Arizona*, in which the U.S. Supreme Court struck down the professionals' Canons of Ethics prohibiting advertising, and, by extension, any kind of frank marketing. *Bates* ultimately changed the nature of all of the professions, and made fertile the ground that created the very problems for accounting and law firms raised up by the Andersen disaster.

Bates, in creating the ability to do frank marketing, brought that new word—*competition*—into the professionals' lexicon. In the first attempts to compete, battalions of advertising, public relations, and marketing people were hired, only to discover that marketing a professional firm was very different from marketing a product. After all, how do you distinguish one accounting firm from another when you can't say, "We do better audits"? Or a law firm from others when you can't say, "We write better briefs?"

Thus, the competition had to be fought on a different level, causing great confusion among marketing professionals. The MBA marketers had no solutions, because they had no precedents. The traditional marketers could only bring classic marketing vehicles into play—the press release, the brochure, the seminar, and so forth—without any great sense of marketing strategy or perspective, nor understanding of the intricacies and nuances of the professions. Ironically, it was the accountants and the lawyers—the very same who had swooned at the idea of frank marketing—who came up with the answer.

That answer was to recognize that the audit services alone, as well as legal services, offered little foundation for competing. Therefore, professionals began to compete by concentrating on new kinds of advisory—*consulting*—services. *Help your client install a new computing system. Help your client build a new cash flow system. Do executive search work for your clients. Help your client structure new subsidiaries or acquisitions.* And so forth.

Consulting enabled accounting firms to do what traditional auditing could not do—differentiate themselves from one another by focusing marketing efforts on the consulting services. It worked so well that the consulting work began to overwhelm the auditing work, until the larger firms—those that do the most auditing—persuaded themselves that they were really business consultants that also did audits. When was the last time anybody has seen a large firm tout its CPA credentials?

Law firms, a little better able to distinguish themselves—at least in most areas—from other law firms, also developed a new aggressiveness in seeking to increase market share. They, too, moved in nontraditional directions. Many became investment advisors or management experts. Many moved into areas traditionally held by accountants, such as financial planning, and financial management in estate planning. Firms with specialized practices, such as construction, hired engineers, and then targeted the market based on construction management skills. Law firms with medical malpractice activities (as well as accounting firms serving the health care industry) hired nurses and doctors as staff. And ultimately, accounting firms began to buy law firms as subsidiaries and profit centers, wherever local law didn't strictly prohibit it. Prior to the Enron scandal, the accounting giant Arthur Andersen became the largest law firm in Europe, through acquisition of European law firms. (Not to be overlooked is the acquisition of accounting firms by American Express, to build one of the largest accounting capabilities in the United States.) And while law firms could hardly say, "Hire us because we win more cases," there were many other ways, including advertising and public relations, to promote litigation skills and success.

And so arose the concept of multidiscipline practice—MDP. While the concept of practice beyond the traditional bounds of a law or accounting firm has long run counter to the Canons of Ethics of both professions, the boundaries separating the two practices—law firms can't practice accounting or share fees with nonlawyers (or make them partners), and vice versa for accounting firms—those boundaries are eroding. They are breaking down, not by mandate (both professional bodies continue to reject measures supporting MDP), but by osmosis through the boundaries' membrane. While the scandals of the first years of the twenty-first century brought regulation that slowed down the process, it is ultimately the needs of the clients that will dictate the course of professional practice.

At the same time, the growth of accounting and law firms began to cause serious internal management problems. If the growing companies they served had to learn new management skills to cope with new size and business configurations, so too did the burgeoning accounting and law firms. Management skills, unfortunately, are not taught in accounting or law schools. There's no management tradition and there's no management training, as there is in corporations. The collegial nature of the traditional partnership began to prove itself inadequate to managing the new demands placed on growing professional firms. The traditional partnership structures began to pose more problems than they solved, and in fact, the total implosion of Arthur Andersen, in which the misdeeds of a few partners destroyed the equity of all the partners, as well as the thousands of staff people, foretells the ultimate erosion of the system. There are now too many issues in professional firm governance for a firm not to look to professional management to replace collegial management.

As the body of knowledge within a firm became vast, internal communications broke down, as seen so clearly in the firms serving Enron, Tyco, and the like, and, obviously, Arthur Andersen. Too much was going on internally that wasn't known by others in the firm who should have known. Failed internal communications has now become a significant cause of major catastrophes of Enronic proportions.

The internal communication and management crisis in today's large international professional firms is also a major reason why merely imposing new regulatory structures alone will solve few of these new problems. Without significant changes in internal communications structures, it's impossible to enforce any new rules that seek to protect against obsolete accounting methods. It seems that as firms grow, and as the need to communicate internally becomes more acute, less thought is given to the process than ever before, a situation that later chapters in this book might well serve to rectify.

The music to accompany this chapter is more martial than romantic, so bleak and chaotic is the situation. After decades—generations—of the sanguine and patrician life of the professional, and practice uninhibited by external regulation and fostered by a purity and integrity matched only by Caesar's wife, the professions now find themselves in turmoil.

What, then is the future? What then is likely to work?

PART II

CLIENTS— WHO THEY ARE AND HOW TO FIND THEM

2

WHAT A CLIENT REALLY WANTS

Listening to the Client for Fun and Profit

It seems so perfectly rational that if you don't offer what the client wants and needs, then the client will go elsewhere.

—Bruce W. Marcus

And if offering clients what they want is so rational and obvious, why should there ever be a dissatisfied client? Why should clients ever leave one firm to go to another?

What, in fact, is it that clients want? And why should it be so difficult to give it to them?

Conventional wisdom gives some pat answers, and they are not news. Clients want help in growing their businesses. They want a relationship that gives them comfort, and the feeling that their professionals really care. They want to know that their professionals are the most skillful available. And on and on and on. It's all true—these are indeed things that clients want. If every professional knows this, why, then, should it be so difficult to give it to them?

Add to this the traditional concepts of client service. Be concerned. Be courteous and helpful. Serve with a cheerful and willing staff. Answer phones cheerfully and courteously, and return phone calls promptly. Be responsive and deliver services in a timely manner.

These concepts are in the service inventories of every accounting firm and every law firm, and as old-fashioned as they may sound, they are still applicable. Why, then, do clients leave one firm for another?

Let's go back to basics.

Consider, first, the difference between professional firms and manufacturing firms. It matters.

13

People buy the products or services they need. Nobody has to be persuaded to buy butter and the bread to put it on, or milk, or even toothpaste. When the taxman comes calling, or the banker or the government demands an audited statement, or the agreement needs a contract, nobody has to be persuaded to call an accountant or a lawyer.

But a manufacturer can persuade you to buy an SUV you didn't know you needed, or an electric toothbrush, or a high-priced cosmetic. Can a lawyer persuade you, as a happily married person, to get a divorce, simply because that's the service he performs? Can an accountant persuade you to get an audit when a government agency or a financial institution does not demand it? Not likely.

Clients come to lawyers and accountants, in the first instance, because they have to cope with a problem that's beyond their knowledge or experience. They know that the law and its regulations, as well as the intricacies of accounting and auditing process, are beyond the capabilities and experience of the nonlawyer or the nonaccountant. What they are looking for, in the first instance, is a *professional*—someone trained, experienced, and qualified in the skills they need to solve a problem, or to enhance the ability to seize an opportunity. Someone who is credentialed in those skills, and thereby subject to the discipline of a larger body, such as a bar association or a state or national accounting body, or regulatory agency.

Today, though, three things temper these needs . . .

- The complexity of business in today's economic environment.
- The wide choices available from within each profession.
- The changing perceptions of accountants and lawyers by the public.

These three factors alter and redefine the nature of client needs to a degree that go beyond the traditional needs of clients. They refine and increase client needs beyond the classic definitions of the demands for the services of a professional. And most significantly, they define the needs of clients that, in many ways, differ from one client to the other. There is, then, no longer a single tent encompassing everything clients want.

The intricacies of business today transcend the one-size-fits-all solution to legal and accounting problems. The lessons of the scandals of the early years of this decade demonstrate that even a legitimately run business can be more complex than ever before.

One measure of this complexity is the erosion of boundaries that separate the legal and accounting professions, boundaries that were once sacrosanct, and mandated by both legal and accounting bodies. Now, from estate planning to taxation to financing and business structure, there is growing incursion by one profession into the realm of the other. Inhibited by regulation, and deterred by tradition, the incursion moves forward nevertheless.

This means that what today's client needs and wants is not only greater sophistication and skill, and more imaginative applications of those skills, but a more meticulous understanding by professionals of these needs and wants, and how best to meet them.

Furthermore, the dynamics of today's business accelerates the rate at which those needs change, demanding that professionals now pay closer attention to the dynamics of each client's business.

As you've seen in Chapter 1, the world served by professionals today is a different environment, with a tempo established by the speed at which information travels, by the intensity of competition, by the flow of capital. It's a world dominated by a regulatory environment that, as you've seen, puts unprecedented external strictures on professionals. It's a global environment, for even the smallest company.

Globalization is now beyond the choice of the contemporary business leader. You can't decide you won't be involved when technology makes it possible to go beyond borders for your capital or your raw material. For the larger company, capital, which knows no boundaries, can come from anywhere in the world, and invariably does. Even the smaller company may not realize that the local bank that helps finance receivables may be getting some of its capital from abroad. Larger companies—and not that much larger at that—may be selling abroad. Public companies may find that shareholders don't always come from domestic investors.

There is a cross-pollination of ideas that reaches deep into the domestic economy. Quality concepts and just-in-time inventory systems came from Japan, for example. Israel's Checkpoint Software protects more than half the Internet sites used by American business. Other countries contributed a good deal of the technology now an integral part of domestic business.

To function competitively, today's accountant and lawyer must be aware of these changes in the clients' businesses.

Today's professional must recognize that today's client knows that there are options. In the past, client loyalty was a tradition, free from intrusion from professional competitors. *Bates* changed all that. Competition moved the reins of the relationship from the professional to the client. It educated the client, who was once willing to accept credentials and skills unquestioningly. Not anymore. Today's client knows what he or she wants and knows the right questions to ask to get it. Yesterday's client could accept a larger measure of client *relationship*. Today's—and tomorrow's—client demands more *service* than *relationship*. For the sophisticated client, golf and basketball tickets are not enough. Clients may enjoy the perks, but in the end, quality of service counts.

While there may ultimately be a shift back to trusting the professional unquestioningly, it will be difficult to overcome the effects of the scandals of 2002 and 2003, in which not only companies, but lawyers and accountants were culpable for the adverse affects of those scandals. And while it's true that only a very small portion of lawyers and accountants were involved, the adverse effect on the entire profession was chilling. Thus, today's client is more wary. The professional will have to do more than ever before to inspire trust.

The time is past when just the presence of the professional was its own comfort factor. It's long been believed that the concept of *the professional* was so exalted, and so trusting, that people accepted advice unquestioningly. No more. The scandals of 2002 and 2003 seem to have bred a diminished—if unwarranted—respect for professionals. Traditionally, professional services have been a seller's market. Now they are a buyer's market.

This new perception of professionals plays out in a number of ways . . .

- Because clients are more sophisticated in the ways of the law and accounting, they no longer accept the advice of the professional without questioning, challenging, demanding more reasoning and detail.

- Because of the complexity of business today, clients demand that their professionals know more about the clients' business and industry than ever before.

- Professional services always function best when trust is at the heart of the relationship, but the corporate scandals of recent years have eroded that trust. That trust must now be regenerated. "The key to professional success," notes David Maister and his coauthors in their book, *The Trusted Advisor,* "is the ability to earn the trust and confidence of clients. Creating trust is what earns the right to influence clients; trust is also at the root of client satisfaction and loyalty." And, note the authors, the workings of trust are more important in the new economy than in the old.

- Where once the narrow structures of a profession were sufficient to serve clients, clients now demand a broader spectrum of capabilities. The more broadly educated and well-rounded professional is the one with the greater advantage in meeting the needs of today's client. Clients demand that lawyers know more than the law and that accountants know more than the basic skills of accounting.

- For the professional, competition is now a fact of life. Clients understand that there are many qualified professionals in each discipline—that they have a choice. It falls to the lawyer and the accountant to attempt to influence that choice—to demonstrate a firm's capabilities as better than those of the competitors'. In other words, to market better.

- Sophisticated clients know the difference between marketing promises and professional services delivery. While clients have always enjoyed the fuzzy warmth of client relations, today's client wants—needs—more service and solutions to go with that warmth.

And so today's law and accounting firm clients are no longer the naive, accepting businesspeople or individuals, gratefully receiving the professional's mystical process or words of wisdom. Today's client is a participant in his or her legal or accounting process. Any accountant or lawyer who isn't willing to accept this new relationship—this new demand for participatory skills—is going to lose out to the professional who does accept the new paradigm of client service.

3

ARE WE A CLIENT-CENTRIC FIRM YET?

Organizing to Meet Client Needs

Who the hell wants to hear actors talk?
—Harry M.Warner (1927), Warner Brothers Pictures

Silent film mogul Harry Warner's question was answered by the public, which is why movies now talk, and do it in color. As Warner's miscalculation teaches us, it's the public that decides. And it's the clientele that defines the professional practice, not the other way around. Obviously, then, there's no professional practice that's irrelevant to the needs of its clients. But for professional firms to be relevant to their clients' needs, particularly in a complex economic environment, they have to be properly organized to meet those needs. The imperative to organize is further compounded by the fact that in today's economic environment, client needs are constantly changing.

DEFINING A PRACTICE

Defining a practice is a process that goes well beyond simply being a professional firm—a collection of professionals whose services and professional skills are available to those who need the services. That process goes farther than merely getting and serving clients, and can make the difference between success and failure in the marketplace. This is particularly true in the new competitive arena, in which consumers of professional services are more knowledgeable about how the services function, and are more aware that they have choices in selecting professionals to serve them.

Defining a practice begins with understanding the needs of the clients in your market, and then structuring your firm to meet those needs. It's not an abstract exercise—it can be done effectively only in terms of the prospective clientele.

There are two choices for a professional firm in today's competitive environment. A firm can allow itself to grow by randomly accumulating clients, and then fitting the services to meet their needs. It's haphazard growth, in which the practice becomes shapeless, the service capability arbitrary, and success can be achieved only by luck or labor that's harder than it has to be.

Or a firm can structure itself by meticulously defining its market, focusing, defining, or developing its skills in terms of the needs of that market, and then projecting its ability to meet those needs. It is the firm with this kind of focus, this kind of understanding of the value of being relevant to the needs of its market, that succeeds and grows.

WHAT IS A MARKET?

It's interesting that almost every textbook on marketing will give a different definition of a market. Ultimately, these definitions all boil down to...

- A market is a cohesive group of consumers—individuals, remember—with a generally common need or opportunity, and for whom your services are appropriate and needed, or whose members can be persuaded that your services are needed, and that your services are preferable to those of your competitors.
- A market is a cohesive group of consumers that can be reached by common media.

A market can be defined by demographics, by industry, by type of problem, or by opportunities that demand specific skills. It can be broad or narrow; it can be small or large, depending upon the criteria you meticulously define.

Keep in mind that with notable exceptions, professional services can't be sold to people who don't have an immediate need for those services. Marketing professional services, then, is generally not focused primarily on simply selling the services—it addresses instead the attempt to persuade prospective clients that you can better serve their needs than can your competitors. *Simply describing the services you perform is not the major objective of marketing. Marketing is the process to communicate your firm's greater ability to deliver these services.* The differences between marketing a product and marketing a professional service firm are what make the definition of marketing for professionals distinctively different from other forms of marketing.

THE ELEMENTS OF A MARKET

How do a group of prospective clients become a viable market? Beyond the broader definition of a market are a number of specific factors that turn a group from a collection of prospective clients with a spectrum of needs into a focused and cohesive group that can be reached more effectively—and cost effectively—with a sound marketing message. These factors include...

- *A common need for specific skills.* For example, tax services, personal financial planning, litigation, negotiation, corporate or regulatory compliance, and so forth.

- *A common industry*, such as real estate, manufacturing, financial services, retail, and so forth.

- *A geographic area.* How far are you willing to travel to serve clients?

- *Demographics,* such as age, economic category, local economy, and so forth.

- *Common media,* capable of reaching the greatest number of prospective clients in your chosen market, including availability of mailing lists.

- *A practical size,* including enough prospective clients in the market group to offer an acceptable return on investment in marketing to that group.

- *Competition.* Some potential markets are saturated by competition with significant market share, thereby increasing the difficulty and cost of penetrating that market. The size and intensity of competition directly affects your marketing strategy.

- *Economic maturity or viability of the prospective clientele.* For example, what percentage of the prospects are in declining, static, or emerging industries?

- *Cost and return on investment.* How much will it cost you to reach and penetrate that market? What kind of pricing structure will that market bear? What is the potential return on your investment in penetrating that market?

- *What are your skills to serve that market?* Are they currently adequate? Will more or other skills be needed? If so, how will you acquire them, and at what cost?

- *What opportunities do you see* to serve a market that may not be immediately profitable? For example, is there a new technology (such as genomics) that is not yet a market, but may ultimately be a good one? Or are there companies you are willing to serve below cost because they are flagships to other companies in that industry?

These factors are often intertwined, and each must be considered in order to define the market as a whole.

Obviously, no professional, no matter how skilled, no matter how general your practice or experienced you are, can be all things to all people. The experienced and specialized divorce lawyer would not likely want to take on an intellectual property matter. The dedicated tax accountant might be wise to stay away from a regulated utility audit.

Not knowing your market in great detail can lead to a vast amount of wasted effort, time, and money. The definition of a market, remember, is not what you have to sell, but what individuals in the market want to buy. Generalizations, such as *the middle market, high-net-worth individuals, real estate industry*, are too broad. For example, if you perceive a market for *high-net-worth individuals*, some clarifying definitions are in order. How will you define *high net worth*? Some practitioners might say, individuals with net worth from $500,000 to $1 million, while others might define the market from $10 million up.

DEFINING PROSPECTS

In viewing each of the prospects in a market, it helps to understand that not all prospects in a category are the same. By understanding the differences, you can use your marketing capabilities more effectively, and can allocate different degrees of effort—and urgency—to prospects in each category. The urgency in chasing down a lead from a reliable source is greater than it is for a client you're carefully nurturing for the future. Let's look at the categories, in order of the urgency of your response.

- *The prospect at the threshold.* This is the prospect who's hooked, but not yet reeled in. It could be a problem deciding between you and several of your competitors, or a failure to understand the real nature of the prospect's problem. The trick is to find out what the holdup is, and respond to it. Sometimes a simple note with an article or advisory you've written on the subject works. It keeps a gentle pressure on the prospect, and reinforces your expertise. Sometimes the best thing to do is simply to ask. Ask about the impediments to a decision and ask about the prospect's problems. The more you understand about the prospect's needs, the better you are able to demonstrate your ability to meet those needs.

   One caution. Don't rely on cosmetics or the age of your firm ("...*a legal tradition since the ice age*"). Focus on the prospect's problem and your ability to solve that problem, and address those needs.

- *The serendipity prospect.* This is the prospect who virtually walks in off the street. It helps to know why that prospect chose your door rather than another's to walk through. You can then reinforce the reasons for that choice. What is the problem that brought the prospect to your door? This is what marketing is supposed to do—bring prospects into your sights. For this category, then, it's a straight selling situation.

- *The "Charley asked me to call you" prospect.* You call, and clarify why Charley thought you could help. You can usually tell in the first few minutes how imminent this prospect is. The call might lead to a meeting. If the prospect's problem or needs have materialized, then you can immediately call him or her a hot prospect, and you can address the problem. If the problem isn't imminent, then you move the prospect into the next category—*I'm here when you need me.*

- *The "I'm here when you need me" prospect.* This is the prospect who doesn't need you now, but will sometime in the future. Pursuing this prospect requires low—but consistent—maintenance. A periodic mailing of clippings, articles, reprints, and advisories helps—the steady stream of material that keeps prospects aware of your knowledge of their problems and your interest in serving them. When that prospect's need for your services surfaces, yours is the first firm that comes to mind, and the prospect moves quickly to the first category—*the prospect on the threshold.*

- *The "I don't know you—you don't know me" prospect.* Here is where your future lies—the prospect who should be your client because you can help, who fits into your long-range plan, who represents the kind of clientele you're striving to build. What you want to do with this prospect, in order of importance and a time line, is...

  ○ Build name recognition.

  ○ Establish your capabilities, particularly in the client's industry and business.

  ○ Ultimately, meet—at which time you begin the selling process and move the client to *The prospect at the threshold.*

For this prospect, this is a process that can take a year or more, unless the configuration of the stars (the prospect's problems and your ability to help) falls into line sooner than that. You can convert this prospect with a routine of mailings (four to six weeks apart), which, with a good mailing list structure, becomes almost automatic and low maintenance. Simple notes with simple enclosures do it. Then, at some point (after three to six such mailings), you call and say, "We've been sending you material for a while now. By now you know a great deal about us, but we know too little about you. Can we meet next Thursday so that I can learn more about you and your company?" If the mailings have been simple and low pressure, and informative, as many as 50 percent of your calls should result in a meeting.

CRITERIA FOR GROWTH

A significant element of organizing to meet client needs is to determine those criteria that are necessary for a firm's success. Obviously, each firm and its partners will have different objectives for the firm—some that are structural and financial; some that are responsive to the partners' personal desires. The objectives affect the way each of the criteria is applied. Defining these criteria is important to reach the firm's objectives. Understanding these criteria is necessary to measuring the firm's success in terms of its objectives.

The criteria are neither vague nor arbitrary, although each of them is affected by the others, depending upon your firm and your objectives. They are the building blocks to create a successful firm. They include . . .

- *Market share.* Market share reflects the portion of business that the firm has in a given market. For example, a CPA firm that specializes in law firm management issues knows that there are 1,500 law firms in its geographic market. The firm currently serves 85 firms. The firm has 5.6 percent market share. The firm can now determine if it wants to increase that share, or devote its efforts to other markets.

- *Geographic reach.* This defines the geographic boundaries you feel your firm can serve. Your geographic reach may also include the number of offices you need to serve that defined geographic area.

- *Profitability.* Ultimately, the size of your practice is irrelevant if you are not profitable. But the degree of profitability is a matter of choice. You can choose any degree of profitability you like, if you're prepared to define your practice in terms of costs, the amount you are willing to invest to develop the business and to serve it, pricing, and the margins you believe are appropriate to your practice and to the market you serve. Client profitability measures the net profit of each client. It can also measure the profitability by target segment or practice group. One firm we know tracks the cost to acquire each new client by partner. This includes both the hard costs (proposal preparation cost, etc.) and opportunity cost (the time spent to acquire the prospect).

  Don't confuse client satisfaction with profitability. Beware the partner who gets the highest client satisfaction results in the firm, but with the lowest realization on work and the highest accounts receivable with the greatest number of days outstanding. Just because clients are satisfied doesn't necessarily mean that they are profitable for your firm.

That is why firms need to measure profitability on a client-by-client basis. It does no good to be so client obsessed that you put the firm in financial ruin. The more you measure client profitability, the more you can determine which market segments are more profitable than others and why. Entering each professional's cost into your time and billing system is the way to determine client profitability. Ron Baker, in *The Professional's Guide to Value Pricing*, observes that there are two elements that make professional services firms more profitable. "It is the price they charge for the engagement that is the first-arm profit driver, and the second-arm driver is the cost of resources—primarily labor—that go into producing the outcome," he says. "Entering each professional's cost into your time and billing system is the first step in capturing and determining."

- *Client acquisition.* This is the rate at which you attract or win new clients. This is a measurement that captures the amount of new business you brought in from targeted segments. There are several ways to track this. Most firms track the revenue that comes from new targeted clients or the number of new clients from the target market. As with any measure, care must be taken. A firm could be acquiring clients with high revenue but very little profit. That is why it's important to look at all measures.

- *Client retention.* This is the rate at which you retain or maintain ongoing relationships with clients. The longer a firm can keep a professional service provider on the engagement, the more profitable the engagement becomes. The longer a firm can keep a client, the more profitable the firm becomes. Most firms will want to measure client retention year over year. A low client retention ratio would normally indicate that the firm is not organized to meet the needs of its clients. If a firm loses 10 percent of its clients each year, in five years 50 percent of former clients are on the street talking about your service (or lack thereof) to other potential clients, referral sources, and even existing clients. Firms can't afford to have that type of negative publicity. High turnover is also very costly because higher client profitability tends to come in later years.

- *Client satisfaction.* The aim of good client relationships, built on good client service, is client satisfaction. If clients aren't satisfied that their problems are being solved, that you aren't of one mind with their business and plans, then all your skills and professionalism are for naught. You will lose those clients to a firm that can satisfy them. Client satisfaction can drive client retention and future client acquisitions, and obviously has an impact on client profitability. Client satisfaction measures tell you how well the firm is doing with its target markets. Client satisfaction forms the basis of the other core measurements.

Firms have been measuring client satisfaction for some 20 years now. While we talk of measurement in Chapter 16, it should be noted here that client satisfaction is dynamic—it can change like the weather, which is why it should be measured and addressed frequently, and adjustments made as measurement indicates.

- *Number of partners.* The size of your firm, including the number of partners, is a function of the kind of practice you want to have and the partners' personal wishes, as well as the profitability and return on investment of each partner. A real estate or tax practice requires a different size firm than does a matrimonial or SEC practice. It's not realistic to plan for the size of the firm without understanding this.

- *Wallet share.* This indicates what portion of the clients' dollars is being spent with your firm. For example, say a firm finds that each of its 85 clients is spending an average 80 percent of its consulting dollars with the firm. That amount would indicate that there is not too much upside in trying to get more business from the existing clients. The firm might be better off putting its marketing energies into getting new clients.

- *Emerging/static/declining.* There is a matrix (*see Chapter 4*) to help you measure the number of clients you currently have in industries that are emerging, static, or declining. The matrix helps in planning by analyzing your practice in terms of the number of clients you currently serve in each of the three categories. While most firms have clients in each of the categories, the future of the firm may depend upon having a preponderance of clients in emerging industries, and fewer firms in static or declining ones. The matrix of your current clientele tells you where your marketing efforts must be directed.

Finally, your growth is a function of the degree to which your clients feel that you can bring value to their businesses. It should be noted, too, that for all the importance of client relations, it's ultimately client service that generates value.

VALUE

What is the value of your service to your clients? Only the client can determine that value, which translates into the fee that he or she is willing to pay you. Ultimately, that determination is measured by the client's perception of benefit.

Value, which is often subjective, can still be defined in business terms. Richard C. Reed, in *Win-Win Billing Strategies: Alternatives That Satisfy Your Clients and You,* defines value as "the measure of what benefits the client perceives have resulted" from the professional's effort. The emphasis is on the word *benefit.*

August Aquila, in his book, *Breaking the Paradigm,* wrote, "Client centered firms realize that they have to understand the client's perception of the firm's services and the benefits they receive from the services. A basic shift in our focus needs to take place. The shift is from the services we provide to the benefit the client receives."

From the client's point of view, that benefit begins with an accurate understanding of his or her problems or needs, moves to a perception of not just the solution, but how the solution will help, and finally, the degree to which the professional firm contributes to that solution.

In determining an accurate understanding of a problem and perceiving a solution, the successful professional uses skills to get to the core of the problem, and to help define a beneficial solution. But ultimately, it's the client that determines value.

At the same time, there are significant activities and attitudes that the professional brings to bear to enhance benefit and value. They are based on service. Real service, and not just a perception of it. It begins with an intensive understanding of the client and the client's needs, followed by enhancing the client's perception of the professional's ability to serve those needs. The professional accomplishes this with . . .

- Depth and breadth of the services
- Quality of personnel, including an effective team
- Technical skills
- Understanding of the client's business and industry
- Attention to the client in every way that's relevant to the client's needs
- Sensitivity to changes in the client's business
- Timeliness in delivering service
- Price
- Service quality
- Adding value beyond the original engagement
- Cost effectiveness

The concept of *quality* is often cited as consequential to a successful professional firm. But realistically, quality is inherent in all professionalism. A manufacturer may choose to make a cheaper version of a product, but there is no such thing as a cheaper version of an audit, or litigation, or any professional service. Any professional who tries to cut corners is not only violating professional canons of ethics, but is subject to civil or regulatory sanctions.

REPUTATION

The chastity of Caesar's wife was a benchmark for virtue, and so too is integrity and honesty a given for the successful professional. Reputation is earned. It's earned by being skillful, reliable, professional in the classic sense of the word, and scrupulously honest. You can't fake integrity.

The word *image*, so often used in this context, is a dangerous word and concept. It implies that manipulating symbols can control a perception of your firm. Not so. The acoustics of the business community are terrific, and so what you are speaks so loud that I can't hear what you say you are. If you don't like the way in which you're perceived, by either your clients or your competitors, you don't change that with a public relations campaign—you change what you are.

The problem with pursuing *image* is that you're spending your time and money on the wrong things. The best way to improve your reputation is to improve your skills, your reliability, your professionalism, and your integrity.

RELATIONSHIP

A significant difference between marketing a product and marketing a service is that if I sell you a product, the product stays and I go. If I sell you a service, I stay. There may be 1,000 people behind the manufacture of a tube of toothpaste, but the interface between the company and the consumer is the tube of toothpaste. The interface between the client and the professional firm is the individual who serves the client. (This, incidentally, is why an increasing number of manufacturers are developing service concepts. IBM, for example, not only makes the machine, it offers consulting services on how best to use the machine in a business context.)

And if I stay, I want to be a good guest. That, essentially, is what good client relationships are about. Social skills. But social skills that translate into business. People enjoy doing business with people who are professional, knowledgeable, and congenial. If each client meeting is pleasant, it is more likely to be productive. And if each client contact is congenial and productive, then more people will want to do business with you.

Defining how and what you want the client relationship to be is a significant element in the success of your practice. Consistency is a must, most certainly in professionalism in the way in which clients are treated by everyone in the firm—whether the client is dealing with a receptionist, mailroom personnel, or a partner.

While professionalism and courtesy are assumed, here are a few attributes of good client relations...

- Courtesy, of course
- Personal sensitivity and respect, in both dress and personal name recognition
- Responsiveness and timely delivery of services
- Timely access to appropriate staff and partners
- Promptness to meetings, and prompt response to inquiries
- Good personal and timely communications
- Team approach and support
- A consistent sense of personal service

CULLING YOUR CLIENT BASE

It's a basic tenet of marketing that it serves not merely to acquire clients, but to shape a practice to a firm's desires. This means recognizing that not every client fits the practice.

As you begin to integrate marketing into your firm, you realize that everything that you do, every decision that you make, is ultimately done because of the type of client you've identified as belonging to your target segments.

Obviously, you'll want to evaluate clients that are not only unprofitable, but show little hope of being profitable in the foreseeable future. Other clients may be in industries you no longer want to serve, because they are inconsistent with the directions in which you want your practice to go. There are clients who may be too obstreperous, and though they may be profitable, they may be too disruptive of your firm's operations or too abusive to your staff.

There may be clients that are currently unprofitable, but fit the pattern of your firm's plans by virtue of their role in an emerging industry, or because they bring a new technology.

The point is that culling clients for the right reason, like pruning trees to improve the shape of their growth, is a prudent business practice. It should be done with the larger picture in mind.

GETTING ORGANIZED

If you are to shape your firm to meet your definition of what that firm should be, if you are prepared to organize your firm to address and serve the needs and opportunities of your defined markets, there are useful questions to ask yourself and your partners that will help. These questions might include...

- Which services are really needed by this market?
- What is the urgency of these services? When a client receives a tax audit notice from the IRS, or is being sued in a product liability matter, you can be sure there is urgency. If the client is planning a new pension plan, the urgency will be less, although the need for your services is not diminished.
- Are these services needed by the market, or are you offering them simply because those are the services you offer?
- Can the market be served by new services that address the changing needs of your clients?
- What do we offer that our competitors don't?
- What are they offering that we don't?
- How will we delineate and distinguish our firm from others? What is our position to offer the market? (See Chapter 5.)
- How can we best deliver our services in a way that meets our clients' needs?
- What is our service strategy?
- What can we do to ensure client satisfaction and to ensure that we sustain a long-term relationship?

Answering questions like these should lead you deeper into the process of keeping clients at the core. Given a clear view of the firm you want to be, this process will bring you closer to that vision.

4

NOW, HERE'S MY PLAN...

Defining the Right Client for You

*Those people who develop the ability to continuously acquire new
and better forms of knowledge that they can apply to their work and
to their lives will be the movers and shakers in our society for the
indefinite future.*

—Brian Tracy, American trainer, speaker, author

There's an old joke about the man who was on his hands and knees under a street-
light, looking for his contact lens. A stranger asks, "Where were you standing when
you dropped it?"

"In that dark alley, back there."

"If you dropped it there, why are you looking here?"

"Because," the man replied, "the light's better here."

And there you have a classic example of an all-too-common marketing and
strategic planning syndrome. Looking for clients in the wrong place.

Strategic planning begins with a market analysis, and not, as conventional wisdom has it, with the firm's ambitions, financial goals, or skills. Without an understanding of the market for a firm's practice and expertise, the firm's goals are little
more than dreams. This becomes particularly acute in today's complex market for
professional services, as well as in an increasingly intense competitive arena. The
tendency to build a strategic plan based upon the dreams and ambitions of the partners, rather than on a realistic analysis of where the clients are, is like fishing in a
mud puddle because it's easier than driving to the ocean.

In fact, despite the traditional view of the independent and exalted professional,
it's the client, not the professional, who's at the core of every practice. The success
and growth of any practice, then, is a function of understanding the client base, the
potential client base, and the firm's access to that base. But how do you define the
right client for you?

31

It's here that targeted marketing serves best, by going directly—and efficiently—to the likeliest prospects, and the ones that can best serve the firm's own practice objectives. For the smaller firm, directly targeting the marketing effort to a specific group—whether that group be geographic, economic, or one that's defined by a common need for the services a firm can supply—is frequently the most effective and cost-effective way to market. For the larger firm, with the means to mount a broader marketing campaign as a backdrop, targeted marketing is equally effective and powerful to focus the message of that campaign to a specific audience.

While target marketing is not a new process—indeed, many progressive firms do it in a number of ways—it's not generally used as part of a firm's strategic planning. Part of the reason for this is that the strategic planning process itself is, for most firms, just emerging.

What can be most difficult, though, is the process of determining the target group. This is crucial, and key to successful marketing for any firm. Without this deterioration, time, effort, and money can be wasted.

There are several approaches to finding the target group. The very knowledgeable consultant Sally Schmidt suggests these criteria...

- Whether the market represents a realistic target (for example, building a sports law practice in a community without a professional franchise).

- The perceptions of the target market (for example, in highly competitive industries, clients may not want their lawyers to work with like companies).

- The strength of the competition (for example, does anyone "own" the market?).

- The ability to reach the market (for example, are there publications, organizations, lists, or other vehicles that will allow the group to identify and contact the targets?).

- The size of the market. For example, is the market segment sufficiently large (for example, transportation vs. railroads) or, conversely, should there be additional segmentation within the group (for example, shopping centers vs. commercial real estate)?

A new way to determine the target market as part of the strategic plan is the *Practice Profile Matrix* developed by Bruce Marcus©.

Some years ago, Marcus developed a matrix based on some work done by General Electric. That matrix is a particularly powerful tool in understanding the health of any law or accounting firm. It is even more valuable in strategic planning for a law or accounting firm of any size, because of its flexibility in profiling the practice in a way that helps define new pools of prospective clients.

The big international accounting firms measured their success in terms of the number of Fortune 500 companies they had as clients. On one axis, the existing clientele of Fortune 500 companies was sorted into three size categories. On the other axis, the clientele was sorted into three growth categories—declining industries, static industries, and emerging industries.

By filling in the boxes for each of the Big Eight firms, we discovered that the most successful of the firms had a preponderance of Fortune 500 clients in emerging industries, and the least successful firms had a preponderance of clients in declining or static industries.

That same matrix, adapted to a planning mode, can accomplish two valuable things for any firm. It can map a firm's health, and it can indicate where the new business effort must be directed.

It works this way...

A firm makes two subjective determinations that are significant to it—the size of its clients, by any measure (*sales volume, fee size, profitability, etc.*), and the designation of each of its clients in each of the three categories (*emerging, static, declining*). Large firms will likely have different criteria than small firms.

By sorting each of its clients into the appropriate box in the matrix, a picture of the firm's present condition in its business environment becomes clear.

Because the profile of every law or accounting firm is different, the determination of each category on each axis is different, and to a degree, subjective. For example, the range of company size can be within billions of dollars for one firm's clients, or hundreds of thousands for the smaller firm.

The categories on the other axis are also subject to a number of variables that can be flexible. Industries that are emerging, static, or declining change with changing economic conditions (particularly in a global economy). A few years ago, for example, the dot-com industries were emerging, as was the telecommunications industry. That, obviously is no longer the case. Economic conditions, locally, nationally, and worldwide, may cause a static industry to either decline or to increase in importance and growth potential. An industry such as biotechnology may be emerging, but not necessarily in the near term.

But industry opportunities are measurable both nationally and locally, and what might be an emerging or declining industry nationally may be just the opposite locally. The real estate development market may be static nationally, but emerging locally. Good business judgment counts for a lot.

Ideally, an economist is the best source for this information. But for the smaller firm, there are other reliable sources. The Internet is a major source of industrial information, and most companies today have their own web sites. *Business Week* and *Fortune* frequently have articles on the nature of specific industries. Publications such as *The Wall Street Journal* and *The New York Times* regularly report on the progress of specific industries. Libraries have up-to-date data. Regional and national Chambers of Commerce and industry associations are a major source. Assessing which industries are growing and which are not is not too difficult, and worth the effort to seek the information out.

In fact, no business—and no professional practice—can be managed without some understanding of the business climate in which it functions. Assessing the industries for the *Practice Profile Matrix* is just one more step.

With these factors in mind, you can shape the *Practice Profile Matrix* to serve a firm in strategic planning. And most significantly, it can be an effective tool in determining the target groups for targeted marketing.

Following is an example of a firm that's significantly healthy, with the bulk of its practice in the second price category in emerging industries. For the future, the firm may want to target more companies in emerging industries in that, or possibly the higher-price, categories.

Firm A...

	$X–X1	$X2–X3	$X4–X5
Emerging	***	******	**
Static	*	****	*****
Declining	**	***	****

Another firm might find the following configuration, with a preponderance of clients in static or declining industries. While that firm might currently be profitable, its weakness in the future is foretold. This matrix offers a warning that it needs to target its marketing efforts to more firms in the emerging industries, of whatever size it's capable of serving.

Firm B...

	$X–X1	$X2–X3	$X4–X5
Emerging	*	***	*
Static	*****	*******	********
Declining	****	******	********

This matrix format is also useful as a competitive intelligence tool, if it's possible to develop a matrix for competitive firms, by giving you a sense of how your firm is doing, compared to your competitors.

There are, of course, some caveats...

- The definitions of emerging, declining, and static industries are subjective, in that they vary from market to market, as well as nationally. Carefully define the foundations for your own criteria. Consistency helps.

- Understand that the economy—internationally, nationally, regionally, and locally—is dynamic. Random events and elements can change the dynamic at any time. The best way to deal with that dynamic is alertness. As we've seen, today's emerging industry can become tomorrow's declining industry (for example telecommunications and dot-com start-ups).

- The size figures used in the matrix vary from firm to firm, and are predicated on each firm's experience and ability to deal with clients of specific sizes. A firm geared to dealing with local retailers will use one set of figures; a firm serving national companies uses a different range.

- The *Practice Profile Matrix* doesn't suggest firing clients in declining or static industry categories. These clients may be profitable, they may help offset the cost of your staff people with special skills, they may be influential in getting other profitable clients, or they may be flagships in a particular industry. It does mean that a major expense or marketing effort to pursue other clients in those industries is not warranted.

- The matrix may also indicate where new skills are needed and investment in training in those skills warranted. More will be said about developing a learning and growth organization in Chapters 10 and 12.

- The profile of your firm shown by the matrix allows you a distinctive view of the firm, offering a number of different factors that should go into your planning.

- While the matrix was originally developed from the General Electric model for the accounting profession, it works just as well for law firms.

- In larger law or accounting firms, a different matrix would be needed for each practice group or area, as well as for the entire firm.

- Above all, your view of all elements of the *Practice Profile Matrix* must be realistic. A wish list is not a plan, fudging the sizes of your clientele fools nobody, guessing the status of the industries available to you will cost you more than doing it right, exaggerating your own sense of what your firm can do will waste your time.

- Any strategic plan, whether using the *Practice Profile Matrix* or any other kind of matrix, must be revisited frequently. Practice will lead to corrections. Conditions change. As your own business grows (or declines), you may have to rethink the elements of your plan. Anything dynamic needs attention, care, and feeding.

- While a key value of the *Practice Profile Matrix* is to improve the use of target marketing as a marketing device, other marketing activities should not be overlooked. They serve as a backdrop to target marketing, in that they enhance your name and reputation, and project your firm's values and capabilities.

Given this kind of information, long-range planning takes on a very different configuration. Rather than basing a plan on a wish list, or even an inventory of your skills, the matrix focuses on your client base in the context of the business community you serve. It is, as it should be, client-oriented.

The matrix shapes your marketing program by focusing it on specific targets and targeted companies, which means that your resources are better utilized and costs are better controlled.

Long-range planning for professional firms is one of the least understood activities of professional firm management, which is why so many plans are misdirected and focused on factors that prevent the plan from becoming a working tool.

This matrix approach works, and has been demonstrated in practice for both accounting and law firms. It allows you to fish where the fish are, and not in swimming pools.

START-UP PRACTICE OR SMALL FIRM

Small firms and start-up practices face a real dilemma when it comes to defining what clients they want to work with. There is a substantive problem that these firms first face—it's called *survival*. Firms have bills to pay, and any paying client looks good. Marketing at this stage is often called *caveman marketing*. The practitioner goes out, gets a client, pays some bills, and when bills start to pile up again, goes out hunting for another client, like the cavemen who went hunting when they got hungry.

The sooner a firm or sole practitioner can define the right client, the sooner it will be able to move into a growth mode. Here is a list of questions that you should ask yourself in defining the right client for you ...

- What types of firms or individuals do I want to work with?
- Are the owners the type of people I will enjoy working with?
- Are the industries those that I have a real interest in?
- Are the client's needs and my talents in sync?
- Will I want to travel throughout the state, country, or world?

- Does the market represent a realistic target (for example, building a sports law practice in a community without a professional franchise)?

- How clearly do I perceive the target market (for example, in highly competitive industries, clients may not want their lawyers to work with like companies)?

- What's the strength of the competition (for example, does anyone *own* the market?)?

- Am I able to reach the market (for example, are there publications, organizations, lists, or other vehicles that will allow the group to identify and contact the targets)?

- What's the size of the market? For example, is the niche sufficiently large (for example, transportation vs. railroads) or, conversely, should there be additional segmentation within the group (for example, shopping centers vs. commercial real estate)?

- And ultimately, how can I serve these clients profitably?

Sally Schmidt, of Schmidt Marketing, Inc., points out in her newsletter to clients that "McKinsey and Company reported that firms that are perceived to be among the top three within a market niche get the opportunity to 'sell' 70% of the time. Opportunities for the firm perceived to be fourth drop to 40%. Yet while the concepts of niche marketing, target marketing and segmentation seem obvious to marketers, they still require a great deal of effort to implement in law firms."

"Sometimes," Schmidt says, "the best way to get a good idea implemented is to start small. Instead of reshuffling the entire firm into new marketing teams or creating a dozen target groups, the firm might consider identifying a willing 'pilot' group or two. After working with the lawyers who are most interested to shape and implement a focused plan, the enthusiasm generated from the resulting successes will undoubtedly spread to the rest of the firm."

A well-conceived group, Schmidt notes, properly structured and staffed, makes marketing a snap. "It allows the firm to identify the places it needs to have a presence (e.g., media, trade or professional organizations), craft messages that resonate with a particular audience, and create marketing forums or vehicles that are enthusiastically received by the targets. The resulting marketing plan will position the team so the firm makes the 'short list' for consideration. It will also focus the lawyers [*and accountants*] on relationships that lead to business, such as clients who can be introduced to a broader range of firm services, potential referral sources for the particular work, and prospects to be developed."

PART III

MAKING YOUR VISION A REALITY

5

I CAN SEE YOUR FUTURE
FROM HERE

Vision? A Working Tool?

Vision is the ability to see opportunities, and the will and the capability to seize them.

—Bruce W. Marcus

There is no concept so dangerous as one that appears the most simple. One such concept, in managing a professional firm, is *vision*. Most firm managers have an idea of where they want to take their firms. The danger is that they call that idea a *vision*, without really being able to articulate it. They hang it on a rack, like an old coat, and forget about it.

Too bad, because a vision, used properly, is an invaluable management tool.

It's valuable if it isn't a vague, unarticulated dream (*"I'd like to have the biggest firm in the region"*), or if it's not based in reality (*"My partner and I would like to be global by this time next year"*). A vision isn't a wish, or something that can be made to come true by waving a wand.

A vision isn't a mission statement, which may be the worst invention in the history of marketing and management. (*"Our mission is to give the best client service possible"*), to which the response is, *"Don't speak of love—show me."* A vision certainly isn't a vision *statement*, which can be as hollow as a drum, designed only to persuade somebody (Your partners? Your clients? Your prospective clients?) that you run a high-class operation. It doesn't work.

Nor is a vision a business plan.

Vision is the ability to see opportunities, and the will and the capability to seize them.

A vision is a useful management tool if there's a blueprint to accomplish it. It's useful if it's realistic, and if you're willing to take the arduous and meticulous steps

41

to make it a reality. It's a guide to developing a business plan—and a marketing plan—that accomplishes the vision.

A vision must be rooted in the realm of reality, or if you believe you can pull off a miracle, in the miraculous.

A good working vision starts with a clear understanding of the kind of firm you want to be, measured in terms of . . .

- Your partners' personal conception of what they want from the practice, collectively and as individuals
- The investment you and your partners are willing to make, not just in dollars, but in time and effort
- The kind of clientele—and industries—you intend to serve
- The kind of satisfaction you want, individually and collectively, from your practice
- Your understanding of performance levels you mean to sustain to serve your current and prospective clientele
- Your understanding of how you mean to be perceived by your clients, and what you are prepared to do to enhance that perception.
- Your view of staffing, and staffing skills, and the quality of work you're most comfortable with
- Your ability to manage the firm to seize opportunities

The responses to these factors define a vision that you and your partners can enthusiastically pursue, and make a reality. They help define the objectives that must be reached in order for the vision to become a reality.

OBJECTIVES

Objectives, like visions, must be concrete and realistic, if they are to have any value at all. Not wishes—save those for birthday cakes—but goals to be achieved to make a vision a reality. Well-formulated objectives are the next step in making a vision a working tool for a firm's growth and success. It's crucial, then, that the objectives be precisely defined, in terms of the realistic ability of a practice to meet them. They are, in fact, business decisions. No strategic plan—nor any marketing plan—can be developed without a clear view of objectives. After all, if you don't know where you're going, how do you know how to get there?

DEFINING FIRM OBJECTIVES

In defining firm or practice objectives, two specific elements are paramount…

- *Market.* There are three aspects of a market that must be considered—its needs, its size, and its location—and all three must be viewed carefully in formulating objectives. What are the parameters of the market's needs—and opportunities—that you're prepared to serve effectively? Where is the market going, and are you in tune with it? How large a market can you realistically serve? What geographical limitations are realistic? How do you plan to stay relevant to a market's changing needs? Today, marketing is as important an element of firm management as is any other.

- *Firm environment.* Nothing—not even profitability—is more important than the kind of firm you are or want to be. Without a firm environment that's satisfying and fulfilling to its partners and staff, there will be no sustained growth or profitability.

With these two elements defined, consider, then…

- *Size of the firm.* Businesses rarely grow substantially by accident. Business growth is almost invariably a conscious decision by its partners or owners, who then take steps to implement that decision. It should be recognized that in order to plan to contain growth, or to grow larger, determining size must be a conscious decision. Nor is size arbitrary. Determining size is not merely arbitrarily choosing a numerical count; growth is a function of the ability to serve the needs of a market, to staff appropriately, and to use staff productively.

- *Time frame.* The ability of a firm to meet its objectives must be defined within a realistic time frame.

- *Profitability.* Profitability is as much a function of margins as it is of volume, and so it's useful to know your costs as precisely as possible—a particularly difficult task in a professional firm. While much of a firm's profitability is measurable, the wild card is productivity. Two products made in a factory are the same. Two accountants or lawyers dealing with the same matters for the same fees produce different results at a different pace. Profitability becomes, as well, a function of the kind of service you're offering, and the kind of market you want to reach. Price, too, is a wild card in determining profitability.

- *Pricing.* Pricing is as important an element of defining a practice as is advertising or promotion. Pricing affects revenues and profitability, but it also affects positioning. For example, do you charge less and go for volume, or do you charge more and go for a more affluent clientele? What are your prices based on: costs? competition? custom? value added? In today's competitive climate, pricing is finally being recognized as a marketing function. As in other forms of marketing, pricing is often set competitively, where it had once been relatively arbitrary. New pricing concepts are slowly emerging in the professions.

• *Share of market.* When a firm is in a rapidly growing market, or functioning in an era of rapid growth, share of market is not primarily significant. Market share will come from the market. But when that market or industry slows its growth, and competition for existing business is the only possibility for growth, then share of market is crucial. If the only way to grow is to capture your competitor's clients, then obviously, your share of market grows as your competitor's diminishes.

• *Share of wallet.* How much of each client's available professional services dollar does your firm receive? Increasing the share of wallet may require you to create new services and prospects, and certainly requires you to develop an effective cross-selling culture.

• *Service concept.* As a professional service, your relations with your clients dictate that they are served personally. But even within that function, there are degrees and options. A firm may decide to give impersonal service to each client, particularly those not on retainer, or it may decide to devote a considerable amount of time and effort to client relations. It may be a 9-to-5 operation, or it may be willing to function around the clock. The service option is the firm's, but it should be made a specific choice.

• *Skills and staffing.* The decision to add or develop staff and skills is a function of both the firm's partners' own vision and the needs of the marketplace. The decision should be a specific element of defining objectives. There's always the danger, too, of successfully achieving marketing objectives too soon, thereby outrunning your ability to serve a new or growing clientele. It makes little sense to do a successful job of increasing your tax or audit business if you can't find a sufficient number of tax or audit specialists to serve your new clientele. That way lies disaster.

Consider, as well, those elements that are beyond individual control. One can't control, for example, the national economy, which can throw the best-formulated objectives awry. An accounting or legal practice can be enhanced or diminished by a new law or regulation or a new Financial Accounting Standards Board change.

Opportunities for professionals are generated or obliterated regularly. This is why objectives, whether in marketing or otherwise, are never more than guidelines that serve to define a course of action.

FORMULATING MARKETING OBJECTIVES

If the marketing program is to succeed, if the *firm* is to succeed, marketing objectives must stem from, and serve, firm objectives. They are the guides to the instruments that fulfill the firm's objectives.

Examples of marketing objectives, in this context, are...

- To change the structure of the clientele and the nature of the firm

- To get new clients, or to strengthen relationships with existing clients

- To sell new services to existing clients, as well as to new clients

- To introduce a new service or enter a new market for a specific service

- To broaden a geographic base

- To change a perception of a firm by its market

- To increase visibility in a niche or industry

Within these goals, the key elements to consider in setting marketing objectives are:

- *Publics.* The target audience must be clearly defined. But it must be defined in the context of both the market's needs and opportunities, and the service offered or planned to be offered. In any market there are several publics. There are existing clients, whose needs for service must be constantly addressed, as must be their needs for new services. There are the prospective clients, who constitute as many publics as there are services you can perform for them. Your firm may serve one public with corporate services, another in the same market group with financial services, and a third in the same market with personal financial services. The three groups may be contiguous, but each may still be separate and distinct.

  Defining a target audience is a function of determining those universal characteristics of the target group to which your services are most profitably addressed. The universal characteristics must include the ability to reach them in a uniform and economical way.

- *Client perception.* How do you want to be perceived by your clientele? Remember that marketing alone cannot develop *images*—a perception that belies reality. No marketing program can convey an image of high service at low cost if, in fact, you are not *delivering* high service at low cost. The acoustics of the marketplace are extraordinary, and what you are speaks so loudly that people can't hear what you *say* you are.

- *Time frame.* A practical and realistic time frame in which to achieve specific goals is essential to establishing marketing objectives. Marketing must be given a reasonable time to work. Unreasonable expectations, in terms of both results and time frame, are a clear danger. Rome, as every schoolchild knows, was not built in a day, and neither will your practice be built without a reasonable time to achieve marketing results.

- *Revenues and return on investment.* Presumably, the objective is to increase revenues by increasing the clientele or the services to existing clients. But at what cost? In designing a marketing program, the cost of achieving a revenues goal—the return on investment—is a primary factor.

  Merely to set an arbitrary figure or percentage increase, without asking pertinent questions about what must be spent to achieve that goal, is insufficient. Nor is the expenditure in marketing dollars alone a gauge of expected performance. The increased revenue, presumably from increased volume, must be serviced. Will new staff have to be added? How much will new staff add to expenses, in both salaries and support costs—space, secretarial and clerical help, support services, and so forth?

  It should be noted, however, that in marketing, diminished effort results in losing impact. There is no sustaining recollection by the market, no matter how effective the original marketing campaign may have been. Other competitors move in, and the value of the earlier efforts is lost.

  At the beginning of a marketing campaign, the return on the investment is smaller. But if the investment and the effort are sustained, the penetration of the effort for the same dollar improves, and so the return on investment is greater.

- *Budget.* There are a number of techniques for determining marketing budgets. But remember that in budgeting, effectiveness—and therefore return on investment—will increase as the marketing program gains in penetration.

- *Share of market.* If share of market is a significant element in your growth or competitive picture, then it must be generally quantified, and marketing plans must reflect the competitive values in your efforts.

THE FINAL TEST

The final test of the efficacy of objectives must consider…

- How realistic are the objectives? Can they be achieved? Is the market really there for what you want to offer? Can the firm really deliver what it plans to market? What will be the key obstacles the firm will face in achieving the objective?
- Is the objective measurable? When will you know that you have achieved the objective? (*See Chapter 10.*)
- Does the firm really understand the cost of meeting those objectives, in terms of staff? Dollars available? Commitment? Professional staff time? Risk of failing in any particular marketing effort or activity?
- Has the firm realistically assessed its commitment to its strategic plan, and to marketing, in terms of supporting the creative effort, the staff, and the program?
- And most importantly, does it fulfill the firm's vision? If not, think hard and twice about doing it.

Not facing these realities, not understanding what's involved in moving into the marketing arena, and not measuring effectiveness of the key processes have caused more than one firm to fail in its marketing.

Once you have developed financial, marketing, and client objectives, then you can go on to examine those internal business processes that will help you achieve them.

6

SEIZING THOSE OPPORTUNITIES

Making the Vision a Reality

*Every great work, every great accomplishment, has been brought into
manifestation through holding to the vision, and often just before the
big achievement, comes apparent failure and discouragement.*
                    —Florence Scovel Shinn, American artist

And now you have a fine vision of the future you want for your firm, and a mar-
velously defined set of objectives. How, then, do you get from where you are to
where your vision says you want to be?

The answer, of course, is a realistic and assiduously pursued marketing program.

Marketing, as we've said before, is a strange and mysterious process, particularly
for professional services. We don't know all we need to know about the market for
our services, nor exactly why people buy. (Although Larry Smith, in his superb
book *Inside/Outside*, came up with more answers than anyone has before.) We don't
know much about motivating professionals to participate in the marketing process.

What, then, do we know?

We do know that marketing is more than just the sum of the marketing tools.

We know, as well, that the differences between marketing a product and marketing a professional service are profound, and defining.

You may not be thinking of buying a motorcycle, but a good marketer may be
able to persuade you that the change in lifestyle engendered by buying one is well
worth the price. But can a lawyer who is a super salesperson persuade you, as a happily married individual, to get a divorce if you are otherwise happily married? Can
an accountant who is a marketing genius persuade you to get an audit if your bank
or the government didn't ask you to get one? Not likely. Nor does anyone wake up
in the morning and say, "What I really need today is a good audit," or "What a great

day to draw up a contract." Here lies, then, a significant difference between selling a product and selling professional services. But there's more.

If you sell me a vacuum cleaner, the vacuum cleaner stays and you go. If you sell me a service, you stay to perform that service.

The next tube of your brand of toothpaste you buy will be exactly like the last one. With each legal or accounting matter different from the last and next, and each legal or accounting matter handled differently by different professionals, where is the possibility for consistency?

We know, as well, that no two lawyers or accountants, even in the same firm, will deal with the same problem in exactly the same way. We know that no two problems faced by a client are likely to be the same from one time to the next.

Why, exactly, do these differences between selling a product and selling a professional service matter? Because when you're selling a product, you can sing the praises of its virtues. You can compare those virtues with those of your competitors. You can promise consistency and reliability of quality from one product to the next. Obviously, these are not the selling points for a professional service. Not only is making these kinds of claims not ethical, they are not provable.

The marketing program for a professional service, then, essentially precludes the product approach. It does, however, attempt to distinguish one firm from another, despite the fact that, by law and custom, most professional firms perform the same services as all the others. Still, there are differences.

Unfortunately, you can't say "We do better audits." Or "We write better contracts." What you *can* do to distinguish your firm from another, then, is to . . .

- Demonstrate skill. This is done not by making claims, but by actually exposing skills to a prospective target audience.
- Identify by market segment the target market for each service you perform.
- Clarify the kinds of problems that can be solved, or the needs that can be fulfilled, by professional accountants or lawyers.
- Build name recognition, preferably within the context of skills.
- Enhance your reputation for skill, reliability, and integrity.
- Invent a new methodology for doing the same thing. A more detailed and robust audit, for example. A method to better organize the facts for litigation. Use technology to manage information more successfully.

Ultimately, the secret to successful professional firm marketing, we know now, resides in the well-wrought and executed plan.

THE MARKETING PLAN

There are four basic elements of a marketing program designed to keep your firm relevant to the needs of your prospective clientele, and to succeed in the marketplace. While there are many ways to plan a marketing program, the most straightforward and responsive addresses these four elements...

- Define your market.
- Define your firm.
- Define your marketing tools.
- Manage your marketing tools.

The wrong direction is to begin with objectives that are more a wish than a reality, or to start with an inventory of your skills and experience, and then trying to fit those skills into a market need that may or may not exist. If the client is indeed at the core of the marketing program, then that program must begin with a clear definition and understanding of the market.

DEFINE YOUR MARKET

No, a market isn't simply everybody who might retain you. A distinctive characteristic of professional services is that people seek the services of a professional only when there is a problem, the potential for a problem, or an opportunity. The government requires an audit, or a periodic report of financial condition. Somebody wants to sue, or you want to sue somebody. A company has grown to a point where it needs better financial controls. A business deal may require a carefully drawn contract and a clear and accurate set of financial statements. And so on.

The point is that while it may be relatively easy to define a market for children's furniture or diaper services, it's not that easy to define an audience for professional services. At least because, within the canons of professional ethics, you can't create demand where there is no perceived need.

The real problem—and the real opportunity—resides in understanding how to refine and define a market and its segments, and to do it in ways that allow you and your service to be relevant to the needs of that market. This goes well beyond the superficial the general category—for example, real estate, audit, insurance, and so forth. Or, you may have a real estate practice that addresses all aspects of real estate. But you know that within that practice, developers have different legal and accounting needs than lenders, who have different needs from brokers, and so forth. What you are doing, in market segmentation, is defining a micromarket whose needs are met by your specific skills and experience.

It may be useful to consider a definition of a market. A market is . . .

- A group with a common need for a specific service
- A group that's reachable through common media
- A group that you can serve profitably

But beyond that general definition, one specific consideration may alter the nature of the market. Without that definition, all marketing activities are either clichés or exercises in futility. For example, do companies in a declining or static industry define a market in the truest sense? Is a market an abstract idea—a place or a bunch of people who buy something? Is a market a reality, or an academic abstraction?

The basic philosophy behind defining a market is that the larger market for your services is really comprised of several smaller markets, or segments, each of which is significantly different from the others. If you can define the needs or opportunities of one of those segments, and if you have a specific ability to meet those needs, then you can tailor a program to that segment.

We live in a world of specialists—so much so that the general practitioners are often competing against specialists in their own profession. The general public may go to a generalist for a simple real estate closing, but not for a complex commercial closing. Within that realm, a housing developer will likely find a professional with specific experience in real estate development, rather than a practitioner with general commercial real estate experience. Therein lies the reality of seeing the market in segments and reaching out to the market segment by segment.

Market segmentation, or *niche marketing*, as it's sometimes unfortunately called, is one of those tools of marketing that sound simple, but can really be very complicated.

In the early days of professional services marketing, we thought of it in terms of industry competence. For example, if one of your specialties is real estate law or accounting, you could market your expertise to prospective clients in the real estate industry. It's a rational idea, and when done right, it really works. Your expertise and experience are, after all, your major competitive tools.

As often happens, sad to say, people trim the shell off a sound idea to use only the idea's most superficial aspects. In the case of industry competence cum market segmentation cum niche marketing, the shell has been assiduously fostered by special interests. These are the people who produce prepackaged material, such as newsletters and brochures to which you simply add your own name. While some of this material is useful, most of it is so canned and trite, produced by people who have no real sense of the needs of specialized markets, that it turns out to be a waste of money. Moreover, your competitors have bought and are using the same material. Where's the competitive edge in that?

How can you target an effective campaign at a specific market if you don't know what the market is in the first place? And yet it's tried every day.

Consider the definition in terms of the answers to the following questions, and see where that leads you...

- Does the segment of prospective clients you see as a market have a commonality that's responsive to your service? For example, do they all want essentially the same things that you have to offer? Every business, and most individuals, need tax services. Does everybody who needs tax services need long-range tax planning? Or tax shelters? Or defense from the IRS? *The market for tax services, then, is only that segment of the population or business community that has a common need for a specific and narrowly defined service within the broader definition.*

- Is the segment of prospective clients you see as a market easily reachable and accessible with a common medium? For example, are there trade journals or other publications specifically targeted to that segment? Do they all belong to the same trade associations? *If you can't reach them easily, then they're not a market—they're a collection of isolated individuals.* You may be able to reach them individually with your message, but only at great expense. The return on investment is substantially diminished.

- If you should succeed in penetrating a specific segment of prospective clients you see as a market, what will you actually have achieved? *Will they be profitable?* Or will you have succeeded in winning the business of a bunch of buggy whip manufacturers? Is the return on investment worth the chase?

- Are you capable of serving that market if you should succeed in getting its business? *The market may indeed exist, but can you effectively meet its needs?* Will you have to add staff or learn new capabilities? Is it practical? And again, is the return on investment worth the chase?

For the astute marketer, the number of ways in which a market can be segmented is infinite. For the professional services marketer, capable of greater flexibility in adapting services to meet the needs of a dynamic market, the potential categories are extraordinary. For example...

- *Economic.* The range of economic definers, including class, incomes, and lifestyle.

- *Geographic.* The area that defines the location of the service.

- *Nature of the prospect's industry.* Every industry has different cycles, as well as other distinguishing characteristics.

- *Regulatory.* Specific groups are subject to a distinctive set of regulations.

- *Time sensitive.* Economic or other defining circumstances may put a time sensitive window of opportunity on a particular market.

- *Type of available communication.* Different groups may be susceptible to different kinds of communication, whether it be media or word of mouth.

- *Age or sex.* A demographic characteristic with its own needs and opportunities.

- *Potential profitability.* Can the group afford your services, at prices that are profitable for you?

- *Technical.* Is this market defined by some technical characteristic?

- *Potential joint venture.* Often, a market arises that is best served by a joint venture with another—and sometimes competitive—firm or company.

Does this kind of definition matter? Of course it does. Consider, for example, the cost of buying an ad in a publication of which only 10 percent of its readers can use your service. Ninety percent of your money, then, is wasted.

Consider the cost of a direct mail campaign to a market segment that can't possibly see any value in your high-priced accounting or legal services. Or that's so geographically dispersed that even if you sold them, you couldn't afford to service them.

But it all starts with point one—*Know your market.* In its entirety, and segment by segment. Know it in terms of your ability to meet each segment of the market with specific skills and experience.

And if you see a potentially profitable market segment for which you have neither the skills nor the experience, then get them. Hire them. Buy them. Or learn them. But don't compete in any market segment that you're not capable of serving. You'll lose to those who really can serve it.

DEFINE YOUR FIRM

No, you're not in the accounting or law or consulting business. You're in the client getting and keeping business. Law or accounting or consulting is part of what you do to get and keep a client.

In managing a professional firm, you have two major choices. You can either reshape your firm to meet the needs of the prospective clientele, or you can ignore the needs of the clientele, and simply run your practice predominantly with the needs of the firm in mind. The first is an exercise in growth. The second is an exercise in imminent disaster.

Every firm has its skills and experience, and every lawyer and every accountant has preferences and passions for a particular kind of practice. A litigator may be completely turned off by real estate contracts, and a tax accountant may want nothing to do with auditing. These are legitimate wishes, and the accountant or lawyer who denies those passions may be in for a very unhappy life.

But then there is the market, and the opportunity to grow by serving that market. Given a prospective market that has little need for the practice you feel passionate about, you can...

- *Move.* Go somewhere else to find the market for your particular skills and experience.
- *Adapt.* Educate yourself in the kind of practice your market needs.
- *Hire.* Bring in someone with the skills and experience your market needs.
- *Merge.* Find a firm with complementary skills and merge or acquire it.

What you can't do, as a professional firm, is something the product people do very well—change the needs of your market to match your skills. That's a singular disadvantage of professional firm marketing.

For a long time, the word processing program of choice for lawyers was Word-Perfect. Microsoft coveted that market, and began a campaign to win over the legal profession. Microsoft started by improving Microsoft Word in ways that would match and exceed WordPerfect's features. It began an intensive program to promote those features to lawyers, using advertising and a dedicated web site for law firm managers. It concentrated on getting corporate managers to use Word and then merchandised that fact to the corporate users' law firms. What put Microsoft over the top was that it helped law firms understand the advantages of using the same word processing program that their clients used. Within a year or two, Microsoft had captured the legal market and virtually eliminated WordPerfect from the scene.

Can you imagine a law firm that specializes in corporate law persuading companies in a market dominated by small privately held entities to go public? Or an accounting firm specializing in construction accounting converting companies in a market dominated by factory workers to go into the construction business?

Within the context of each profession, there are many ways in which a firm can remake itself to enhance the ability to serve the needs of its particular market. For example, a firm can...

- Restructure itself into practice groups. The practice group structure, in which all of the professionals in a firm serving clients in the same industry, or offering a specific practice, function as a separate entity, is fast becoming the firm structure of choice in both accounting and law. Each group is, essentially, a mini-firm, dealing with the same problems and opportunities. It has proven successful as both a communications structure and as a marketing platform. (See *First Among Equals, by Patrick McKenna and David Maister*.)

- Modernize its governance structure.
- Reexamine its fee structure.
- Establish joint venture programs with other firms or other professions.
- Adapt its culture to match that of the market it serves.
- Build a market research function that supplies valuable data to clients in a particular industry.

Given the ability to serve a market with accounting or legal services, there are many things a firm can do to promote itself.

- It can strive to understand the character of the community, and find ways to fit in. Local public service activities help. Joining and supporting local organizations help.
- It can build reputation and name recognition.
- It can find ways to better serve its community. For example, not all communities are fully professional in managing finances or investing its money.
- It can, if appropriate, find unsolved problems, and communicate the firm's ability to help. For example, a corporation may not be fully aware of all of the requirements of Sarbanes-Oxley, and may not know how to meet those requirements effectively and cost effectively.

The point is that a professional firm is shaped by its market—not the other way around. To understand your firm, and to shape it, you must first understand the market you serve. Otherwise, there is a vast gap in your connection to your market— one that your competitors will quickly exploit.

DEFINE YOUR TOOLS

When you consider that there are a finite number of marketing tools, and that each of your competitors has access to those tools that's equal to yours, how can you develop a program that outperforms your competitors'? The difference between your marketing program and those of your competitors is the artfulness with which you execute each aspect of the program. And artfulness—the thoughtfulness and the originality with which these tools are used—is indeed the word.

The tools available to you as a professional firm marketer are, on the face of it, the same old marketing tools, which means that for the tools of marketing to function effectively for you, there are two considerations—the context in which the tools are used, and the skill with which each tool is used.

The context for marketing tools is the program itself—the market, the objectives, and the way in which each tool reinforces the others. It's a cake, which is more than the sum of its ingredients, but which reflects the taste and the quality of each ingredient.

Effective marketing programs are synergistic—the strength of the whole is greater than the sum of its parts. While it's true that any marketing tool alone can be helpful in affecting the market's view of the firm, only the integrated program will have an impact that fully achieves marketing objectives.

Only within the context of the total program does the individual marketing tool achieve its greatest impact.

While any two marketing programs may use the same marketing tools, if the objectives are different and the market is different, then each program will be different.

The marketing tools themselves are basic building blocks of a program. Articles. Brochures and other collateral material. Public relations. Advertising. Sales, including telemarketing. Web sites and e-mail. Web casts. Networking, including seminars and speeches. Newsletters. Direct mail. Issues campaigns.

Every marketing professional understands the rudiments of these marketing tools. But why these tools don't always work well, or contribute substantially to the overall success of the marketing effort, is a function of the marketer's not seeing the basic elements of each tool in the context of the total marketing program and its objectives.

Each marketing tool has its own purpose and its own nuances. The point is to understand each tool well enough to go beyond the basics. More of that in the next chapter.

POSITIONING

If you think of marketing as a process to move goods and services to the consumer, there are two ways to view the process—either you sell people what they want, or you try to persuade people to buy what you want to sell. The second is an almost inevitably fruitless exercise in egocentric behavior. *I can make you buy anything because I'm a good salesperson.* It's an uphill trudge, and yet, it seems to be the way to which most people seem to gravitate.

Selling people what they want is obviously the better way, although it's not without its rigors. How do you know what they want? How do they know what they want? When nylon was invented in the 1940s, could you have asked women who had never heard of the stuff if they wanted nylon hose?

We do know that people buy what they need. They are sold what they're persuaded they need. And if you have to persuade people that they need something, isn't that the same as selling what you want to sell?

Not quite the same—if you can cast your product or service in a context that addresses the consumer's needs or concerns. Du Pont solved the nylon problem by asking women who had never heard of nylon, "Would you be interested in hose that were as sheer or beautiful as silk hose, but wore like iron, and didn't cost any more than silk?"

And that was *positioning* before the word was ever used. Du Pont, and other good marketers of the day, did three things...

- They defined consumer expectations.
- They figured out how to meet those expectations with a product they had developed that nobody had ever heard of.
- They asked themselves, "What fact or value can we communicate to the market that would address those expectations and concerns?"

From those three points they developed the marketing campaign that sold nylons. That's *positioning*.

And these three points define the clearest approach to positioning that might be used by an accounting, law, or consulting firm today—no matter what the size of the firm.

But articulating a position is hardly a total marketing plan. A number of elements must be addressed to turn a position into a marketing plan.

A caveat. There is a distinct difference, too often ignored, between a position and a mission.

A mission is a projection of objectives. It defines what the firm thinks its purpose is—where it would like to go in the business context...how it would like to serve its clients...how it would like to be perceived by the community it serves. It is, essentially, a wish list and a blueprint for the company. But a mission is the company's business, not the consumer's. I say to you, "I would like you to be my friend and for you to love me." That's my mission. And you say to me, "That may be what you want, but what's that got to do with what I want? Why should I be your friend, and what have you done for me that's lovable?"

No, a mission statement is not a position.

Nor is it a niche. In fact, positioning enhances both niche and target marketing.

A position says, "I understand what you want and need, and what concerns you most, and I'm going to give it to you."

In practical terms, how does positioning work? More caveats.

- The position must stem from the best possible understanding of the needs, aspirations, and expectations of the prospective clientele. There should be a perception of what your market most wants of a firm like yours—and ideally that perception comes from research. Many of the large accounting and law firms have spent several million dollars each on just this kind of research. If you don't have that kind of money—or commitment—do your own survey. Ask your existing clients, your friends, their friends—anybody. But don't guess. Know.

- The position must be based on reality. You may take the position—and advertise—that you do better audits, or write better briefs. But if you can't prove it, or it just isn't so, you're ultimately going to lose more than you gain. Don't promise what you can't deliver. The acoustics of the marketplace are magnificent, and if your promise is not deliverable, you'll get caught and hanged.

- The position you choose must spring from—and be driven by—your own business strategy. You've got to look at your firm . . . see who you are and what you want to be . . . consider partner aspirations . . . weigh skills, strengths, and weaknesses. If you ignore this step, you stand in danger of not only selling a mythical firm, but of being unable to deliver what you sell.

- There are at least two ways in which a position can be determined. The first is a perception of the market needs, however that perception is arrived at. The second is to choose market opportunity. The first is a careful analysis of what the market wants and needs, and that you can supply. The second sees an opportunity that may not have existed before. Either way, the position must be reinforced in a proper marketing campaign.

- Either work with available skills, or develop new skills before the positioning program begins. It's one thing to recognize the opportunities for your firm for helping small companies because of government proposals, and to choose a position based on the needs of small businesses. It's another thing to have a real ability to serve those needs.

- Choose a single position point. Diverse positions are impossible to sell effectively, and each position, instead of reinforcing the others, dilutes them all. One point, one thrust. Examples cited by one expert, Paul Cole of Decision Research, are based on the observation that a customer's overall impression of a company is one-dimensional. "Pepsi, for example, is associated with youth. Volvo with safety, Burger King with flame-broiled food," he says. "American Airlines stressed comfort and leg room in its planes. Only when a market has fully accepted the unique position," says Cole, "should a company attempt to build positioning extensions. Now that BMW is fully associated with full performance, it can begin to extend its positioning to luxury as well."

- Al Ries and Jack Trout, in their landmark book, *Positioning,* point out that the only company with a predefined position is the market leader—the number one company in the field. It tells the market that the market itself prefers that company. It also defines the market from which competitors must capture a share, if possible.

- Emphasis, in positioning, must always be on how the public will perceive the firm, and not on how the firm perceives itself, or would like to be perceived. The position must stem from the reality of the firm and the market, and not from an arbitrary notion of what will sell, regardless of the reality of what the firm is. Reality counts, not image. The danger in the concept of image is that it implies that symbols can be manipulated to control any image—even one that's not rooted in reality. It simply isn't true. If you don't like the perception that the public has of your reality, change your firm, not the symbols. As the old man said, what you are speaks so loud I can't hear what you say you are.

- When the position is determined, it must be communicated internally, even before it's communicated externally. Simply, if you're going to tell the world who you are, don't you think you should tell your own staff and colleagues first? After all, they're the ones who have to breathe life into the position, aren't they?

Given the defined position, three things must be kept in mind . . .

- Positions are dynamic. They should be rethought periodically, in every aspect, to be sure that they still apply. The market may change, or you may change.

- No position will work if it doesn't, in some way, differentiate your firm from others.

- The position is ultimately nothing more than a platform to project your firm's ability to meet the needs and expectations of a prospective clientele. The marketing program, in all its aspects, must be used to make that position live and viable as a marketing device.

The marketing program may be as elaborate or as simple as your budget and marketing objectives will allow, but if the position you select is to be effective, the program must spring from that position.

In professional services marketing, the tools of marketing are used to project that platform—that singular reason for people to want to do business with you—in an integrated and concerted effort. Advertising, even when millions are spent on it, and even if the ads perfectly reflect and project the position, won't produce a single client if there isn't a well-rounded support program that includes some projection of specific capability.

And no positioning program, nor any marketing program, will work if it doesn't lead directly to the opportunity for a lawyer, an accountant, or a consultant to make a personal presentation. Which brings it all down to effective sales training.

The profound difference between product and professional services marketing poses some interesting obstacles. Bufferin can project, as its position, that it gives the relief of aspirin without irritating the stomach, because it knows that there's a vast audience of people who are concerned about the stomach problems that might be caused by aspirin.

But without making unbelievable or unsustainable promises (*we do better audits/ we do better briefs*), how does a professional service devise a viable position?

Based on the foregoing positioning principles, there are always specific concerns that prospective clients of professional services have. Small business owners may feel that they know how to manage their businesses, but may be concerned about cash management, or financial statements that will help at the bank, or about tax returns that not only save money but also are sustainable under audit. People are concerned that they are too small to get proper attention from a firm your size, or that they'll get the right individual in your firm for their problems, or that your firm has the breadth of experience or technical skills to give them the best possible help. All businesspeople are concerned that you don't understand their business, or that you're more concerned with your business than with theirs. Addressing concerns such as these are valid and useful positions.

A position, as with any aspect of marketing, or reputation in marketing, is only as good as the way in which it's used. If it isn't constantly reinforced, it's useless. It's like a hoop. As long as you keep beating it with a stick, it keeps rolling. When you stop, the hoop falls over, and the distance it's gone is lost.

Can you market without a position? Of course. But it's like cutting thick steak with a dull knife. It may work eventually, but it isn't worth the effort.

THE IDEAL MARKETING PLAN

Based on the four tenets of knowing the market, knowing the firm, knowing the tools, and managing the tools, the effective marketing plan for a professional services firm is one that . . .

- *Builds name recognition*, in terms of skills and ability to solve specific problems. While all tools serve to meet that end to one degree or another, public relations and advertising serve best.

- *Demonstrates skills.* Here, articles, speeches, and seminars are most effective.

- *Affords direct contact.* Direct mail and telemarketing work best here, by getting directly to the individuals in the target market.

- *Sells.* Selling is the point of contact with the individual that allows person-to-person selling, where the sale is actually generated.

- *Leads to the proposal and presentation,* which is the final step in the selling process.

These are the steps of a plan. The smaller firm, on a limited budget, may use only a few of the tools, but the process is the same, and should include these five points. And no matter the size of the firm, the aim is to build relationships that lead to the selling process, and to the opportunity to sell face-to-face with the prospect's decision maker.

BRANDING

The concept of branding, long accepted as valid in product marketing, is now heard more and more in the corridors of professional firms. Has something changed? Is it now a valid concept where before it was not? Have marketers—and those they serve—become more sophisticated in the advanced concepts of marketing?

Or is it just a fad to make important marketing characteristics, such as name recognition and reputation, seem more urgent and important? Is it just a gimmick for marketing consultants to sell their services?

Many years ago, in the early days of generic branding for products, marketers discovered a keen reluctance by consumers to give up the more expensive name brands of products they were used to. The perception was that the familiar brands were better and therefore worth more, even though the perception wasn't necessarily true. It was only when house names of generic products were marketed as brand names on their own, with full promotional efforts, that consumers began to accept them.

In the early days of marketing professional services, the concept of branding was thought to be irrelevant. People don't buy a firm—they buy an individual service or an individual accountant or lawyer or consultant whom they believe has the specific expertise to address their needs or problems.

The answer to the puzzle of branding for professionals seems to be that there are now circumstances under which branding concepts make sense in professional services marketing, and conditions under which branding may be irrelevant.

The very real results of successful branding, however rare in a professional service, come at the invitation to bid. There is strong evidence that a firm looking for a particular legal, accounting, or consulting service will ask for proposals from only the top two or three firms known to specialize in those services. Other firms may be invited to submit proposals, although they may be just window dressing to assure other executives in the company that the choice was made from among many firms, but only the firms perceived to be the best at the particular service needed will make that final cut. The invited firms that make the final cut may be assumed to be those that have successfully built a brand concept for their services. Certainly, reputation. But brand? Maybe, but not necessarily.

What, exactly, is a brand? In product marketing, the textbook definition (depending upon what textbook you read) is that it's a consumer's perception of a product or company or institution that sees that product, and so forth, in a way that's distinctive, unique, and offers more to the consumer than do other brands of the same product. Truth told, it's really an attitude built on a perception. It's not the product or company itself. The product is sold by the company. The brand of that product is bought by the consumer, predicated upon the consumer's perception that the brand of a product he or she buys differs sufficiently from another brand of the same product to warrant choosing one particular brand over another. And, by the way, to warrant paying the price for it.

In fact, there may be no real distinction between the different brands of the same product. But if the customer perceives a difference in his or her own mind, then the concept of branding really works.

In brand marketing, the marketing effort is dedicated to imbuing a product with those distinctions, real or imagined, that give the brand substance, validity, and acceptance.

Ken Roman, in his book *How to Advertise*, describes Unilever by noting that "Unilever is in the business of marketing brands, not products. What is the difference? A product is merely a category—a whole class of goods, e.g. cars, cameras, detergents, toothpaste, margarine. Unilever, therefore, often markets several brands in one category."

Where marketers gather to ruminate, the discussion about the meaning of branding takes on the texture of discussions of how many angels can dance on the head of a pin. But this is clear...

- The value of the brand exists not in the product, but in the customer's mind. This value is measured beyond the usefulness of the product (or service) to include perceptions of quality, consistency, reliability, and simply getting one's money's worth. It would be easy to dismiss the concept of a brand as an intangible, except that tangibility is irrelevant. To the customer with a specific brand of choice, the brand is very tangible.

- There's a difference between reputation—even a favorable one, with great name recognition—and a brand. The reputation may serve as a backdrop for receptivity for other marketing efforts, but other marketing efforts there must be. Reputation and name recognition are not the same as the array of perceptions and emotional attachments that consumers have for a brand. Subtle distinctions, perhaps, but very real ones. Everybody knew Pricewaterhouse-Coopers by name, because they audited the highly visible Academy Awards and had for years. But without a great deal of marketing activity that seems almost irrelevant to the name recognition, PricewaterhouseCoopers might not have gotten another client.

- Branding for a professional service may very well be different from branding for a product. Which is not to say that there isn't some viability in branding for a professional service. But different it is.

Joseph Vales, a leading and thoughtful marketing consultant formerly with PricewaterhouseCoopers and now head of Vales Consulting Group, enhances the definition. "A brand," he says, "is more distinctive than a product. It is, first of all, a name—a means of identification. Second, it is a set of added values, values that offer both functional and psychological benefits to the consumer, such as performance in use, price, packaging, color, taste, smell, shape and form, associations, and the perceptions formed by advertising."

For the product, it might be said that establishing a brand is the ultimate aim of marketing. When all of the devises of marketing—including strategy, advertising and other marketing tools, and distribution—add up to win the customer's heart and mind, then share of market increases, sales increase, and the marketing manager gets a raise from a grateful company. People go out and ask for the product by brand name, and will accept no substitute.

But wait a minute. A major factor in successful branding for products is consistency. Revisit the distinctions between marketing a product and marketing a professional service. You can choose one brand of toothpaste over another because you know that the next tube of that brand you buy will be the same as the first one you bought. Can you say that about a service? Is the next tax return you do for a client going to be the same as the last one? Is the last deal you structured for a client going to be the same as the next one? Of course not. And in many cases, the specific service is performed only once for each client, unlike the tube of toothpaste, which is bought over and over again. The question, then, is will the service be performed for one client in the same way as it was performed for another? In view of these differences between a product and a service, how, then, can you have a brand name for an accounting or law or consulting firm?

If IBM or Xerox can build brand strength that carries forward to all of the IBM or Xerox products, why can't an accounting or law firm do the same?

In fact, it can, if some clear distinctions are made—and acted on. Some factors...

- In professional services, an entire firm is rarely capable of becoming a brand name, in which all of its services, without distinction, are accepted and preferred on the strength of the firm name alone. Name recognition helps, but only to serve as a backdrop. Name recognition is not the same as a favorable attitude. You can remember a firm's name unfavorably, and not want to do business with it.

- At the same time, the scandals of the first years of the twenty-first century touched, to one degree or another, every one of the Big Four firms, and many of the next 10. In fact, since the explosive demise of Arthur Andersen, whose name and reputation oozed trust and probity to make it virtually a brand, how much harder is it now to think of branding in the professions?

- A firm's *specific services*, on the other hand, can be developed as a brand, but only if certain steps are taken. And those basic steps may just be a starter.

  o The specific service must have a name that distinguishes it. *Pricewaterhouse-Coopers Change Integration Service*, for example. It defines their specific approach to company reengineering. The emphasis is on approach—on process. This is an important distinction in branding for a professional service.

  o The service must be positioned specifically to meet the needs of its market, as defined by the needs of the market, not by the wishes of the service provider.

  o There must be a sense of consistency in performance of the service—a track record, a methodology, an implied or real manual of performance that suggests that, like the tube of toothpaste, the next time you hire the firm to do that job, it will perform for you in the same satisfying and successful way as it did for someone else the last time it performed the service.

  o The brand can be established only with the full force of marketing. That means clearly defining the service, advertising, public relations, direct mail—the full marketing arsenal.

  o And the marketing activity must be as consistent as the service. Nothing is as fragile as a brand value, and if it's not constantly sustained and polished, it quickly tarnishes, diminishes, and dies.

- It seems quite possible that a service of a firm that becomes a brand may well share an aura with other of that same firm's services—but not without strength in those other services. Look at Arthur Andersen Consulting (now *Accenture*), which was probably one of the first real brands in professional services marketing. (McKinsey and other consulting firms did it first, however.) Certainly, Andersen Consulting enhanced perception of the Arthur Andersen, the somewhat separate CPA firm. But the CPA firm helped by having a reputation for being superior in everything that it did. Which, ironically, may be an exception to the statement that firms don't become brands. But name three others.

- Still, Arthur Andersen's ability to develop Andersen Consulting's name—now *Accenture*—as a brand doesn't insulate it from marketing attacks on specific services offered, with a brand's marketing force, by other firms. In fact, the firm's brand may make Andersen Consulting vulnerable to marketing attacks from the branded specific services of other consulting or accounting firms. Here, the success in marketing is derived not from the firm's overall reputation, but from any firm's ability to project a specific service and its ability to provide a solution to specific problems. John may have a reputation for being a great carpenter, but he loses business to Harry, who is known (or perceived) to be a great window installer.

- Of all the things a brand is, what it isn't is a reputation, a niche, or a position. And if you try to build a marketing program without understanding the distinction and the realities of the differences, you might just as well burn your money. At least you'll enjoy the light of the flame.

On the face of it, it would seem that the concept of branding may be useful for only the largest firms. Quite possibly, if for no other reason than the cost of promoting a service for brand identification. But the beauty of marketing, and the joy of it, is in finding ways to imaginatively transcend the obstacles.

The smallest accounting firm in town, for example, could conceivably develop a brand identification for, say, its succession planning concepts. A small law firm could do the same for, say, its method of real estate closing.

It could well be argued that branding has long existed in the professional services by the tax clinics (H&R Block, for example) and legal clinics. In both cases, however, it would seem that the menu of services that each offers is so consistent that they pass into the definition of commodities, and therefore products.

Two questions remain . . .

- Is branding necessary for successful marketing?
- Is branding valuable to a professional service?

No, branding is not necessary for successful marketing—except where a competitive service is being marketed as a brand, such as the Arthur Andersen situation, which ultimately burst into flames by violating the basic tenets of its own reputation for quality. Then for competitive reasons, there is no option but to do the same.

And yes, it can be valuable, if the effort is made to develop—and sustain—a true brand.

There is still yet another nagging question. Why has it taken almost two decades (since *Bates*) for a marketing concept as old as branding to be considered in professional services marketing?

Who knows? Maybe because professional services marketing is maturing. It would certainly be nice to think so. More likely because there is a growing professionalism among professional services marketers, and selling branding is more exciting than merely selling reputation.

TARGET MARKETING

Professional services marketing always comes down to selling the individual clients—one by one.

You can talk about *strategies*, and *image*, and *niche marketing*, and *branding*. You can talk about *articles*, and *brochures,* and *press releases,* and *seminars.* But it always comes down to selling the individual clients—one by one.

One of the greatest ads of its kind, for McGraw-Hill, says it all. It showed a dour, forbidding-looking man, seated in a chair, glowering off the page straight at you. He is saying, *"I don't know who you are...I don't know your company...I don't know your company's product...I don't know what your company stands for...I don't know your company's customers...I don't know your company's record...I don't know your company's reputation. Now, what was it you wanted to sell me?"*

This is why marketing efforts, prior to the face-to-face contact, are important.

All those tools and strategies of marketing build a context to facilitate getting to the individual client prospect, and supplying a background to selling the individual client. In the highly competitive arena that now constitutes professional services, all of the mass marketing techniques build reputation and name recognition. They attract prospects, and define a firm as a foundation for moving those contacts into your arena. Then target marketing comes into play, enhanced by preselling.

What does target marketing mean? It means identifying and choosing your prospective client by name, and going after that prospect with a broad spectrum of techniques, all of which are supported by a mass market campaign.

Let's take it step by step.

- Define the client you want. A lot of ways to do this. Location. Size. Industry. Specialized need. Your fee range. An industry configuration that requires a specific service. Industry-related arena. Your definition, but do it in great detail.

- Identify the company or individual that fits your prospect profile—the one that best defines the kind of client you want for the kind of practice you want. Identify what it is you want to sell (assuming that you've already determined that a market exists. Don't try to sell labor law to a community of individual entrepreneurial farmers who use machines instead of people). Then identify the companies in your market area that you think would be great clients for you, because they fit your client profile. You find these prospects by...

  o Scouring your own lists of existing clients and prospects. There's more gold there than you think. *Why existing clients? Because the chances are that you've got clients for some of your services who don't have the slightest idea that you can do this new thing for them, and that they need it.*

  o Doing some simple secondary research. Go to a library or get online—or hire a research firm—and look up companies that you think might fit the bill. Use simple research sources, such as Dun & Bradstreet, Standard & Poor's, and so forth. It only takes a hundred or so companies to start with. And how many of those companies, turned into clients, does it take to make the whole effort worthwhile?

  o Prospecting. Have a good agency do a great series of inexpensive ads that include requests for literature. If the ads are well done, and placed in the right publications, and if the material you're offering is worthwhile, you will quickly assemble a terrific list of targets. Under some circumstances, telemarketing is a good prospecting tool. Or do a mailing offering a brochure.

  o Holding a seminar, with material aimed at the kind of client you want. The attendees not only comprise a mailing list, but they become your first contact in a networking program.

- Devise your campaign strategy.

  o If you're playing off a specialty you have, then use that skill for a kind of mass marketing campaign. But remember, that campaign is only the backdrop for target marketing. You're still going to have to go after each company individually.

  o Identify the key people who make buying decisions in the prospective company. These are your targets.

○ Deal directly with those people to establish a relationship. Write. Phone. Do a seminar and invite them. Set up a regimen of regular mailings—articles, reprints, brochures, newsletters, etc. Client advisories. A newsletter. Advertise in trade journals read by prospects. Your objective, ultimately, is to build a relationship that facilitates a prospect's getting to know you and your skills and what you have to offer.

○ Do it. Strategy is a wonderful word. It rolls nicely on the tongue. But to make strategy more than a buzzword, you've got to...

• Have a plan that's realistic. No wishful thinking. Know what's doable, and who's going to do it. Don't identify and market to 500 companies if you can't cover more than 50 in one crack.

• Be precise in your profile of your prospective client. Start with the clients you have, as a guide to what you do for them and what you can't do.

• Be realistic about your partners' commitment. Everybody wants new clients. Everybody wants to be in the swing of marketing. Not everybody is willing to do it, or has the self-confidence and eagerness to do it. It's easy to say yes to a strategy, and then get busy with billable hours.

• Be professional in your marketing tools. Writing a direct mail letter isn't the same as writing a letter to a client. And even the newsletter you buy from a service should be looked at carefully to be sure that it's specific to your firm, your service, your market, and your needs.

• Be organized. Get it down on paper. Who does what, and by when? More good plans slip away undone for lack of drive and organization and a good manager.

There's a large element of networking in targeted marketing, as there is in any professional services marketing. It can't be done from a distance, in the abstract, like product marketing. Somebody has got to get out there and meet and court the prospect, in order to make it happen.

There is one more important factor in target marketing, one that's perhaps the most important of all, especially for a growing firm.

A manufacturing company is defined by its products. A professional firm is defined by its client base and the services the firm offers those clients.

Target marketing—choosing your clients and then going after them with whatever it takes to win them—defines your practice and defines your firm. If you are what you serve, and to whom you serve it, then you should hand pick your clients. That's why target marketing matters.

MANAGING THE TOOLS

The literature on professional services marketing is replete with exhortations to write articles, hold seminars, issue newsletters, send out press releases, make speeches, and use direct mail—all of which are valid and important tools of marketing. Except for one thing. Only in rare instances do these activities, of themselves, produce clients.

There are two reasons for this. First, people rarely hire an accountant or lawyer or consultant from an article or seminar, or even a direct mail piece. This is a major difference, by the way, from selling a product, in which the product's features tend to speak for themselves.

Second, people cannot be sold a service they don't need at the moment. Nobody wakes up in the morning and says, "What I really need today is a good audit," or "What a great day to sue somebody," or "Help me solve a problem I don't have yet."

To expect the tools of marketing to create a client is a recipe for disappointment.

If these tools don't sell, what, then, is their purpose? At best, and with rare exceptions, they build name recognition and reputation—a backdrop against which to ultimately sell your services. They help define your firm, in terms of its expertise and the expertise of its individual practitioners, its quality in the areas in which it focuses, and the overall nature of your practice. With seminars, or in dealing with prospects you may meet under other circumstances, the purpose, other than to display your expertise, is to develop and expand relationships, not to sell. And since the tools themselves don't sell, the ultimate objective of the campaign is to get the invitation to propose.

But most significantly, each of these marketing tools is, ultimately, the first step in networking—in building relationships that lead to the selling process. Properly used, properly focused, these devices should lead to an opportunity to a face-to-face meeting with prospective clients. It is at these meetings that the selling is done. A relatively simple—but important—process. Some caveats...

- The best way to sell a firm is to sell it by its parts—individual skills focused on a single practice—rather than to try to sell the whole firm. A litigation practice with a strong concentration on risk management, for example, shouldn't try to sell all of its litigation capabilities to a broad audience, but rather just its risk management capabilities to a targeted audience.

- Each market segment is defined by a need or prospective need for a single service. Don't try to project your capabilities in risk management litigation, for example, to a white-collar crime market segment by assuming that any litigation is all litigation. Different audience—different message.

- All marketing activities for the defined audience should be positioned to that group. You may have a great wealth preservation practice, but the risk management audience doesn't want to see your capabilities in wealth preservation.

- Choose a target audience. Choose a position based on that audience's needs and your ability to meet those needs. This is the foundation for all your activities to that target (articles, seminars, newsletters, press releases, direct mail, etc.).

- Clarify your mailing list for each target audience. Not every market segment is interested in everything your firm does at any given moment. Focus.

- Now use your tools to begin a networking process.

The point is that merely to rely on the articles, advisories, seminars, and so forth, to do the job can give you a long wait between new clients.

7

MAKING MARKETING
A NICE WORD

Building a Client-centric Marketing Culture

*The aim of marketing is to know and understand the customer
so well the product or service fits him and sells itself.*

—Peter F. Drucker

In the deep, dark, dismal days before professional services marketing became legal, circa 1977, the very thought of marketing was considered obscene by lawyers and accountants. The word *competition*, which began to creep into the boardrooms of austere professional firms, so deeply steeped in tradition, was something real professionals didn't indulge in. Gentlemen—which most professionals were then— didn't steal other gentlemen's clients. Shawn O'Malley, a senior partner (and later managing partner) of Price Waterhouse said, then, "We will advertise over my dead body."

But somehow, the realities of the marketplace have a way of creeping in, uninvited but persistent. It's taken more than a quarter of a century, but marketing is now an integral part of professional firm management. The nagging problem, however, is whether the need to market, and the willingness to do it, have penetrated the ranks of law and accounting firms below the firm management level. To an overwhelming number of professionals, marketing is something done by that person down the hall. Even today, in many professional firms, the nonaccountant and the nonlawyer still meet inhospitality in accounting and law firms.

Part of the problem is that there's no marketing tradition in professional services firms. A manufacturer, whether it's IBM or a maker of small gadgets, understands on some level that the business it's in is marketing. The product is what they make to fill the channels opened by marketing. Moreover, everybody who works in a manufacturing company understands, on one level or another, the role played by

73

marketing, even though marketing may not be his or her specific job. To cite Peter Drucker yet again, they understand that the purpose of a company is to create a client. There is no comparable attitude in the traditional accounting or law firm. Firms may have their *rainmakers*—the partner who could go into a telephone booth alone and come out arm in arm with a new client—but in today's competitive marketplace, one or two rainmakers are not enough to keep the firm vibrant. The firms themselves must be turned into marketing machines—to have a culture that understands and supports a marketing effort.

What makes marketing professional services more difficult is that in professional services, the final sale that converts the prospect into a client must be done by a professional who performs the service, even when a nonprofessional generates the lead.

Today, the firms that compete best in the marketplace are those that might be said to have a successful *marketing culture*, a structure—and, more importantly, an attitude that grants enthusiastic hospitality to marketing.

DEFINING A MARKETING CULTURE

A firm may be said to have a marketing culture when its professional staff . . .

- Understands and recognizes the role that marketing disciplines play in firm management and development
- Realizes and respects the professionalism of the marketing professional and the marketing staff
- Recognizes the relationship between what they do and the needs of the marketplace
- Appreciates and accepts its role in the marketing process
- Understands and accepts that nonbillable hours spent on marketing are an investment in the future of the firm
- Participates in specific marketing activities
- Retains and supports competent professional marketing staff
- Structures the firm to develop and pursue a marketing program
- And ultimately, is managed by people who understand and enthusiastically support the marketing effort

A firm that meets these criteria is one that will compete successfully, function profitably, and grow.

BUILDING A MARKETING CULTURE

With no tradition in marketing, and certainly no training in it, how does a firm overcome a culture in which the very concept of marketing is anathema to the very people who most need to participate in the process? It takes more than exhortation. Building a marketing culture is not done with 1-2-3 steps. It requires...

- Top management support
- Good marketing professionals
- Education
- A marketing structure within the firm

Ultimately, building a marketing culture requires a measure of behavior modification, which sounds worse than it really is. It's not a Pavlovian exercise so much as an understanding that for marketing to succeed in a professional firm, every professional must participate. And every professional must understand the competitive advantages of participating.

TOP MANAGEMENT SUPPORT

Top management support is crucial. Merely to have the managing partner say "OK, let's do it" is not enough. Whatever the management style—lead by example, exhort, mandate—it's not the same thing as being able to understand and then explain why marketing activities are essential for the growth of the firm; that people will be rewarded for marketing activities; that a measure of nonbillable hours applied to marketing is not only acceptable but cherished; that marketing activity is a factor that contributes to measuring partner, associate, and professional staff compensation. Top management support means inculcating into the firm the concept that in all professional activities, the client is at the core—that without clients there is no firm.

The managing partner must recognize that the element of competition, long absent in an overt form from the professions, is now integral to firm management. For today's firm, there is no growth, and likely no survival, in thinking of marketing as something somebody else does.

Professionalism is not an arcane philosophy that serves the professional alone—it's a service that addresses the needs of the clientele—a crucial distinction. Top management support means more than acceptance of marketing. It means leadership.

GOOD MARKETING PROFESSIONALS

Someone once said that if you're smart enough to be a lawyer or an accountant, you're smart enough to do your own marketing. Sure. And you're probably smart enough to be a nuclear physicist—but that doesn't make you one.

In fact, marketing isn't nuclear physics, but it is a profession with its own practices, experiences, skills, and techniques. The good marketing professional is trained in the tools and mechanics of marketing, in its ideas and concepts, in its highly focused point of view. Experience tells the marketing professional what may work and what may not work. If the marketer is imaginative and deft in using imagination, you get a program that's thoughtful and specifically relevant to your needs. And the good marketer understands your profession and its needs.

The firm must recognize the professionalism of the experienced and knowledgeable marketer. Ultimately, the professional marketer is as great an asset to the successful professional firm as is any partner or other professional in the firm. This means, of course, hiring the best available.

The good marketer understands the distinctive nature of lawyers and accountants, and is capable of working well with them. As a professional, the good marketer belongs to, and is active in, the association of law (LMA—Legal Marketing Association) or accounting firm marketers (AAM—Association of Accounting Marketing), benefiting from the experience of peers, and contributing as well. He or she is also a teacher, who knows how to impart the meaning and techniques of marketing skills to professionals who are not themselves trained marketers. The good marketer is a leader, capable of leading professionals in marketing activities and concepts, and of managing marketing staff.

Remember, the tools of marketing are available to everyone. What counts, then, is the experience and imagination the marketer brings to those skills. It's more than the sum of the skills and mechanics, it's the artistry with which they're used. When you're hiring a marketing professional, then, don't hire the mechanic—hire the artist.

EDUCATION

Since the *Bates* decision, people have been trying to turn professionals into marketers. It rarely works, and it's never going to happen. And when you try, the professionals dig their heels in defiantly. "I didn't go to law (or accounting) school to be a salesperson." What, then, should a professional learn about marketing?

The first thing to learn is that ultimately, nobody can close a deal with a new client but the professional. The marketing professional can build the marketing program that enhances name recognition and reputation, and that can project the law-yers' or accountants' skills and special capabilities, but ultimately, the client has to meet the person who's going to perform the service. The bond between client and practitioner, the trust needed in a professional relationship, is a personal relationship that no salesperson can engender for a professional.

Some measure of sales training may be useful. This need not be an elaborate at-tempt to turn an accountant or a lawyer into a salesperson—that never has worked, except in rare and felicitous cases. Rather, the professional can learn the four basic tenets of turning a prospect into a client...

- Learn the prospect's business problem.

- Demonstrate that you understand that problem.

- Demonstrate that you can help solve that problem.

- Arrange a starting date to put the solution in place.

But the marketing things that the lawyer or accountant can do, particularly under the aegis of the marketing professional, are important. For example...

- The professional, with the marketer's help, can write articles, can run semi-nars, can make speeches.

- Under the marketer's guidance, the professional can improve networking skills, particularly under a carefully devised networking program.

- The professional can learn to contribute to such marketing activities as writ-ing articles for a firm or firm practice newsletter.

- The professional can learn how to follow up a contact made by direct mail, by attending firm seminars.

- While the professional who is not an instinctive salesperson is not likely to become one, any intelligent professional can learn the selling skills necessary to convert a prospect into a client.

- A professional can learn how to keep a client, once the client is in the house.

- A professional can learn to understand the broader marketing program, and his or her role in it, without having to become a professional marketer.

These are things that merely broaden individual intelligence and education, at no cost to professionalism, and without going beyond the boundaries of normal busi-ness practice.

THE STRUCTURE FOR MARKETING

If we have learned anything in the quarter century of professional firm marketing, we've learned that with rare exceptions, you don't market the firm, you market its services and practices.

This is the trouble with branding, as we've noted elsewhere. Every tube of toothpaste from a manufacturer is the same as every other tube of toothpaste. Is every lawyer or accountant in a firm the same as every other? Is every practice in a firm the same as every other? Of course not!

Nothing should prevent you from promoting your firm as a firm, but if you do, you'd better be prepared to be confused with every other firm that does exactly what you do. And remember, you can't say "We do better audits," or "We write better briefs." You can't prove it, it's unethical, and it's certainly not credible.

What you can—and should—do is promote each skill, each practice, each market segment you serve. While this doesn't preclude a general marketing campaign that enhances name recognition, presence, and firm prestige, segmented marketing designs programs that go straight to target markets, and that give you more latitude in promoting individual firm skills.

While there are many approaches to structuring a firm for marketing, perhaps the most successful, as defined by Patrick McKenna and David Maister in their masterful book, *First Among Equals*, is the practice group. For any firm with more than a few lawyers or professionals, the practice group structure is proving to be the most effective way to manage a practice. It recognizes that each practice area has a different target audience, and each requires different skills and techniques. The practice group allows the professionals in that group to address the specific practice and marketing problems of the practice, and to manage them effectively. Among the advantages of the practice group are...

- It's defined by a specific practice within a firm, or a specific target audience. It could be a real estate group, or a tax practice, or a group offering computer services—anything defined by a discrete market that's served by professionals within the firm. The advantages are that every member of the group shares a common set of skills with the others in the group, addresses a common market, and most significantly, has the intellectual capability to develop a distinctive marketing program to attract that market.

- It can enhance the skills of its members, all of whom share a common market, with common needs.

- It can share the burden of a marketing effort. For example, if the group publishes brochures or newsletters, each member can participate in writing. Each member can participate in seminars or speeches. Each member can address one of several organizations that are part of a networking plan. Specific tasks in each practice segment's marketing program can be assigned to each individual in the segment or group. These tasks can be as simple as writing an article for the group's external newsletter or segment of the web site or as elaborate as helping write a brochure.

- It can be a superb vehicle for communication with other practice groups within the firm, thereby eliminating unnecessary communication, while sharing ideas for a common goal.

Managing the practice group, as McKenna and Maister point out, requires its own set of management skills. However, not only is this not the purview of this book, but also it's superbly handled in *First Among Equals*.

If the nature of your firm doesn't lend itself to practice groups, you might consider designating one partner as the marketing partner, with the responsibility to oversee the program, coordinate the efforts of marketing professionals with the partnership, and act as a monitor and motivator to oversee participation in the program by individuals in the firm.

THE MARKETING PROGRAM

There must be a cogent and appropriate marketing plan. It must be relevant to the needs and objectives of the firm. Be sure that everybody in the firm who must make the plan a reality understands it, and understands that each individual must play a part in making it work.

One word that should guide the marketing program is *realistic*. As we point out in Chapter 9, the tools of marketing are not a program—they are simply tools.

A marketing program, then, is not simply a catalog of tools. It's a plan . . . a strategy, and attendant tactics. It's the sum total of all relevant activities, supporting one another, and not just random activities designed without objective or relevance to the needs of a prospective client.

It begins with an understanding of the needs and opportunities of the markets you serve. It defines your abilities to meet those needs. It develops a strategy to persuade your market that you can serve its needs. And it formulates the tactics needed to make that strategy functional.

The word *realistic*, in this context, means that you have to assess the markets, and your ability or willingness to meet the needs of these markets, realistically. The relationship between assessing the market and assessing your ability to serve the market is crucial.

In marketing a professional firm, as we've noted, it's important to recognize that with rare exceptions, and notably the big international or national firms, you can't market the entire firm beyond building name recognition. The range of services offered by even the smallest firm is too wide, as is the audience for each of those services.

This is why the major strategy should be to market practice by practice and service by service.

Marketing the entire firm, whether it's through advertising or other means, is necessary to some degree for the name recognition (forget image—it's a myth and a cliché). But if you want to compete with your skills in expatriate taxation, then you market expatriate taxation, or real estate closings or any other of your specialties. And the firm itself will benefit as well, in the best possible way—with credibility.

You can't say, "We have great skills, so hire us." That kind of statement doesn't distinguish you from your competitors, nor is it credible. You can't say, "We believe in client satisfaction" for the same reasons. And that's why you can't expect any effective strategy to market your skills and ability to serve clients by marketing the entire firm. Each practice, each skill set, must have its own marketing program.

By defining the target audience first, you can devise the strategy to address that audience, by...

- Defining the needs and opportunities of that market segment
- Designing collateral material addressed to that audience
- Writing articles and developing other media activities for media that serve that market
- Networking through organizations that serve that market
- Running seminars for companies in that segment
- Doing specialized newsletters
- Using carefully targeted direct mail

TACTICS

Tactics are the most difficult part of a professional firm marketing program, because so much of what must be done depends upon the scarce, nonbillable time of partners and professional staff. If the firm management hasn't made clear that participation is an integral part of recognition and growth within the firm, you can scrap the marketing program.

The marketing professional can do a great deal. Your marketing director may be able to write an article or a brochure, but still needs the input of the practitioner. The marketing professional may be able to design and run a seminar, or arrange for a speech, but the practitioner must supply the content. The marketing professional may be able to place the story in the media, but the practitioner must supply the story.

The firm that understands this process, and participates in it, is one that can be said to have a successful marketing culture.

All of these activities must be managed. They must be prioritized. They must be made to happen, whether at the behest of a marketing professional or of a partner in charge of marketing. They must be timed and coordinated.

As the program shows results, you should merchandise those results to the rest of the firm. Let the firm share in the pride of a successful interview or article or ad. You should, of course, reward successful participation. Give credit to the professional who participated in the successful effort.

And the major objective of the well-designed marketing program?

First, to get the opportunity to meet the prospect face to face, in order to sell. Then the objective, and the only ultimate objective, is to get the client.

CLIENT RETENTION

Getting the client is only half the battle. The other half is keeping the client. It's done with more than just doing good work. In fact, most clients, surveys tell us, don't really know how good or how bad your work is. Why should they? It's not the business they're in.

Independent studies also show that a large percentage of professional firm clients are dissatisfied with the levels of service from their accountants and lawyers. They are given no basis for understanding what's being done for them, nor are reasonable expectations defined. What basis do clients have, then, for being satisfied?

The reality is that this new world is competitive in ways that it's never been before. Ask your clients how many times they've been approached by your competitors, and pursued aggressively. And then ask yourself if you can continue to be sanguine about keeping your clients happy, on a day-by-day basis.

There are, of course, some things that are clearly necessary in client retention. Significantly, getting the right client in the first place is important. Doing good work, obviously. Being responsive, obviously. Being timely in delivering promised reports and material. Being polite to clients.

But these are things that should be taken for granted—things inherent in the meaning of *professional*. It's what the client is paying for. You get no credit for doing them, but you lose clients for not doing them.

The larger picture of client retention is predicated upon recognizing the competitive and changing nature of the marketplace.

Sophisticated marketers have a strong handle on who the client company is, what the company does, what its needs are, and how to address those needs in marketing approaches.

Which means that if you don't have that same knowledge, and the kind of relationship that means total involvement in the client's concerns, then you're in imminent danger of losing that client.

Client retention, then, requires more than the obvious factors of doing good work and delivering it on time. And in fact, in a dynamic business world, it's often more than a personal relationship. It's at least...

- *Being immersed in a client's business and industry.* While the professional has a stake in some aspects of arm's-length relationship, this doesn't preclude knowing enough about a client's business to anticipate problems in your professional area, and to seek new ways in which other of your services can help the client.

- *Frequent contact points,* beyond the engagement. You do, of course, what you've been hired to do. But you help both the client and yourself when you send a brochure on a subject of mutual interest. Or a copy of a clipping in which you've been quoted on a subject the client might care about. Or a simple newsletter, either your own or one of the excellent packaged ones, covering information of interest or concern to the client. The client should know you exist between contracts, between matters, between consultations.

- *Maintaining personal relationships.* Not just drinking and dining to keep the client happy, but establishing and reinforcing a sense of mutual understanding and trust. The degree to which the client calls on you for business advice is as much a matter of personal trust as it is professional trust.

- *Visible quality control systems.* You may have internal quality control systems, but if the client doesn't know that, then the client has no reason to believe they exist. More important, the quality control systems should relate to the client's business, not yours. This is increasingly pertinent, following the accounting and corporate scandals of the first years of the century, and in many respects, it's mandated by such laws as Sarbanes-Oxley.

Quality, a buzzword frequently used in business, relates to the client, not the professional firm. If the client doesn't perceive quality in terms of the client's needs, then your service can be the best there is, but not for that client.

The *client-driven,* rather than the *practice-driven,* firm is the only safe way to compete in today's market. A major professional firm once took a highly conservative position on a client's matter. The problem was not the position, but that the position was taken for the firm's protection, not the client's—and the client became aware of this. There went the client.

Keeping in touch with your client is crucial because needs change. Your services change. By constantly reviewing the client's needs, you not only assure that you're giving the client the best service, and that you're maximizing the relationship, but you're also telling the client that you're concerned.

Regular client surveys help. New York's former mayor Ed Koch used to walk the streets of the city, asking people, "How'm I doing?" He didn't always like what he heard, but he always knew. Anybody who doesn't take active steps to keep aware of client attitudes toward the firm is somebody who likes surprises. A simple one-page survey, annually, goes a long way. Frequent personal conversations between the client and the managing partner are even better.

Successful professionals are those who've learned the difference between *client relations* and *client service.* Both are important, but one is not the substitute for the other. In client retention, you have to have both.

It's the peculiar nature of professional services that *quality* plays little or no role in getting new business, except perhaps in terms of reputation. It plays a crucial role in client retention, however, if you define quality as giving the client what the client needs, wants, and expects. Most frequently, in order to know what the client needs, wants, and expects, you have to be immersed in the relationship. And you have to ask. Here *quality* is not an abstraction or a hollow boast—it's a reality.

Those who are most successful at client retention are those who actively work at it. They have programs and checklists. Even small firms that are aware of the need for it have programs that focus on paying attention. They listen. They contact. They understand the economics, and know what kind of return they're getting on their investment in it.

And they know, at firsthand, why it's true that keeping a client is still cheaper than getting a new one.

CLIENT RELATIONS

Keeping in touch with clients is not—and cannot be—a casual matter. Today's business is too dynamic, and things change constantly. At the same time, your competitors aren't resting from pursuing your clients, so you may not rest.

And inherent in every client may lie a way to mine as much as 20 percent more business than you have now. That mine is a source of more business that you should expect to get from existing clients.

The technique is a process that you should be using anyway for client service, client relations, and client retention (which, by the way, are three different things). Four simple steps...

- Identify the appropriate client.
- Find a basis to hold a conversation (particularly if you're dealing with someone you don't deal with frequently or whom your partners service).
- Carry the conversation from a client satisfaction inquiry to a service information inquiry, to a frank selling situation.
- Perform the service.

One thing you may find is the need for a service that you don't normally perform. That means that you'll have to consider whether to add that capability before the client goes elsewhere for the service.

THE APPROPRIATE CLIENT

There are clients for whom your service potential is at a maximum. Either they're too small, or they have in-house capabilities, or they need things you just don't do. There are clients whose businesses have changed with the economy and new technology, but for whom your service has remained the same. There are clients whose businesses have grown, while your relationship with them has not.

In fact, almost every client offers potential for growth, but time may limit you to only the likeliest candidates. These might be...

- Your larger clients. It seems to be a truism that 80 percent of your revenue comes from 20 percent of your clients. Obviously, they're the most dynamic, and have the most going for them. At the same time, no large company can ever be sure that it's getting every possible tax advantage, that its cash management systems are the most effective, that its financials are always telling what it (or its banks) need to know, that its computer systems are still equal to the needs of the business. In fact, every new tax law, and many other laws, afford an opportunity for contact, and a potential upgrade in your relationship.
- Clients whom you or the current engagement partner know firsthand are susceptible to an expanded program.

- Clients in dynamic industries that you know are subject to regulatory change, or are affected by the new tax law.
- Clients whom you feel might be feeling neglected or underserviced.
- Clients for whom you're performing a limited range of services, no matter how small.

There may be other parameters, but the point is that it's worth taking some time to list and prioritize before you start the process. Go with the likeliest candidates first (unless you'd like to try one or two training calls with the less likely prospects).

Initial Contact

Essentially, you want an approach that seems rational to the client, particularly if it's someone you haven't been in touch with on a regular basis.

If you are the managing partner, it's not only appropriate for you to contact any of the firm's clients, it may also be flattering. The point is that you don't want to have a client put off by the notion that your only purpose is to sell. And as managing partner, you have to take a special responsibility for those 20 percent of clients that supply 80 percent of revenues.

The appointment can be set up by either you or the engagement partner, and in some cases that may be done easily. Send a letter first (conspicuously CC: to the engagement partner, unless it's a client you're directly responsible for), that's something like . . .

Dear _____:

Dave and I were talking about your company the other day, and we realized that while you've been a client of our firm for four years now, you and I haven't talked lately, and I haven't had the opportunity recently to thank you for your business.

I'd like to take that opportunity now. Can we sit down for a few minutes at your convenience?

We're also very concerned that we're serving you well and efficiently, and meeting your [accounting—auditing—tax, etc.] needs thoroughly and effectively, and I'd like to talk to you about that as well.

I'll call you in a day or so, to arrange a meeting at a time convenient for you.

Yours truly,

The Follow-up

The trick is to avoid having the client ask, on the phone, what this is all about—in a way that forces you to deal with him or her by phone. *The purpose of the follow-up phone call is just to get the appointment, not to answer questions.* Very important. The following is a worst-case scenario...

> *"What do you want to see me about?"*
>
> *"Well, as I said in my letter, we haven't talked recently, and as the firm's managing partner, I really want to know our firm's clients better. And while I assume that you're happy with the service you're getting from Dave, you should know who I am, too, and that I'm always available as a backup."*
>
> *"OK, I've met you. I'm really too busy to socialize."*
>
> *"I'm with you on that, which is why this is a business call. It's quite possible that our spending a few minutes together might offer another perspective on what we're doing for you, and how we might improve our service to you."*
>
> *"What did you have in mind?"*
>
> *"Nothing complicated, but I'd really like to meet you and discuss this in person. Is next Tuesday at 10 all right?" (Always move to the specific time.)*

Most calls will be a lot easier. The point is that you have to move to the appointment as quickly as possible, and avoid discussion on the phone that can foreclose a face-to-face meeting.

The Meeting

The meeting itself should be informal. The objectives are simple...

- To lead the conversation to a discussion of the client's business and industry.
- To listen. And not just listen, but to look for opportunities to better serve that client.
- To reach a point at which you can ask the magic question, "If you could resolve that problem, how would it help you?" Not *would it help you,* but *how would it help you?*

If the client starts to answer that question—How would it help you?—that client is going to sell himself or herself to the point where you can say, "Let's start on that first thing in the morning."

The script for the meeting can't be literal—you've got to be at ease with it. Whether you spend time on pleasantries or not is a function of what you're most comfortable with.

The crucial point to remember is that you're not there to sell—you're going *to ask questions*—systematically, and in ways that lead clients to persuade themselves. The client persuades—you don't—and that's why this system works.

LIVING WITH THE MARKETING CULTURE

Some quarter of a century since the *Bates* decision breathed life into professional services marketing, the professions have gone from an arcane, firm-centered, elitist culture to the beginnings of an understanding that at the core of every successful practice is the client. We've gone from groping to sophistication in marketing, which was as new to the professions in those early days as were the first live pictures from Mars.

We've learned a lot about marketing the modern professional firm. But we've learned nothing with greater certainty than that the firm with the best marketing culture is the firm most likely to thrive in the coming decades.

8

IT'S THE END GAME THAT COUNTS

Contact—Turning the Prospect into a Client

It's the bottom line that counts...

—Ancient professional saying

When all the tools of marketing have been used effectively, and the world is persuaded that your firm is among the best available, there still remains the problem of finding yourself face-to-face with the prospect and then moving the prospect to a client. This is the point at which you come to the stark reality that the marketing process, up to this point, can't sell a client. What it can and should do, however, is put you in the same room with the prospect, and do so in a context that enhances the prospect's understanding a great deal about you, your firm, and its capabilities. There are almost always three more stages following a supportive and effective marketing program...

- *Selling the prospect.* In many cases, particularly with smaller firms, that sales call can bring the prospect into the fold. In most cases, however, the best you can hope for—and what you should prefer—is to be invited to submit a proposal. The good thing about a written proposal is that it gives you an opportunity to present your firm, and your sales message, in a carefully thought out process, rather than simply presenting your firm orally.

- *The proposal.* This is a document that requires artistry, must address the prospect's business needs and interests, and must set your firm apart from other bidders, particularly if you find yourself in a competitive situation. This is the document in which you can write, edit, consider, ponder, and bring others into the selling process.

- *The presentation.* Here is where the client is brought to the decision point. If the client's company is small enough, a few individuals, present at the presentation, can make the decision. If the prospect company is larger, the information and impression at the presentation may have to be passed on to others in the company, or a board of directors, or an audit committee. This is why the proposal document is so important—your story may have to be read by people who were not at the presentation, because the ultimate decision may have to be made by people who were not part of the early selling process.

Depending on the size of your firm, the size of the prospect, the nature of the problem, the prospect's management structure, and a few other random factors, the process may vary. But essentially, in one form or another, these three elements are an essential part of the end game of the marketing process.

SELLING

More words have probably been written about selling, and with less comfort to the people who have to do it, than on any other aspect of business.

In professional services marketing, in which the ultimate selling must be done by accountants, lawyers, and other professionals who, "if they wanted to become salespeople, wouldn't have become accountants/lawyers/consultants," selling has become a mystique—a *bête noir.*

One problem with selling is that to many people, it's an art form. In professional services marketing, it's an art form that most professionals would rather stay away from, because of its underlying implication that you're persuading people to do what they don't want to do, which therefore makes it unacceptable—and certainly, unprofessional. Fortunately, the intensity of competition in the professions is altering that attitude.

And perhaps the more serious problem, particularly for nonprofessional salespeople, is the fear of rejection. Hearing *no*, which you hear more frequently in selling than you hear *yes,* can be very painful. Professional salespeople don't take *no* personally, which is a key to successful selling.

To a large degree, these and other stigmas in selling are the vestigial remains of the classic techniques of selling products. Reading a modern book on how to sell, you find it says the same things—albeit in different ways, sometimes—that were said in the 1920s—The "chat 'em up... pitch your product's advantages... close quickly and often" school. In other words, how to persuade... how to exert the power of your personality... how to outtalk and razzle-dazzle your customer. No wonder the accountant or lawyer—the professional—shies away from traditional selling. Selling, says tradition, is for silver-tongued devils.

But suppose you were to think of the process in terms of...

- Identifying the prospect
- Identifying the client's problem or need
- Being sure that the client realizes that you understand the need or problem
- Being sure that the client realizes that you can resolve the need or problem
- Getting the client to agree to start Monday

At no point was the word *selling* used. At no point was the word *persuade* used. What is apparent, though, is that this approach is entirely geared toward satisfying the *client's*—not the *seller's*—needs. Moreover, it seems irrelevant to the classic (and now outmoded) selling techniques. Here it's a straight business approach.

There's no question that, in marketing professional services, any selling technique is better than none at all. The woods are full of training courses that are derived from one technique or another, usually with catchy names, but usually all adding up to the same techniques of persuading and closing. The question is not merely what works—a lot of selling techniques work to one degree or another—but what works *best*.

As in so many aspects of professional services marketing, what works or doesn't work is a function of the differences between product and professional services marketing. Here, the important differences are...

- In product sales, the product stays and the salesperson goes. In professional services, the seller stays.
- In product sales (except for very-high-ticket items), the decision can usually be made by one person, on the spot. In professional services (except for small engagements), getting to a buy decision usually involves several people, and therefore several meetings. This, incidentally, is why the standard closing techniques are so often irrelevant—you can't even think about standard closing techniques when you're dealing with more than one person.
- In product sales the product is visible and usually has a track record. The next tube of toothpaste you buy is going to be exactly like the last one you bought, and you can rely on that. In professional services, each project or engagement is brand new, and the professional's ability to deal with it may be assumed, but is really unknown before the performance. Faith and trust is significant—*which*

is why the ultimate sale must be made by the professional who performs (or is responsible for overseeing the performance of) the engagement.

If we think in terms of the client and the client's need, then we see a somewhat different approach to selling than the classic charm/persuade/close algorithm. It's an approach based on the SPIN Selling techniques developed by Neil Rackham, of Huthwaite, Inc. in his book, *Spin Selling*. What we are after is asking the prospect the kinds of questions that will lead to his or her understanding, without external persuasion, that...

- You understand the nature of his or her need or problem.
- The prospect sees the need or problem in a highly focused way.
- The prospect understands the ramification of not serving that need or solving that problem.
- The prospect understands what you can bring to serving that need or solving that problem.
- The prospect understands the value of not only the solution, but of *your* supplying that solution, and *persuades himself or herself* that you should be retained.

Persuades himself or herself that you should be retained. That's the crux of it. You don't sell the prospect—the prospect sells him- or herself. And it's done by asking questions the answers to which lead to an inevitable conclusion. No selling. No glibness on your part. No promises you can't keep or representations that just aren't so. It's all business, and all businesslike.

The secret is in two things—the basic thrust of thinking like the client, and the questions you ask.

The questions are in four different categories, asked progressively, to lead to the ultimate objective—the sale. The four categories are...

- *Situation questions,* designed to elicit basic information regarding the prospect's needs or problems. *Situation questions*—such as, "How would you describe your product line?" or "What are the principal competitive factors in your business?"—allow you to...
  - Turn up potential problem areas that you can help resolve
  - Give you the opportunity to be a good listener and build rapport
- *Problem questions,* designed to move the discussion to focus on the real needs, and most urgent problems, faced by the prospect. The emphasis here is on

focus. Problem questions—such as, "Do you find yourself losing market share?" or, "Are you satisfied that your current reporting systems are giving you adequate information, on a daily basis, to allow you to make fast business decisions?"—take the information you've gotten from the situation questions, and turns it into a probing of the depth and gravity of the problem or the prospect's needs. While there may be a tendency and urge to offer solutions, it's too soon; the prospect isn't ready to hear them. Problem questions, on the other hand, focus on the prospect's real problems and needs—frequently more concisely than the prospect has done him- or herself. By clarifying the problem, by seeing it more clearly, the prospect frequently sees a greater urgency to solve it. Vague and ill-defined problems tend not to be urgent.

At the same time, prematurely suggesting a solution can lead to a prospect rejecting the solution or offering excuses why the proposed solution won't work. This approach also deprives the prospect of the sense of participation in the solution—the *ownership* of the solution—so crucial to this kind of selling.

Problem questions also allow you to learn more about an opportunity, problem, or potential problem, and allow you to demonstrate—through the relevant questions you ask—your ability and experience. Better to demonstrate through questioning than to describe that expertise.

- *Implication questions,* designed to focus on the implications to the prospect of not addressing the need or solving the problem. Implication questions—such as "How much do you think it's costing you, in expenses or lost opportunity, not to have a firmer grip on your day-by-day company performance?" or, "How will not solving this problem affect your competitive situation?"— magnify or quantify the significance of a problem. They ask, in effect, "What are the implications to your business of *not* solving these problems?"

Implication questions bring to the discussion the ultimate realization that the problem is clear, that the need for solution is urgent, and that you understand the nature of the problem. This context serves as a platform for successfully bringing the prospect to the conclusion that you are capable of solving his or her problem; of filling the need.

- *Need-payoff questions,* designed to focus on the benefits to the prospect or client of your addressing the need or solving the problem. It's at this point that the prospect is made to understand your service, and how it can help solve the problems. Need-payoff questions—such as, "If you could figure out a way for you to acquire that company without more debt, how would that help you?" or, "If you could install a reporting system for you that would keep you up-to-the-minute on the crucial data you need to run your company on a day-by-day basis, how would this help you run your company more effectively?"—bring the prospect into a receptive mode for your explanation of how you can help.

If the three prior groups of questions are properly handled, the answers to *need-payoff questions* will invariably be in your favor.

Need-payoff questions also tell you whether the prospect has any unresolved concerns, and how seriously the prospect sees the problem and the need for solution. They lead to a distillation of his or her vision of the client's company. Favorable answers are the clues to tell you that the prospect is prepared to discuss your services, and the terms of engagement. And by having established the value of the solution, you have a better context for pricing. Because the return on the investment in your service is so clear, the price is less arbitrary, and less of a concern to the buyer, in terms of the value offered by your services.

SPIN Selling is a system designed to generate eagerness to accept your solution, a willingness to believe that you can serve the prospect's needs or solve his or her problems, a demonstration of proof that your solution works for the prospect. It remains, then, only for you to describe your services, and how they will contribute to the prospect's business in ways that are acceptable to him or her.

This is selling based upon leading prospects to their own conclusions that you've identified the problem or opportunity; that you understand it; that you can help resolve it. And by leading prospects to those conclusions, rather than bulling your way to the conclusions by arduous persuasion, you've moved the selling process from a heavy-handed process to a business consultative conversation that's very much within the realm of your professional training and background.

Does the system work? Based on extensive experience, it works to a far greater degree than any other selling system now being taught to professionals.

Selling, even for full-time salespeople, is tough. For professionals trying classic selling techniques, it's too often inimical to both training and personality. The client satisfaction selling approach, however, uses only those skills of thinking and interpersonal relationships that are inherent in every professional's training and makeup. It uses business conversation, rather than the kind of persuasion that too often leads to rejection, and it uses the professionals' technical business skills in a comfortable context. It's clearly the technique of choice for training professionals to sell.

USING OUTSIDE SALESPEOPLE

What was once unthinkable under the traditional Canons of Ethics for professionals—using outside salespeople to sell professional services—is now increasingly standard. But while there is no tradition for doing so, there's a growing body of knowledge about how to do it successfully. It's not as cut and dried as it is in selling a product, because with rare exceptions, no matter how skillful the salesperson, no matter how effective the marketing campaign, the ultimate sale must be made by the professional who performs the service.

The problem is twofold—determining what an outside salesperson can and can't sell, and finding and training the right person.

You must recognize that to a very large degree, all the salesperson can do is produce the opportunity for you to make a presentation, and ultimately, the sale. Virtually nobody hires a lawyer or an accountant without meeting the professional who will perform the service. The exceptions may be in the very routine tasks of both accounting and law—perhaps those services, for example, that can be performed by an off-the-shelf computer program for, say, bookkeeping, or for writing simple contracts. But for any service about which the client might feel sensitive, even the best salesperson can't do it. Also included in the exceptions may be clearly defined consulting services that are so standard as to transcend anxiety by the client. For example, installing off-the-shelf software for some applications, or selling standardized training programs. But these are indeed exceptions.

You have to understand as well that no salesperson—no marketing program, for that matter—can sell your firm. All that can be sold are your firm's services—very specific services, geared to the needs of the prospective client—not to the services you want to sell. If your services don't meet the needs of prospective clients in your market area, change your services, not your sales pitch.

You must be careful of your expectations. If you think that a hotshot salesperson is going to sell up a storm, and that you don't have to do anything but service the clients that come cascading in, and that you can abdicate all responsibilities for marketing and selling, then you're due for a serious disappointment. Don't bother to even consider hiring a salesperson.

It will pay only if you're prepared to back the sales effort with good marketing. It needn't be elaborate, but it should be organized and consistent with your firm, its services, and your market. It may be a newsletter, or some articles, or a few seminars, and probably some printed material, such as brochures. But don't think you can send a salesperson out cold and expect results.

HOW DO YOU MAKE IT WORK?

Assuming that all the foregoing is in place, you should do at least this to make outside salespeople work...

- *Hire right.* It's difficult to bring somebody into your firm from a culture that's different, and with skills you've never had to use before. And salespeople are indeed different. They are, generally, outgoing, gregarious, energetic in a physical sense, and have egos that allow them to hear the word "no" without taking it personally. Not all salespeople are equal—in skills, in experience, in intellect, in temperament. Silvia Coulter, chief marketing and business development officer for Dorsey & Whitney LLP and a pioneer in using outside salespeople, says, "Hire someone with solid sales experience who lived off commissionable dollars and worked toward a significant revenue target. This individual will know how to help lawyers [and accountants] build prospect lists and close business."

  There must be the ability to understand the nature of your practice. Not just accounting or law, but the specifics of your practice, and your strengths and weaknesses. Your salesperson must be able to understand the differences between selling a service and selling a professional service—to make the prospect understand why your firm, and no other, should be chosen to supply the service he or she may already know is needed.

  The salesperson must be able to grasp the crucial concept of addressing a specific service or need, and not just trying to sell the whole firm generally. No matter how large or multifaceted your firm may be, only one service can be sold at a time at the initial contact.

  Your salesperson must be able to recognize that all that he or she can sell is the opportunity for you to make a personal presentation. More salespeople fail by saying too much at an initial meeting, by trying to move the whole ball of wax in one call, by answering questions that you should answer as part of your presentation—thereby allowing the prospect time to build resistance and to think of reasons why not. A clearly demonstrated ability and experience in integrating the selling effort with other marketing activities is important. Your salesperson should be able to accept that he or she is part of a team effort, and part of a process—that in selling a professional service, unlike selling a product, selling doesn't stand alone.

- *Train right.* You may not know anything about selling (which, by the way, can be as professional in its tenets as law or accounting), but you do have a sense of what you do, and what you want your clients to know or think or feel about you, or what your clients expect of you. Somebody who's never sold professional services before may be a great salesperson, but not without a lot of orientation about you, your firm, and your services.

- *Communicate internally.* Let your partners and staff know what you're doing, and get their input. Certainly, enlist their aid. Your salesperson needs all available help and cooperation. It will pay off for you to think in terms of a team. And keep your partners and staff clear on expectations, lines of authority, and so forth.

- *Listen to feedback.* Selling opens up two-way channels. Your salespeople are out there selling. But they're also listening. A good salesperson is as valuable as a listener as he or she is as a persuader.

- *Compensate fairly and realistically.* This is an interesting problem. There are more questions raised than answered. How do you pay, for example, if salespeople only produce leads, but are not responsible for results? How can you calculate a basis for commissions if you have to do the final selling? How do you get the best salespeople without your having a track record that offers them some sense of how much they can earn? Experience in different approaches is growing. Talk to others who've done it.

- *Create a prospect list at each seminar the firm produces,* suggests Coulter. "Sit with the attorneys who spoke at the seminar and assign each prospect to an attorney for follow-up. Add these names and follow up dates to the sales forecast spreadsheet that is sent to management," she says.

- *Develop a major client/strategic account plan.* "Select 10 to 15 clients for whom the firm does work," Coulter suggests. "Assign a team leader to 'the account' and meet with them to develop an annual strategic account plan for each client." Identify annual revenue goals, she says, and discuss those goals with the core account team and leaders.

- *Master the database technology.* "Keeping track of key clients and other important firm clients' needs, likes and dislikes, along with sales activities, is critical to the process of developing new business," Coulter points out. Carefully tracking activities, she says, is critical to avoid missteps in the process. "Everyone needs to know who at your firm has had contact with any given client or prospect to avoid the appearance of being disorganized to the buyer. Very few sales organizations can thrive without the use of automation to help track sales prospecting activities." Firms should consider using CRM—customer relationship management software—such as ACT!, Goldmine, or Microsoft Outlook.

- *Train yourself and others to sell.* No way around it—you're going to have to learn how to sell. OK, don't call it selling, but you've still got to learn these five points, noted earlier...

  ○ How to identify a prospective client

  ○ How to understand that prospect's needs or problems

  ○ How to make the prospect understand that you understand his or her needs or problems

- How to make the prospect understand that you can help meet his or her needs or solve his or her problems

- How to get the prospect to agree to start working with you on Monday

Now, at no time did we use the word *selling*. And not one of these five things can be done by anybody but you.

- *Manage the process.* You don't hire a salesperson and then walk away, feeling that your responsibility is over. In addition to all of the foregoing, the sales process must be managed in terms of territory, process, sales message, coordination with marketing efforts, integration into the firm, processing feedback, and on and on—a long list of management issues that contribute to the effective sales process. It doesn't happen by itself.

Yes, there is a difference between using outside salespeople and relying on the firm's professionals. The process of using professional salespeople to sell professional services is really just emerging. There are successes, but there are more failures. Unfortunately, too many of the failures derive not from inadequate efforts of the salesperson, but from the inability of the firm's partners to grasp the meaning of the function and the process—to expect the wrong things, and thereby, to manage the process badly. An expensive waste that derives from impatience.

Is this the whole story? No, of course not. The concept of using professional salespeople to sell professional services is still new. But it's a great start. Pay attention to the future.

THE PROPOSAL

It would be nice if professional services could be sold like vacuum cleaners. The salesperson makes a pitch; the pitch is accepted by one individual, money changes hands, the vacuum cleaner stays, and the salesperson leaves.

But obviously that's not how it works. Whether it be through one marketing effort—an article or a seminar—or as the result of a massive marketing campaign that informs, that builds reputation, and that enhances name recognition, you or a representative of your firm is invited by the prospect to discuss your firm and its capabilities. That's where the selling process comes in.

If the sales techniques work well, you may be asked to submit a written proposal. This is certainly standard for large firms, and it's become increasingly so for smaller firms, particularly in competitive situations, or where several people must make the final buy decision. At the same time, large-scale proposals are not always in order, and because they can be tremendously time consuming and expensive, many firms are opting not to do them.

All that may be required is a simple letter, showing that you understand the prospect's needs or opportunities and describing your ability to help and that you have the techniques to do just that. But simple or elaborate, the proposal is still a selling document, and should be written under the guidelines outlined in this chapter.

In fact, even if you're not asked for a proposal, you should consider doing it. Why?

Because unless you're a super salesperson, who can carefully and precisely articulate your sales message, the written proposal is your opportunity to think out the reasons why you should be hired, and then, having set it all down on paper, rethink your message, edit it, and hone it. This is the blessing of the written proposal.

This is a judgment call, in which you evaluate as best you can whether advantages outweigh the effort and cost of doing a written proposal.

If the decision to retain your services is to be made by several people at different management levels, the proposal may be the only way to get your message through to a decision maker who wasn't at your original sales presentation. And even if you are dealing directly with the ultimate decision maker, the proposal document enhances the ability to make a considerate decision. To be thoughtful in making the buying decision. To review points that help make the decision.

Certainly, in a competitive situation, the ability to write a good proposal may be the winning edge.

THE REQUEST FOR PROPOSAL

In many cases, and particularly where your firm is one of several being considered, a prospect may send you an RFP—a Request For Proposal. You are being asked to give reasons why your firm should be hired, what you would do, who would do it, and how much it would cost. What you do next can cost you the assignment, or give you the competitive edge that makes the difference.

The RFP may be as simple as a verbal request for a proposal, or it may be a document of many pages, delineating precisely what information is needed. But regardless of the nature of the RFP, the criteria for deciding to pursue the client, and the criteria for responding, remain the same.

Your first step upon receiving the RFP, according to Gilbert R. Parker of Parker Consulting, is to review it with your associates to consider whether you should accept the opportunity or reject it.

Parker, who has directed, managed, and written more than 225 successful proposals for the largest accounting and consulting firms in the world, suggests that the criteria to use in deciding to accept or decline the RFP should be based upon such factors as . . .

- Business opportunity
- Strategic fit of the prospect's company to your firm
- Significance of the work
- Practice building potential
- Resources required
- Start-up investments needed
- Inherent risks of serving the company (management integrity, financial performance, engagement profitability, and company survivability in its industry)

Consider also that it's a not infrequent practice to invite several firms to submit proposals even though a selection has already been made. Thousands of dollars have been wasted in doing proposals under these circumstances. While it may be difficult to do, try to determine the legitimacy of the request.

If you and your associates agree that this can be the right client for you, and after you've done a great deal of homework to confirm the foundation for your decisions, Parker suggests, "Be one of the first firms, not the last, to call and write the company contact confirming your strong interest in proposing." It's perfectly appropriate, he says, to ask which other firms are proposing, and what the company's criteria are for ranking and selecting service providers, so you can assess your qualifications and chances for success.

It's extremely important, Parker emphasizes, that you precisely follow the RFP's guidelines and ground rules that govern the proposal process, including plans for initial meetings, bidder conferences, site visits, written documents, oral presentations, and other deliverables. Follow as well the detailed instructions for completing and submitting proposal documents—including organization of material, content, format, maximum length, section numbering, contract terms/conditions, administrative forms, government compliance, binding, packaging, and delivery specifics. "Make sure that your firm is in full compliance with the RFP," Parker says, "so that you're not penalized or disqualified for being unresponsive."

THE PROPOSAL STRATEGY

Responding to a request for proposal should be thoughtful and considerate, and not simply an ad hoc attempt to display your capabilities. If possible, it should be done as part of a team consisting of your partners and associates—particularly those in your firm who are likely to be the professionals working on that account—your marketing professional, associates and partners whose skills you particularly respect in communicating with skill and originality, and, if possible, an experienced proposal specialist.

Traditionally, before we had experienced the rigors of competition in the professions, it was considered standard to respond to requests for proposals with a catalog of the firm's capabilities, its size, its clients, its personnel, and a raft of other self-serving data that ultimately made each firm sound like every other firm in the profession. After *Bates*, and with the advent of the computer and its graphics capabilities, proposals became elaborate and fancy. Proposals then became over-packaged with all kinds of irrelevant graphics on CDs and on videotapes. None of these attention-getting devices was ever really significant in a competitive situation.

What, then, makes the difference? The difference is in your ability to demonstrate to the prospect that...

- You understand the prospect's problem and the need for your services.
- You convey the fact that you understand.
- You convey that you can specifically address and understand that problem, and resolve it.
- You bring specialized skills and innovative solutions to solve the problem.
- You have the resources and capability to serve the client's specific needs.

In fact, the successful proposal is the one that best demonstrates that the client, not the one who proposes, is at the core of the relationship.

Thus, the winning strategy, notes Parker, will invariably be the one that fully supports each prospect's business objectives, goals, and plans, and one that delivers real economic value and other benefits to the company.

With proposals, as with any written document for your firm, the initial question that should be addressed thoughtfully is "What do you want the reader of this document to know, think or feel after reading it?" Asking that question helps focus the content and thrust of the proposal to more precisely meeting the prospect's needs, and best focuses on your ability to meet those needs.

In addition to demonstrating at the outset that you understand and can address the prospect's needs, Parker adds these elements of a winning proposal...

- *Best engagement individuals or team.* Select the most highly qualified individuals or team in your firm to serve the company, not just the available people. Provide top-management oversight of the engagement; a senior client service executive with strong leadership qualities—a core team of specialists with the right mix of relevant skills and experience; plus any business, industry, and technical advisors. Make sure the personal chemistry is right between team members and company executives.
- *Company knowledge.* Demonstrate in-depth knowledge of the company's business objectives, goals, and plans—based on the RFP and publicly available information previously researched and analyzed. Show a real understanding of

the industry—its business outlook, growth, profitability, competition, pricing, regulation, and trends and developments. Confirm and clarify the RFP service requirements; and ask insightful, probing questions about the scope of work and client expectations.

- *Value proposition.* Develop a compelling value proposition that provides your firm's *best value* solution with all of the strategic, operational, technology, and cost-reduction benefits clearly spelled out for the prospect. Show how your firm's service offerings will help the prospective client compete more successfully in the marketplace—in terms of increasing top-line revenues, accelerating new product development, gaining greater market share, and better serving its own customers.

- *Creative business ideas.* Offer creative business ideas, innovative solutions, best practices, and other initiatives to help the company achieve its business objectives, goals, and plans. Discuss these ideas with company executives during meetings and site visits; test and refine the ideas before including them later in the written proposal and oral presentation. Offer to conduct a special study or consulting project, for free or a nominal fee, to assist the company with an important project and to demonstrate expertise.

- *Best value pricing.* Determine how best to structure the pricing of the engagement to provide the prospective client with the best business and financial value, while providing your firm with an assured contribution to profit, operating margin, and internal rate of return. Pricing options to be considered might include time and materials, fixed price, cost plus, transaction based, incentive based, shared risk/reward, joint venture, operating company, and other arrangements.

- *Competitive advantage.* Conduct a *SWOT* analysis (Strengths, Weaknesses, Opportunities, Threats) of your firm versus major competitors—to help map out a winning proposal strategy. This analysis is not used to run down competitors, but rather to help make a realistic assessment of your firm's resources, capabilities, industry expertise, and core competencies. Decide how to build on your firm's strengths while minimizing its weaknesses.

- *Client service plan.* Develop a comprehensive and detailed client service plan that is tailored to the prospect's business requirements, needs, and interests. The plan should cover scope of work; service level and quality; management oversight; governance; centralized planning and control; organization and staffing; roles and responsibilities; technical approach and methodology; project work plans; major phases and tasks; transitions; deliverables; timetables; milestones; expected results and outcomes; budgets; and reporting.

- *Alliance and partnerships.* Determine whether your firm should expand its product or service offerings, or acquire any specialized resources, or form any alliances or partnerships with specialist firms, to bolster your competitive position, better qualify for serving certain clients, and deliver a more integrated or total solution. Today's service providers are forming bidding consortia more than ever before.

If the size of your firm and the nature of the prospective client warrants it, using external sales proposal consultants can provide independent and objective advice on proposal strategy, written documents, and oral presentations. They can provide guidance on your value proposition, business and technical solutions, competitive positioning, and key selling points to differentiate your firm. Once the selection decision is made, they can interview key executives to evaluate why your firm won or lost, and provide valuable insights on firm strengths and weaknesses. And should you not win the account, it's a good idea, and perfectly appropriate, to politely ask why you didn't get it. The answer will give the best education you can get on how to do the next proposal.

As you gain experience in doing this kind of proposal, and with input from prospects on why you won or lost, you'll build an expertise that will stand you in good stead in future proposals. Having a good proposal team to review proposal drafts and presentation plans helps.

If it's possible and appropriate, try to get personal introductions to senior executives through your firm's contacts with the company's management, board of directors, law firms, accounting firms, and other influencers. Parker suggests that you then develop effective working relationships with these senior executives, as well as with the other executives who are made available for interviews as part of the proposal process. If appropriate, invite them to the firm's offices and facilities as well as to business seminars, social affairs, and special events.

With basic proposal strategy taking shape—it will be refined as you go through the sales proposal process—your client service and marketing and sales team will be better able to manage their selling activities in a more effective way, and to gather the vital information needed to prepare an outstanding written proposal.

The Sales Document

Because the proposal is a powerful sales document, the choice of who should write it is determined by who, in your firm, has...

- The most relevant industry and technical credentials
- The deepest understanding of the prospect's needs
- The most creative, cost-effective business solutions
- The most highly responsive client service plan
- The best business/financial value for the company

The written proposal, Parker points out, has to be a powerful sales document that communicates these messages and really distinguishes your firm from the competition. It has to address the top-management decision makers, their primary reasons for buying your firm's products/services, and their criteria for ranking and selecting a service provider.

The written proposal has to convey a professional view of a firm that delivers superior quality and excellence, he says. It has to be well organized and strong on substance and content. It has to be written in a clear, concise, and readable style. And it has to be customized and tailored to each individual prospective client organization with no boilerplate. Boilerplate—indeed, any show of lack of originality and focused understanding of the prospect's specific needs—is easily recognized and sharply diminishes the prospect's view of your firm.

Parker suggests some practical guidelines for preparing the written proposal...

- *Proposal planning.* Organize the proposal group, no matter the size of the team, with clear roles and responsibilities for the document's development. The proposal team should study RFP questions in detail, and assign questions to those best qualified to answer them. The team should agree early on value proposition, bid strategy, positioning, content, formats, and other elements, and have a clear work plan for document development, review, editing, and production.

- *Proposal cover.* Prepare a well-designed cover (preferably in color, with your firm's name and logo on the first page) with the prospect's and provider's names and logos. It should state the main title precisely and a subtitle as appropriate. It helps to add a positioning or key selling theme to be emphasized throughout the entire document; include RFP reference number and date as required.

- *Transmittal letter.* In the transmittal letter, your firm's senior executives should refer to your firm's value proposition, positioning theme, shared goals and values, expected benefits and results, and resources and commitments. The letter may have multiple signatures to show top-management attention. It should be no longer than two pages, and not preempt the summary.

- *Contents page.* This page should give readers a clear view of the organization of the major sections, subsections, and appendixes. It should use descriptive selling captions and headings, and a clear numbering and lettering scheme. It should have a separate section for RFP questions and answers, and provide a cross-reference subject index as a helpful guide for larger, multivolume proposals.

- *Summary* (sometimes unfortunately referred to as an Executive Summary, which is an unwarranted cliché). This opening section (5 to 10 pages, or even

15 pages for mega-proposals) should literally be a summary of your proposal, demonstrating, as concisely as possible, your understanding of the prospect's needs, your ability to meet those needs, and your ability to add value to the prospect's company. It should give the top-executive decision makers about 10 to 15 persuasive reasons, key selling points, and distinguishing factors for selecting your firm. The summary may be your firm's workhorse sales pitch, because management readers have come to expect it.·

- *Statement of the prospect's needs.* This should be the introduction, because without demonstrating to the prospect that you understand those needs, the remainder of the proposal is diluted. If this introduction is written carefully and thoughtfully, it helps the prospect focus on his or her own need for your services. It's the foundation for the solutions you offer in subsequent pages, and it sets the platform—and the relevance—of the solutions you offer. It is an excellent device to control the course of the ultimate dialogue with the prospect. It should help establish your firm's in-depth knowledge of the company's business objectives, goals, and plans, as well as industry trends and developments that impact the company's competitive standing and future. It should address the executives' special service needs, interests, and priorities.

- *Value proposition.* This section should present a compelling value proposition that provides your firm's *best value* solution with all of the strategic, operational, technology, and cost-reduction benefits clearly spelled out for the company. Discuss exactly how the firm will deliver these expected benefits and results as well as their estimated business and financial value to the organization. Also describe your pricing policies and pricing structure.

- *Best engagement team.* Introduce the engagement team leaders, directors, managers, and staff in a highly personalized way—with their roles, responsibilities, and relevant experience clearly spelled out. Provide similar information on industry or technical specialists with ongoing roles in the engagement. Provide an organization chart showing individual names, titles, and reporting relationships; and prepare customized resumes that really sell each person's relevant experience and accomplishments. Photographs of the team members, along with personal quotes, can, if appropriate, be helpful.

- *Responsive service plan.* Describe the firm's comprehensive and detailed client service plan and show how it is tailored to meet the company's special requirements, needs, and interests. The plan should cover scope of work; service level and quality; management oversight; governance; centralized planning and control; organization and staffing; roles and responsibilities; technical approach and methodology; project work plans; major phases and tasks; transitions; deliverables; timetables; milestones; expected results and outcomes;

budgets; and reporting strategies. Make sure your plan satisfies all of the RFP's statement of work requirements as specified; but also provide alternative solutions and constructive suggestions for better ways of doing things.

- *Responses to RFP questions.* Create a separate section with this name to keep all of the RFP questions and answers together in one place. Type each question in bold or italics, using the prospect's numbering or lettering scheme so that readers unfamiliar with the RFP know what the questions are before reading your answers. Provide clear, concise, and responsive answers to the RFP questions. Answer each question directly before explaining or providing background information. Aim for high marks on each individual question and answer, because firms will likely be scored on each response.

- *Firm experience and credentials.* Demonstrate, in this section, your firm's leadership, resources, capabilities, and expertise in key industries, service lines, technical specialties, and subject matter. Your firm's profile should describe your global organization (if relevant), management team, vision and mission, products and services, relevant experience, and advanced technologies. Provide complete client lists and well-researched client service citations, with engagement summaries and results achieved.

- *References and influencers.* Make effective use of the favorable research/ analyst reports that have been published about your firm by others, including clients (with their explicit permission), bankers, lawyers, civic leaders, and other influentials. These reports provide excellent third-party validation of your firm's leadership, capabilities, and reputation in your field—and carry a good deal of weight in the vendor selection process. If appropriate, include quotes from satisfied clients and executives about your excellent track record of responsive client service.

When the proposal is completed, and carefully reviewed by as many of your staff and partners as reasonably possible, Parker suggests that you hand deliver it on the date it is actually due. Don't try to score points by delivering it a day or two early, he wisely suggests, because your strategy and fees may get leaked to the competition.

ORAL PRESENTATIONS

This is the moment of fire and truth—the point at which the sale is made or denied. This is the culmination of the entire marketing process, and the end of the competition against others or, indeed, yourself. The forum for the oral presentation is the ultimate decision maker.

The objective of the oral presentation, then, is to get the client. To build trust that you are capable of performing and delivering what your proposal promises. To add weight and dimension to the promise of your written proposal.

Parker points out that you need to show the prospect's management exactly how your firm will support the prospect's business plans, and what really differentiates your firm from the competition.

There are some possible obstacles and variables that should be considered beforehand. Presumably, for example, the prospective client will have read the proposal, although that isn't always the case. You must therefore be prepared to reiterate every major selling point you made in the written presentation.

There are your own presentation skills, which should be honed. If you aren't experienced in presentation, or if you aren't comfortable with it, investing in professional training is well worthwhile.

Preparation for the presentation is crucial, and Parker outlines a number of steps that should be taken beforehand...

- *The prospect's executives.* Confirm which company executives will be attending the oral presentation. If it's feasible, you might call executives with whom you've already met, and who have presumably read the written proposal, to ask what topics they would like emphasized in their areas of interest and responsibility. This helps to personalize the presentation and demonstrate responsiveness to their individual service needs. At this point, it may even be possible to ask for feedback on your firm's written proposal. Try to learn what the key decision makers especially like or dislike about it, what questions and concerns they may have, and what topics and issues they want to discuss at the orals. Ask how the proposal ranks against the competition, in terms of people, services, technologies, pricing, and other vendor selection criteria. Be responsive to any company requests for additional clarifying information that may be needed to address critical matters. Assume that any last-minute questions are very important and could be deal-breakers, so figure out what the questions really signify and answer them fully and properly. *The more you know beforehand, the better your presentation is likely to be.*

- *Understand the rules.* Be sure you understand, from either the RFP or discussions with your initial contact at the prospect's company, the company's guidelines, ground rules, and expectations for the oral presentation, including agenda, format, available dates, time allotted for prepared remarks and questions and answers, and other meeting logistics. Be sensitive to the corporate culture and management style—find out what kinds of presentations the management and the board of directors are accustomed to, how formal or informal their meetings are, and what their personal preferences and priorities are. If possible and appropriate, check out the conference room and audio-visual equipment being made available for the bidders' presentations.

- *Distinctive differences.* Recognize that the dozen or so attendees will have different views about your proposal, different service requirements, and different internal political agendas. If you can learn these differences beforehand, you can be prepared to address each person's individual needs and interests, and anticipate potential objections and resistance.

- *Presentation team.* Select the very best individuals in your firm. Try to match the number and level of presenters with the company's executive attendees. Your senior person should clearly be in charge of the meeting, from opening remarks to concluding summary. Your main presenters should be the people who will actually be doing the work, supported by other resources or industry and technical specialists. Whoever participates, they must all be seen as a cohesive team of professionals who work well together.

- *Meeting agenda.* Prepare an agenda that highlights the points of your proposal that demonstrate your understanding of the prospect's needs and your ability to meet those needs, including your service plan, qualifications, and points of the written proposal. The presenter's job is to make the proposal really come alive, with more personal energy, enthusiasm, and commitment than can be expressed in the written document. "Remember, too," says Parker, "that some of the most important senior executive decision makers may have been too busy to read the proposal; they often come to the presentation assuming that each firm will tell them everything they need to know to make their vendor selection decision—so tell them loud and clear."

- *Presentation guide.* Provide a basic presentation guide to the executives at the start of the meeting, so they can better follow the speakers and slides being shown, take notes of important items and questions, and have a convenient summary document to refer to later as they make their selection decision. Emphasis here is on *summary*, simply because you don't want an audience reading while you're talking.

- *References.* If you can, be sure to distribute copies or excerpts of favorable research or analyst reports and articles that have been published about your firm. These reports provide excellent third-party validation of your firm's leadership, capabilities, and reputation in your field. Talk about your satisfied clients and what their executives say about your excellent track record of responsive client service and the results achieved. Third-party endorsement is important to demonstrate that what others say about you is equal to what you say about yourself.

- *Team rehearsals.* Rehearse. No matter how highly you cherish your presentation skills, rehearse. You should count on your competitors to do so, and invariably, the better-prepared individual or team wins. If possible, practice before a panel of colleagues and consultants for their feedback. Consider using a video camera so that individual speakers can critique themselves, because the camera never lies and reveals everything.

- *Questions and answers.* With a third of the presentation time typically allocated to Q&A, you need to anticipate the many tough questions that may be asked and develop the best answers. These questions, and your answers, should be rehearsed. This is a critical part of the presentation, because it's the best opportunity for the prospect's management to get a sense of who you are and what it might be like to work with you. At the presentation, listen to the question carefully, maybe repeat your understanding of it, then answer it clearly and concisely right away. "Give direct answers," Parker says, "as in a legal deposition, and don't hedge, duck, or ramble into negative areas that could weaken your case."

- *Deliver with passion.* You and the presentation team have to show a deep understanding of the company's business needs, and articulate a compelling understanding of both the prospect's needs and your solutions that will support the company's strategic business plan. You and your firm have to distinguish yourselves from the competition as the best-qualified firm, with the most relevant industry and technical credentials, with the most highly responsive service plan, and offering the best business and financial value. Presenters should speak with energy and conviction, establish good rapport with the executives, and engage them in a meaningful dialogue. They should come across as friendly, sincere, trustworthy, and personally committed to serving the company's best interests long term.

As your firm grows, you may find yourself vying with other firms for larger clients. As your competition increases, then so too should your proposal and presentation professionalism increase. You should not overestimate your abilities in both exercises. You should consider, then, working with RFP and presentation consultants. The RFP consultants can provide valuable guidance on the plan, agenda, and format for the oral presentation, which they will normally attend. Also, they can advise bidders on the vendor selection criteria being used and the weighting of the various selection factors, such as firm resources, organization and staffing, business benefits, technical solution, and pricing arrangements.

Proposal and presentation professionals can offer insights about what key decision makers are thinking, how they view various bidders' proposals, what the more important differences are, and what your firm has to do to offer better value and win confidence. They are trained and experienced in understanding new ideas, initiatives, commitments, and services to introduce at the orals, and how to neutralize and overcome any competitive advantages that other bidders may have already gained through the written proposal stage.

THE FOLLOW-UP

Try to find opportunities to follow up with appropriate executives to reinforce key points in your presentation, but be careful to avoid overselling. Certainly, a thank-you letter should be sent, reaffirming your commitment and enthusiasm for serving the company. You might seek further meetings to clarify and negotiate scope of work and pricing to be more competitive with other bidders. Or, if it seems appropriate, you might arrange for satisfied clients to call or meet with key decision makers. Carefully thought out and appropriate postpresentation steps you take could be the tiebreaker that puts your firm in first place to win the account.

In many cases, the final selection decisions are not made or communicated immediately following the presentation. If there are several decision makers, they need time to consider what they've heard, to check references, and to debate the merits of different firms. Meanwhile, stay in close touch with the prospect.

If you haven't heard the results after a reasonable time, it's appropriate to make discreet phone calls to ask.

And if you don't get the account, you should find out why. Few companies will decline your request for the information. The point here is not to try to change a decision—that rarely works. What you want to learn is what you did wrong, and how to do it right the next time. And while a postmortem following the presentation is useful, doing it after you've been told you didn't get the account is even more important.

In recent years, professional service firms have refined their sales, proposal, and presentation practices to a high level of sophistication, as they've gained more experience in winning and losing new business opportunities. Experience, imagination, skill, and professionalism have helped develop skill and sophistication. Competition will always do that, of course. And the winning firm—the client-oriented firm—will be the one seeking and using that skill and sophistication, and the best sales proposal practices.

PART IV

MARKETING TOOLS AND HOW TO USE THEM

9

HANG HIGH THE RAFTERS, CARPENTER

The Tools of Marketing that Build the Marketing Program

It's not the tools, it's the way they're used.

—Bruce W. Marcus

There are three obstacles to competing successfully in professional services. One is that all professional services firms do essentially the same thing as all other firms in the same profession. The second obstacle is that within the sharply defined limits of professional services marketing, all firms have the same finite number of marketing tools. The third is the limitations on the use of these tools, due both to ethical and traditional considerations, and to the realities of professional practice.

But these obstacles are, at the same time, opportunities to be more thoughtful and original—to use the tools more skillfully and imaginatively. It's necessary, then, to understand not only the basic and realistic uses of each tool, but the art of using each tool effectively.

ARTICLES

In a competitive situation, just having your name known is pretty useless, unless it's known for *something*. A good *personal injury lawyer*—not just a good lawyer. A good *audit or tax accountant*—not just a good accountant. In professional services, it's the reputation for expertise that counts, not just the reputation. This is why one of the most effective objectives for any marketing program for a professional service is to project expertise.

There are many ways to do it, but one of the best and most reliable is the article. In a byline article, you don't have to say you're an expert—the fact that you wrote the article, expounding on a particular subject, says it for you. It's your expertise on display.

The reader is concerned with the value of the content of the article—the expertise—and not the size of the author's firm.

An article is the one technique in public relations in which you have control—you can say what you want to say, and say it your way. In most cases, if an article is acceptable on its own terms, an editor won't change the thrust of it. In other aspects of publicity, you propose, but others dispose. Your press release is edited to the editor's satisfaction, not yours. But your article says what you want it to say.

For most publications that might accept a byline article from you, particularly the local or trade journals that might be most useful to you and your practice, you don't have to be a famous writer to write an article that's likely to be accepted. You merely have to know what you're talking about, say something useful to the publication's readers, and be reasonably articulate. An editor may help with syntax and style, but isn't generally likely to touch content.

And finally, the article does double duty. Not only does it have its value when it's published, but as a reprint, it becomes a powerful marketing tool. It says what you would want to say in a brochure, but as a reprint it has the additional sense of the publication's implied endorsement and objectivity. It can be used, then, as a brochure might be, but with added benefits. In direct mail, for example, it can serve as a point of departure for the mailing piece's discussion.

There are seven basic elements to using articles effectively...

- *Identify the purpose of the article.* What do you want people to know, think, or feel after they read the article? What do you want the marketing effort to accomplish, and what do you want the article to accomplish? If the article is part of an overall marketing program, it will be used to support other marketing efforts. If it must serve as the sole effort, it must stand alone in accomplishing its aim. The common factor is to enhance your reputation by allowing you and your expertise to be visible before an audience of the publication's readers, and to do so in a broader context of expertise.
- *Identify the subject matter*
  - What do you know?
  - What expertise do you want to project that will best help you in practice development?
  - What will be the specific subject matter?

You are addressing a specific problem of a specific target audience with the expertise you most want to project. Try not to cover more than one major subject in each article.

• *Identify the publications you will target.* There are several directories available, such as *Bacon's Directories* (Chicago), that list all magazines by category. The chances are, though, that you already know the publications that reach the audiences you want.

• *Place the article.* Think in terms of what the reader wants and needs to know, and not what you want to say. Cast the proposal to the editors in terms of the problem it solves, not merely your solution. Try to relate the magnitude of the problem as large and consequential—as important to the reader, not to you.

When you've identified the publications you want to approach, read several issues carefully to get the feel of the kind of material they use. Then call the editor, and discuss the article you'd like to write. The editor may ask you to put the proposal in writing, but many publications will discuss your idea by phone.

Sometimes a publication's editor will ask to see the article itself before accepting your proposal. This is particularly true if you've never written for the publication before, if you're otherwise unknown to the editor, or if the editor is not convinced of the importance of your subject. It's not a bad thing to do, if you're new to the process. If the article is good, either that editor will take it, or some other publication will. If it's bad, well, you've learned something.

• *Write it.* As an art form, writing has no rules—if the writer is an artist. But for inexperienced or nonprofessional writers, there are some useful guidelines.

   ○ Read several issues of the publication to get a feel for what the editors like and will accept. They, not you, are the boss. They're not going to bend the rules of their publication for you.

   ○ Ask yourself what it is that you want readers to know, think, or feel after they've read your article.

   ○ Do an outline. Even if it's a list of things you want to include in the article. And even if, as you write, you wind up not following it literally. At least you'll have listed everything you want to get in the article.

   ○ Open with a statement of the problem, not the solution, and not the background. Remember that the most important rule in writing is to catch 'em with the opening sentence. If you don't, they're not likely to read the second sentence. If you do, the chances are they'll go through to the end.

- *Know the difference between an academic or legal paper and an article.* An article has to flow. It has to be interesting. Avoid the academic style—*"In this paper I'm going to show..."* Get to the point. Show it.

  o Don't write formally—talk to people. A good trick is to imagine a single reader, and talk to him or her. Tell what you would tell about the subject if he or she were a client and you were answering a direct question. Then the writing is more likely to flow, and to be readable, than if you tried to craft it with words and sentences.

  o Writing isn't the manipulation of words—it's presenting ideas. Words and sentences and grammar are simply the vehicles. Get the ideas down. Write the first draft and don't worry about style or syntax.

  o After you've done that first draft, read it once to see that you've said what you want to say. Read it again to see if your ideas are clear and understandable. Then start editing. Read each sentence for grammar, simplicity, and clarity. Does it say what you want to say? Have you used the right words to convey your meaning? Is your language clear and simple—or have you loaded the article with big and obscure words? Is the grammar right? Do tenses and cases match?

  o And one final reading to try to see it as a reader would. This is best done after you've let it lay unseen for 24 hours, so you can get a fresh look at it. If you're satisfied, send it off, with proper title and identification. Most publications now prefer transmissions by e-mail, so they can work directly with the material.

- *Reprints.* When the article is published, discuss reprints with the publication. First, you may not reprint without their permission, which few publications will deny you. Second, a reprint should be designed, as would be a brochure. Discuss format with the publication. It may include, at a reasonable price, a special layout with the publication's masthead and room to add your own message to place the article in a selling perspective for you. Reprints are a second life for an article, and can sometimes be a better sales tool than was the original article.

If you're in practice in any profession, chances are you've got something to say. Say it in an article. It can only serve you—particularly if it serves the reader.

BROCHURES

There is a peculiar comfort in a brochure. It's easy to feel that if you've got one, you've taken care of marketing. Or most of it, at least.

Brochures, then, are too often done "because everybody has one," rather than as part of a thoughtful marketing plan.

A brochure, in this context, is a pamphlet or booklet that describes a firm, a facility, or a service. It may be used to explain all or a segment of the firm's services, or how the firm functions in a particular industry, or addresses a specific problem.

Despite the values inherent in well-done brochures, there are some pervasive misconceptions that substantially undermine their very real value to sound marketing. Perhaps the most expensive misconception is that brochures *sell*—that a prospective client will read a brochure loaded with glowing adjectives, and sign a contract as a result of it.

To assume, too, that people read brochures thoroughly and carefully is another trap. In fact, a brochure, no matter how attractive or thorough, is usually simply glanced at. It may be read in conjunction with other material, to get an overall impression of a firm. But it's rarely devoured like a novel.

For all that a good brochure can contribute to a marketing program, it's rarely the keystone of a total marketing effort, nor should it be. But as an *adjunct* to a marketing plan, it can be powerful.

THE POWER OF THE WELL-DESIGNED BROCHURE

In conjunction with other marketing tools, brochures...

- Are tangible, with staying power. They give dimension and weight to anything you say about your firm and capabilities.
- Can demonstrate a firm's most valuable asset—its intellectual capital.
- Catalog and describe a firm's capabilities, facilities, expertise, or point of view, all in best light.
- Can supply valuable information, redounding to the benefit of the source.
- Give visual dimension to a firm. A well-designed, attractive publication implies a well-run, efficient organization.
- Define or explain a new facility or service.

THE BASIC QUESTIONS

Thinking about brochures should begin with the very basic questions...

- Who is our audience, and what do we want them to know, think, or feel after they've read the brochure?

- What are we trying to accomplish with this brochure in terms of the overall marketing program?
- How will the brochure be used in conjunction with other marketing tools?
- Will some other marketing tool better accomplish what we want the brochure to do?
- How will the brochure be delivered?
- How should it be positioned? What is the one most important thing about your service that meets the most significant need of your prospective clientele? That *position* should be at the crux of your brochure—the guiding and impelling factor that drives the thrust of your brochure.

The answers to these questions will, in turn, focus the objectives of the brochure, and lead to developing a more effective document.

The format is dictated not by arbitrary choice, but by the role the brochure is to play in the marketing plan. Too often, the graphic designer is called in before the writer and before the brochure's marketing role is defined. This subordinates the message to the design, almost invariably resulting in a visually attractive publication that diminishes or fails to serve the communications or marketing objective. In fact, be sure that the designer understands that the message is in the text, not the design. Let the text do its work.

The thoughtful, and most useful, brochure for a professional firm must solve a major problem—how do we describe our facilities and services in ways that differentiate us from our competitors, and at the same time project quality? Ethics, of course, preclude comparison. How do you get the message across without using the same language that everybody else uses, and saying the same things that everybody else says? How do you distinguish one professional firm from another, when you can't use adjectives?

The answer is always emerging, driven by the imagination of marketing professionals, but we do begin to see some things that work. In fact, what you can do is more interesting.

You can't use hard sell. But you can deal with facts. You can say, "Every client's account is managed by a partner, no matter how small the account." That's a fact that says more than all the adjectives you can summon up.

You can say, "We deal with problems in patents and copyrights with more than just attorneys. We have a full staff of physicists, chemists, and other scientists who work closely with our attorneys." You can say… "that every person on the staff functions with state-of-the-art computer software, to increase efficiency and lower costs of serving our clients." These are statements of fact, and they're more compelling than any slick selling technique.

You can describe specific problems, and explain how you deal with them. "The strategies we design for controlling the flow of commodities to our clients' plants have increased our clients' productivity by 35 percent." If this is true, then it says more to sell than does any selling language.

If being *creative* is really important to you, you can make the point without using the word, by describing several situations in which your innovative approaches solved specific problems.

Perhaps the guiding rule is in the old saying, "What you are speaks so loudly that I can't hear what you *say* you are."

One of the reasons this approach is so much more compelling than the old techniques of adjectives and hard sell is that nobody hires a lawyer or an accountant or a consultant from an ad or a brochure. The marketing devices may generate an interest in a firm that clearly offers a solution to a problem. They may cause a predilection toward a specific firm. But in the final analysis, brochures don't sell professional services, only professionals do.

Hard sell, then, rarely has a place in professional services marketing, and that's good. It forces us to be thoughtful and innovative.

In developing and writing a brochure, some guidelines that may help...

- Clarify the objectives. Again. *Clarify the objectives.*

- Think *positioning*—the guiding and impelling factor that drives the thrust of your brochure.

- Keep it simple. Focus. Limit the brochure to a single purpose. A service. A facility. A single problem and its solution. Don't try to say too much in one brochure. Make one point about your firm and make it well, and you're ahead of the game. Go for the overall impression, and don't try to tell everything in one brochure.

- Always have a plan to use the brochure effectively, before you start to write it. Know beforehand who your audience is to be. You have different things to say to different audiences. How you write anything is a function of who you're talking to, and no one statement is universal. Know how the brochure is to be distributed, publicized, used in both direct mail and personal selling situations.

- Write about your solution or services as if you invented them, even if you know you didn't. It may be the first time your reader has seen that capability or solution delineated.

- The operative word, implied or in fact, is "you." Most brochures die when the first word is "we." Your brochure must be cast, invariably, in terms of the needs of the market—what the prospective client needs, not what you have to sell.

- Don't tell the reader what he or she should think about your firm—demonstrate it. Don't say "We become involved with our clients' business," find a way to demonstrate it. Don't say "We pride ourselves on service," find a way to demonstrate it. Avoid clichés like "honest," or "service," or "creative." *"We give creative service to your needs."* What does *that* mean? Does it mean that you give clients what they pay for? Does it mean that they get their money's worth? Does *creative* mean you make it up as you go along?

- Don't expect the brochure to present an *image*—if by *image* you mean a perception of your firm that's other than reality. If you don't like the way your firm is perceived by the market, don't try to change the perception by manipulating symbols—it won't work. Rethink the business you're in, change the firm accordingly, and then write the brochure—not the other way around.

- Don't cast your brochure in stone. The life of a firm brochure shouldn't be more than two years. If your marketing program works, and your firm grows, it will outgrow the brochure in less than two years. If the brochure is applicable to the firm and still current after two years, then your firm is in trouble. Even if you don't want to be larger in two years than you are today, there's going to be some kind of change and growth. If it doesn't happen, you're in serious trouble as a professional and as a business.

- The best way to describe who you are isn't by describing it—why should anybody believe you? It's to demonstrate what you do, and how you do it differently. As the song goes, "Don't speak of love—show me." The trick is to talk about what you've done, not what you say you can do. "I can leap a thousand feet high" is nothing compared to "Here's a picture of the high wall I leapt and here's a picture of me leaping it."

- Borrow from corporate annual reports. In the attempt to get the reader's attention, corporate annual reports use a number of exciting devices and techniques. A roundtable of financial analysts discussing the company. The CEO interviewed. An illustrated first-person narrative. Boxes and sidebars to depart from the narrative to discuss an important point, or to define an unusual concept.

- Deliberately try to be different. If everybody else plays a major scale, play a minor scale. If you said it this way last time, say it that way next time. Do you want to be read? Work at it. Clichés don't work. If you can't do more than clichés, save your money. Don't do a brochure.

- Purpose alters the format and text of a publication.

- Think carefully about illustration. All professionals seated at desks look alike. Use both your own people and client situations imaginatively. Appropriate graphs and charts can help.

- Be thoughtful about details. For example, how a brochure is to be distributed affects its physical design. If it's to be mass mailed, postage costs are a major consideration. Odd shapes that use custom-designed envelopes increase costs substantially. Consider, too, how long the publication will be expected to do its job. A brochure with an intended long life shouldn't have dated references.

- Work with professionals. You know what you want to say about your firm. You know how big you want the pictures to be. But as effortless as the better brochures look, that's how hard it was to get them to look effortless. Conceptualizing a brochure that really says to your clients and prospects what you want to say to them is an art form, rooted in skill and experience. Designing a brochure is a skill that's as professional as yours, and the difference between a brochure that's a chore to get through (and so won't be read) and one that's as inviting as a chocolate cake is artfulness. Use a professional.

A brochure, in a sense, is no different from any marketing tool. Properly used, it works. Improperly used, it not only doesn't help, but it lulls you into thinking that you're accomplishing more than you really are. Better to take the larger view; to develop the larger marketing context in which the brochure is a working cog.

PUBLIC RELATIONS

Public relations encompasses everything we do to convey information or an impression (favorable, obviously) about a firm and its services. This may include the way your receptionist dresses or answers your phone to sponsoring a major and newsworthy event.

Publicity is the communications part of public relations, and most often functions as media relations. As a function of both new technology and the demands of society, media relations have changed, as has media itself. It used to be all press releases and buttering up editors. Still is, but to a sharply diminished degree. It is now more professional. Richard Levick, president of Levick Strategic Communications, LLC, one of the most effective public relations firms serving the legal profession, says that his firm rarely uses press releases.

Publicity, in fact, is no longer simply a matter of getting your name in the paper, but rather, communicating a clear message that informs, that enhances your reputation for skill and professionalism, that enhances an understanding of you and your firm that's based on reality. Some caveats...

- Publicity has to be about something. It has to report *news*. Not just something you want to see in print (or in any other medium), but something that persuades the gatekeeper of the medium—the editor, producer, or publisher—that the news is genuine and valuable to the readers or viewers. Publicity, then, doesn't begin with the press release, it begins with the news.

- Your news can't misrepresent—the acoustics of the marketplace are too good, and falseness or shallowness will soon be found out. Publicity can clarify and present reality, if sufficient skill is used. Skill without integrity, by the way, rebounds badly. It's the acoustics again.

- *Image* is a myth. It implies that if you don't like reality, you can manipulate symbols to change the perception of reality. It's not so. If you don't like the way you're perceived, change the reality, and the perception will follow quickly. Even if the best public relations program succeeds in creating an image that is not based on reality, it's a bubble. It will burst.

- Journalism has changed, which means that the long-standing practices of public relations may include a lot of obsolete things. The fabled four W's that were supposed to be in every lead paragraph (*who, what, when* and *where*) went out even before dress-down Fridays came in. Just read the front page of a newspaper like *The New York Times* or *The Washington Post.* And remember, every publicity presentation competes against every staff journalist's story for the same space or air time or Internet time, so the presentation had better be good professional journalism, not merely good professional public relations. The motto, remember, is the publicist proposes, but the editor disposes.

- Publicity doesn't work when you confuse a press release with an ad. A press release is a news story, and should be written in a style that would fit comfortably on the front page of *The New York Times,* no matter what paper the release is going to. Remember, you're competing against the medium's professional staff—not other publicists—for limited space or airtime.

- News can't be manufactured, but news-making activities can. Newsworthy stories can't be manufactured out of whole cloth, but the newsworthiness in a story can be focused and highlighted and presented clearly.

- The journalistic styles of print media, broadcast media, and Internet media are different, as are the techniques of dealing with journalists. Long gone are the days of the roll of nickels and the phone book and the Rolodex. Now are the days of professionalism, of media as a target audience, and of new ways to deliver news.

- Publicity and public relations go wrong when the publicist loses sight of their role in a total marketing program. In publicity, as in all marketing, think *you,* not *we.* Think in terms of the medium's needs, not yours.

10 MYTHS OF LAW (AND ACCOUNTING) FIRM PUBLIC RELATIONS

Richard Levick cataloged 10 significant myths about public relations. They effectively define best practices in dealing with the media for accounting firms as well as law firms . . .

- *You don't need to return reporters' calls.* Reporters are like stray cats—if you don't feed them, they go to someone else's door. Call them back first, even if it is to say that you can't say anything. Reporters remember who calls them and who doesn't. Not returning the journalist's call today, no matter what the reason, guarantees that you won't get the call when you do want to be in the paper. By not returning calls, you are forfeiting your right to complain when others are quoted.

- *Reporters can't be trusted.* Reporters have a different job than you do. Their job is to write *a* story, not *your* story. But that doesn't mean they can't be trusted. Of all the thousands of reporters we work with all over the world, only a handful don't play by the rules. They may not always get it right from your perspective, but almost all will work to get the story the best they can. The more often you work with them, the more likely they are to get it right.

- *Moving to new offices and hiring lateral partners are news.* Uh-huh. Sort of like flossing your teeth is news. Look at the publications you want to be in regarding your office move or new hire. Ask yourself how many times they devote more than a paragraph to one of these earth-shattering events. That doesn't mean it's not important or that news coverage of these and related events will not occur. It just means that news is more likely to be made if there is something of significance attached to it, such as a move into an historic building or a named partner or entire practice area moving from another firm.

- *A merger is news.* With the exception of historic mergers between major international law firms, law firm mergers are news, but they are known as one-day stories. Focusing your press efforts on the merger rather than the law firm is like Honda focusing all of its press on only the first day of its new model year. Press efforts have to be ongoing to be effective. Look to get some press from a merger, then give it value by getting press coverage of the partners, practice areas, and firms for the other 364 days of the year. That is, after all, how your clients and prospects read the news.

- *The daily newspaper will mention the name of the firm.* The higher up in the media food chain, the less likely the name of the firm will be mentioned. If you are getting coverage in the industry trades, you will likely get the firm name mentioned and often even a photo. If you get into *The New York Times*, you very likely will not. This doesn't mean don't spend time with the major dailies. It just means that while continuing to push for the name of the firm in the paper, set your expectations on what is realistic. Fortunately, most of the local Asian dailies frequently include the firm name.

- *Advertising and public relations are the same.* Advertising and public relations are the great marketing trade-off. With advertising, you control exactly what is said, where, and how often. But because you do, there is far less credibility than with public relations. Interviews, however, require a third party—the reporter. You cannot make a reporter write something as you want it or see the story exactly as you see it. But when managed, it can be influenced. What reporters write, when repeated often enough, has far more credibility than advertising. It's the power of the third party.

- *Everyone reads the articles as closely as you do.* Lawyers read newspaper articles about themselves like, well, lawyers. Newspaper articles are not legal documents. They are opportunities prospects. With rare exception, that's it. Did they include your quote? Spell your name right? Will the news source call on you again? If the answers are *yes,* then you have a successful interview. Now, do it again and again—and again.

- *Publicity is local.* In the age of the Internet there is no local paper. Producers at the BBC read stories that appear in *The Bangkok Post.* It's called the news stream, and once you get into a newspaper, no matter where, the chances are clients, prospects, and other reporters are going to have access to it.

  That means if there is a bad story in one city, it should be countered by other stories, or you leave it as the only record on that issue. If it is a good story opportunity, take the reporter's call, even though they are "out of market."

- *Publicity begins with a press release.* According to Jim Schachter, *The New York Times* Business Editor, "sending a press release to *The New York Times* is like sending a satellite to Pluto." Press releases written by lawyers have all the appeal, news, and timeliness of white rice. We place 300 to 400 different legal stories every month, using a total of one to two press releases monthly as the tools to place those stories. Press releases, like any legal tactic in a lawyer's bag of tricks, have their place and time, but it is seldom and not always.

- *Public relations should be handled on a project-by-project basis.* Law firms conducting press relations project by project are wasting their money. If Coca-Cola engaged in publicity only when it had a new formula, you would be drinking Pepsi. Publicity requires reach and repetition. That means lots of placements, lots of times. Getting press "every once in a while" has little value beyond soothing the ego. Publicity for law firms is about business development, not ego.

DEALING WITH THE MEDIA

In most businesses, the frequently onerous role of dealing with the press is usually left to the public relations professional. Not so in professional services. The phone call can come to anybody, and frequently does.

The shock is when that nice, rational remark you made shows up in print, looking irrational and outrageous. The usual battle cry is, "I was misquoted."

Maybe, but probably not. This is the point at which you learn that how it sounds isn't necessarily how it reads. Gone from the printed words are the inflections, the half-smile, and the arched eyebrow that gave the nuances to the words. What's left, in cold type, can be harsh, possibly out of context, and a distortion of what you really meant to say.

And this assumes both the goodwill and the skill of the reporter, which can sometimes be more a presumption than an assumption.

There are two general areas in which you might find yourself talking to a reporter. In one context, you may be dealing with a technical matter, in which the contact has been generated by you, your public relations staff, or as an inquiry from a journalist who knows and respects your expertise. Here, it's presumed that you're on solid footing. You've been briefed, or at least had time to think out what you're going to say, and you've had time to anticipate questions and to frame answers. In the other context, there is a fast-breaking and controversial news situation, and you're unprepared for the call or the questions. It can be a naked feeling. While there's no way that every possibility in a press contact can be anticipated, there are some basic elements that can be prepared.

You should know that being interviewed by the press, even with a single question, makes you—sometimes unwillingly—part of the journalistic process. While normally all you see of it is the polished result, you rarely get to understand the process itself. Some basics:

- Except on small weekly papers, the reporter you talk to is only one link in a chain. The reporter usually reports to an editor, who may him- or herself be responsible to a managing editor. This means that the story the reporter writes passes through a number of hands, and may not be the story that gets printed. And, of course, the person who writes the headline may not even know the reporter. He or she works from final text.

- The crucial fact here is that not only is the reporter not likely (with exceptions) to be expert in the subject you're talking about; the reporter also lacks your emotional concern with it. Tomorrow he or she'll be covering something very different. And the farther up the editorial chain the copy gets, the less the knowledge or concern about the subject. It's just not as important to the reporter as it is to you.

- The reporter has time constraints that may conflict with yours. He or she's usually on a deadline. This can make the reporter more curt than you would like him or her to be.

What this all boils down to is that these are facts to be kept in mind during an interview. How to handle it, then?

- *Be well briefed.* This may mean rereading a few memos, or in the case of a major interview, building a briefing book with the help of others in other departments, and learning its contents.

- *Anticipate questions.* Not just the easy ones, but the tough ones, too. In an in-depth interview, you're not likely to anticipate all the questions, but the more the better. Try to avoid curves.

- *Get the answers down very carefully.* This is where you can avoid that "I was misquoted" syndrome. The less you have to say on the wing, the better you're going to like the way the story comes out.

- *Rehearse.* Unless you're a former secretary of state, with experience in being interviewed almost daily, the more you rehearse, the fewer mistakes you're going to make.

- *List the key points* you want to make, in order of importance. You may not get to make them all, nor will you be assured that they all get printed, but that list of points is the spine of the successful interview.

For a successful interview, everything depends upon this list of points, because if you're careful, and skillful, you can lead the interview. How? By visualizing how you would like the interview to read as if you had written it, and by crafting your answers so that those points are made, *even if they are not always directly responsive to the question.* How does it work?

> *Question:* Do you plan to open other offices?
> *Answer:* Yes. (*Responsive to the question. Then add...*) We'll use two criteria to select sites—economic and market needs for our specialized services.

Keep it up, and you'll be very subtly running the interview. And if you're calm and friendly and cooperative, and the reporter brings no inherent hostility, and the editor doesn't cut it or rewrite, the story will come out the way you want it to.

And then there is the press inquiry. "We hear one of your clients is going to jail. Do you have any comment"?

While it's difficult to make hard and fast rules about dealing with the press beyond the normal professional considerations and bounds of confidentiality of client matters, there are a few guidelines you may find helpful in dealing with press inquiries of this kind.

The real problem is with those inquiries from the press that are client-related (or may relate to the client of another firm), or involve your firm. They may be controversial, and are potentially hostile. In those cases, reporters are merely doing their job when they try to solicit a controversial statement on a matter, or to badger you into saying more than is appropriate.

The objective should be to remain politely aloof and uninvolved, without fostering animosity with a member of the press with whom you might want to deal in your own behalf sometime in the future. The following hints may be useful...

- If it's a matter in which you might anticipate a press inquiry, your position should be drawn beforehand. It should be written and distributed to key people in your office who might get a call from the press. Preferably, in such matters, a specific spokesman should be designated, and appropriate personnel should be advised that all calls on that matter should be given to the designated spokesman.

- Because people not used to dealing with the press are frequently surprised when they see that statements made in all innocence look very different in print than they did when they were spoken, there is an advantage in writing out a position beforehand. If a call is not anticipated, always think of how you can minimize your comments, and how your words will look out of context in hard type.

- Usually, it's not advisable to give the press a statement "off the record." While journalists may respect your request, they're not going to like you for it unless it serves as legitimate background for them to understand something that you can say on the record. Journalists, remember, make their living on what they *can* print—not what they *can't* print.

- There is nothing more challenging to reporters than to hear someone say "no comment." It's a red flag. Instead, if you were to smile, and say in a friendly way, "I'd like to help you, but you know it would be a violation of professional ethics (or client confidentiality) for me to discuss that with you," you're asking them to understand that you'd really like to help, but you can't for reasons beyond your control.

- It helps to keep people informed—and to have them keep you informed—of potential situations where the press may be involved. If everyone is alert to potential danger and there's preparation beforehand, then the likelihood of being misquoted—or worse, being quoted accurately in a misstatement—diminishes substantially.

It's all very well to try to reduce press relations to rules, but press relations is life, and life doesn't work that way. Being calm helps, and so does being rational and thoughtful.

SPIN CONTROL

The phrase "spin control" implies that a good media relations practitioner can control the nature and texture of a story in the press—can put the right *spin* on it to get the journalist to tell it the spinner's way. It's really a myth.

It's just not so. For all that the myth implies, when it comes to the media, we propose—but others dispose. Thus it was, and thus it always shall be, as long as we have a free press.

But is the telling always accurate? No. Is it always fair? No. Sometimes, despite all of the public relations professionalism, and despite all the cooperation we may offer the press, the story comes out badly. Disaster, dispensed in the aura of a supposedly objective press, doesn't merely strike, it reverberates.

The picture you so carefully and accurately painted is distorted, the wrong people are quoted and the right people are not, the facts are warped and bent beyond recognition, and the whole piece reads as if it were written by your most malicious competitor. Certainly, it will be relished by your every detractor.

THE EXPERTS' ADVICE

Beyond the first scream of outrage, what can you do? Or more significantly, what has been done most effectively by others who have lived through it—and survived?

Perhaps the hardest factor of a negative story to deal with is that most people who are not professional marketers tend to overreact. At one extreme is incredible upset and anger; at the other is casual disdain that says, "So what, no one will believe it." Neither extreme is warranted nor accurate.

The most useful course, then, is to do nothing until you've recovered from your anger. Even doing the right thing in the wrong frame of mind can perpetuate, not cure, the damage. So...

- *Don't act precipitously.* Think of every action in terms of possible reaction. What seems like a good idea at the moment may be a backfire next week.

- After you've gotten over the emotional impact and the anger, *don't think vindictively.* You may have to live with that publication again someday, and vindictiveness in any event is not profitable.

- *Assess real—not assumed or presumed—damage.* That's where you've got to focus your attention. Much assumed damage at first light disappears when the sun comes up. What's left is damage you can deal with.

It's this last point that's crucial to successfully limiting the damage of bad press. Too often, the defense is predicated on imagined damage, in which case the reaction is an overreaction, and causes more damage than the original article.

Experts rarely concern themselves with why it happened. Unless libel is involved, it doesn't really matter. The reporter could have functioned out of ignorance or laziness. Reporters are people, and are not immune to such foibles as preconceived notions that can subvert the professionalism of even the most experienced journalist. There may have been an adverse chemical reaction to somebody in your firm, or a fight at the journalist's home that morning. It fact, it really doesn't matter, because the reason for an adverse story is rarely an element that can be dealt with in damage control.

There are some specific questions to be addressed...

- What does the article really say? Is it bad because it's wrong—or because it's right?

- Is the article distorted because the facts are wrong, or because they are put in a wrong context that distorts the facts?

- What is the real damage? Is it libelous? Misleading enough to cause real business damage? Or just embarrassing?

- Consider the publication. Is it widely read, or will people you care about never see it? (Consider that under certain circumstances, your competitor may want to make a point by sending a reprint of the article, along with a favorable one about him- or herself from the same publication.) What's the publication's reputation for credibility?

- Is the potential damage internal as well as external? Sometimes an unfavorable article can hurt internal morale more than it affects an external perception of the firm.

THE IMPACT FADES QUICKLY

Staying power is an important consideration. How long after publication will the story, or at least its negative aura, linger? Depending upon the publication and the nature of the story, considerably less time than you think. As one experienced marketer put it, the impact fades quickly, but the impression can linger.

Some time ago, a major professional firm was savaged in the press for nepotism. The impact was shocking. In fact, the firm not only lost very little business, but also continued to grow. Did the story contribute to competitive defeats? Hard to say. An impression may have lingered in a prospective client's mind and contributed to other negatives. But ultimately, the damage was nowhere equal to the impact and shock of the article's first appearance.

RESPONDING TO THE DAMAGE

Assessing the damage accurately allows you to choose the appropriate response. There are, in fact, a number of responses, some, unfortunately, inappropriate. You can...

- Sue, but only if there is real libel and real—and demonstrable—damage. There rarely is.
- Get on the phone and scream at the editor. Good for your spleen, lousy for your future with at least that segment of the press. And you'll never win.
- Write a nasty letter to the publisher. Only slightly better than screaming, but with the same results.

There are, however, some positive things that can be done...

- *Avoid defensiveness.* Plan positively.
- *Warn people.* If you know an article is going to appear that might be unfavorable, alert your own people, so that it doesn't come as a surprise.
- *Have a plan and a policy,* preferably before you need it. This should cover how to deal with the press, who does it and who doesn't, how to deal with

client reactions, how to deal with internal reactions. It should cover how calls are handled, who responds and who routes calls to whom, what to say to clients and who says it, and so forth.

- *A letter to the editor is important,* if only to go on record. But it should be positive, non-vitriolic, and deal only with the facts. It should not sound petulant or defensive.

- *Deal with the real damage.* If the real damage is in specific markets, mount a positive public relations campaign aimed specifically at those markets. If the damage is internal, try to assess the root causes for the negative reaction. It would take a powerful article in a powerful journal to demoralize a firm that's otherwise sound and comfortable with itself.

- *Consider how a competitor might use the piece,* even within the bounds of propriety. It could be, for example, reprints to a particular market. Offset this with positive publicity to the same market.

No story is so bad that it should warrant extreme reaction. No publication that's still publishing is so devoid of credibility that some readers won't accept what they read. The role of the professional trained and experienced marketer is to maintain perspective, to assess the damage appropriately, and to see that the response is equal to—but does not exceed—the damage.

If bad press meant nothing, then neither would good press, and we know that consistently good press means a great deal. But one story—good or bad—rarely has sufficient impact to seriously aid or damage a company (although a negative story is more titillating than a positive one). Most positive public relations is a consistent series of positive articles, interviews, and news stories. If a negative press consists of more than one story, then the problem is usually not the press—it's the subject of the stories.

The perspective of the bad story, then, requires dealing with it as an anomaly. This means dealing with it as a calm and rational business decision. And no business decision, in any context, is ever a sound one if it isn't arrived at rationally and professionally.

ADVERTISING

The role of advertising for a professional firm is obviously different than it is for a product. How do you advertise competitively when you can't say, "We do better audits?" or "We write better briefs?"Advertising rarely works for a professional services firm as it does for products because people may buy products from an ad, but nobody buys professional services from an ad without meeting the people who perform the service.

Advertising, for a professional firm, informs and persuades. But what it persuades is not that you buy an audit or litigate when there was no prior reason for it. It attempts, rather, to influence the choice between your firm and your competitors', since it's unlikely that anybody will hire you based solely on your ad. Still, there are lessons to be learned from what successful professional services advertisers have done successfully.

- The successful firms understand the difference between focusing on a single service to a single market, and what we call institutional advertising. Institutional advertising says, *"Law firms are good for you and ours is a great law firm."* Single-service advertising recognizes that the nature of professional services is that most prospective clients generally can't tell the difference between one firm and another. But when a firm says, *"Our rate of successful real estate closings for major institutional lenders has propelled us to leadership in the field,"* and advertises it to institutional lenders, then the target gets hit with meaning and impact.

- They did market research. They know their audience, and what their audience needed. Then they recast their services to address the needs of that audience.

- They didn't rely on just advertising, which became one tool of many in their arsenal.

- They understood *positioning.* It means working very hard to understand the prospective target audience's needs, demonstrating that they understood those needs, and focusing their message on showing that they understood and could meet those needs. The difficult fact is that no professional firms can successfully be all things to all businesses. Positioning is the technique of focusing and honing your message to a pinpoint precision. In successful positioning, lasers work; baseball bats don't.

- They didn't get hung up on fads, like branding. By focusing, their prospects and target audiences learned who they were and what they could do. Law firms and accounting firms aren't Wheaties, and they didn't confuse name recognition and reputation as branding.

- They, and the agencies that worked for them, knew how to write ads that work—that achieved the ads' objectives. They knew that a good ad campaign starts with a theme that focuses on the perspective client's problems or opportunities. They know how to write headlines that are not only catchy, but also relevant, and stem from the position. They write copy that's not only easy to read, but that fulfills the promise of the headline.

- They used professionals. Advertising—in fact, most of marketing—is like tightrope walking. It looks simple when professionals do it well. It's not. In advertising copy, it's amazing what works and what doesn't work.

If you're an accountant or a lawyer or a consultant with a marketing program, you don't have to know how to write an ad, but you should know some things about how to judge one written for you. You should know also that what you think works may not.

What makes it difficult for the inexperienced is that what you may judge to be great copy because of the sheer poetry, imagery, sound, and lyricism may be inappropriate for accomplishing the mission of the ad.

Nor are copy rules decisive. When the advertising legend David Ogilvy was told that copy should be short and terse, because nobody reads more than a few words of an ad, he wrote the classic ad, *"At 60 miles an hour the only sound you hear is the clock."* It was a full page of text, describing the features of the Rolls-Royce. It sold a lot of cars.

The advertising process is a function of not only training, but also skill, intelligence, and imagination—all of which are what we usually mean when we use the peculiar word "creative." There are rules, and there are ways to break the rules. But like the best abstract artists, who know better how and what to abstract because they are fine realistic artists, it's likely that those who know the rules best are those who break the rules best.

THE LIMITS OF COPYWRITING

The limits of copywriting are essentially those of the medium. You can't write 10 minutes of copy for a 30-second radio spot. The mechanics of writing for one medium are too infrequently translatable into another medium. You can't put 50 words of copy on a billboard alongside a high-speed highway and expect the message to be read.

And yet there are times when originality, imagination, and skill dictate that all rules be violated. Fifty or 100 words on that billboard may be just the ticket if the headline is something like, "There are not enough words to describe..." and you don't really expect people to read the text.

THE OBJECTIVES OF THE AD

Writing advertising copy begins, as you might expect, with defining objectives—of the campaign, of the marketing program, of the specific ad. These objectives will be unique to you and your firm, to each campaign, and to each ad. They dictate that the copy—as well as all other elements of the ad—are focused and relevant.

ELEMENTS OF A GOOD AD

An ad that includes at least the following elements might be expected to work...

- *Attention.* In the clamor and clutter of sight and sound, and the competition for the reader's eye, ear, and heart, it's imperative that you compete successfully for attention. There should be some element in the ad—whether it's the headline or the illustration or the layout—that attracts the eye or ear and arouses sufficient interest to warrant attention to the message. And the copy itself must sustain that attention.

- *Promise of benefit.* Something in the ad should promise the reader or the listener some benefit that will accrue from accepting the ad's premises.

- *Credibility.* The premises of the ad must be believable. (Do you really believe that Exxon put a tiger in your tank? But that campaign sold a lot of gas.)

- *Persuasiveness.* The ad should be persuasive. It should sell or generate the need for the service you offer, and project your service as superior. (What do those Nike shoe ads say that persuade you? But they sell a lot of athletic shoes.)

- *Interest.* Once you've captured the reader's attention, you've got to say or show something to sustain interest, or the message will not be heard.

- *Desire.* The ad must generate a desire to accept what you have to say about what you have to offer the reader, to want to do business with you.

- *Action.* The ultimate aim of an ad is to generate action on the part of the reader or listener; to cause the target to want to do something that you want him or her to do, such as buy your service, or, in the case of professional services marketing, to generate an inquiry or accept a selling situation. Yet just getting a reader to think about you in a specific way is an action, too. That's what institutional advertising is about.

Ads seem to work best when you...

- *Know your prospect.* Not only who your prospect is, but what kind of service your prospective clientele really wants, and what kind of problems they'll depend on your service to resolve.

- *Know your service.* Know your service in terms of what the prospective client is willing to buy, not what you're offering to sell.

There are some other guidelines that professional copywriters also find useful…

- *Talk to the reader, the listener, or the viewer.* Don't announce, don't preach. And don't get carried away by words and lose sight of the message.
- *Write short sentences,* with easy and familiar words. You want the reader or listener to do the least possible work to get your message. Even when you're talking to very bright people, communication is of the essence, not language manipulation.
- *Don't waste words.* Whether you use 3 or 1,000 words, make sure each is exactly the one you need. Make sure each word is exactly the right one to convey your meaning.
- *Try to avoid being formal.* You're talking to people as people. You're not writing an insurance contract for lawyers. An ad is information and persuasion.
- *Use the present tense and the active voice* ("All professional copywriters have extensive experience in preparing material," rather than "…extensive experience in the preparation of material.") If you do want a formal style, it should be deliberate, and you should have a clear idea of why you are using it.
- *Punctuate correctly.* Punctuate to help the reader, and not merely to follow specific rules. The less punctuation the better, within the bounds of clarity, but don't be afraid to use it if it helps the flow of an idea. Don't be afraid to use contractions and personal pronouns, just as you would in chatting informally with a prospect. After all, that's what you're trying to accomplish in your ad.
- *Watch out for clichés.* They turn some people off. More significantly, people don't hear them as they pass mindlessly off the tongue without bothering to visit the mind, and the point you're trying to make is lost. (Again, unless you're doing it deliberately.) Try to use bright, cheerful language that keeps the reader alert and maintains attention. To be enthusiastic and exciting is to be well along on the way to being interesting.

Writing is not the manipulation of words—it's the expression of ideas. Words, grammar, and punctuation are merely the tools and devices we use to express ideas most clearly. To think of copy as a configuration of words is the same as thinking of a symphony as a configuration of notes.

Why do ads that seem well written sometimes not work? Because they miss these points of advertising. Because they attempt to merely translate somebody's idea of persuasive talk into the ad medium, which can sometimes be like wearing a tuxedo to the gym.

And because somebody didn't recognize that the art of advertising copywriting is not the art of literary writing. Different medium, different art form.

PLANNED NETWORKING

There was a time, around the turn of the twentieth century, when Mr. Andersen and Mr. Price and Mr. Waterhouse and Mr. Young and Mr. Skadden and Mr. Cromwell were all sole practitioners. Back then, and during most of the century, they were precluded for the most part by canons of ethics from pursuing what we can now call frank marketing. They couldn't advertise, or solicit one another's clients, or send out mass mailings to prospective clients.

And yet, they surpassed hundreds of other sole practitioners and small partnerships that existed at that time, and they went on to become Sullivan & Cromwell, and Price Waterhouse, and Arthur Andersen, and Skadden, Arps.

How did those big firms grow when they couldn't advertise or do any of those other good marketing things? In their early days, they made a point of getting to know people who were in a position to give them business. Or to know people who could recommend them to others who were potential clients. And Messrs Sullivan and Price and many others expanded their circles of contacts, and kept in touch with them, and found ways to reciprocate favors.

We have a name for this process. It's called *networking*.

NETWORKING

It means, generally, getting to know people who can help you grow your business, or who know people who can help you expand your business. It means letting a great many people know who you are and what you can do for them. It's also called *building contacts*.

It's a business process, not just a social process.

While it's true that an overwhelming amount of business for professional firms is built through networking, a closer look at those who do it successfully quickly shows that networking is more than glad-handing, more than taking a banker to lunch, more than playing golf at the right country club. And certainly, it's more than cynically using your friends and others to further your business.

Successful networking is a carefully planned system of building—and nurturing—a structure of business associates with whom you can work for *mutual advantage* to build your business. And there's more to the success of networking in the *mutual advantage* than in any other aspect of building and sustaining the contracts.

Successful networking means building relationships with people in ways that allow them to know and understand what you do, and that you do it well, and that they can trust you to bring credit to them for having recommended you. It means, as well, building trust that you can deliver what you promise, that you can be recommended safely. At the heart of the process is the concept of *mutual benefit*.

Lester Garnas, a marketing and sales training consultant who is an expert on networking, suggests that successful networking is often impeded by a mythology that restrains pursuing useful relationships effectively. "Too often," he says, "professionals believe that reaching out to people who might help them requires them to be aggressive and pushy, and to be manipulative. Some people seem to feel that networking is only for the extrovert, or the individual with the outgoing, backslapping, hale-fellow-well-met personality."

Nothing is farther from the truth, Garnas says. "If you consider two key factors of the process, networking becomes a significant marketing tool. Those two factors are that you always think of establishing relationships in which there is an advantage that's mutual; and that you recognize that every technique you use in a networking context is a *business* skill, not merely a *personality* skill."

Successful networking, says Garnas, is considerably more than building social relationships based on pleasant conversations. "It's a skill," he says, "and more significantly, it's an acquired skill."

THE SKILLS

The skills of networking are, to the largest extent, skills of organizing and planning. They're the skills, as well, of communications and interpersonal relations. Using these skills effectively requires...

- *Planning.* This is crucial. And there's nothing crass about it if you keep in mind that the element of *mutual benefit* is integral to the process.
- Planning addresses these considerations...
  - How do you define your ultimate target market?
  - What kinds of companies are in that group, and who are the individuals who run those companies?
  - What services do you specifically have to offer those companies, and how have you packaged them (defined services, applicable skills available in the

firm, literature describing the services, other marketing communications tools, such as brochures and newsletters, used to market those services)?

o Who are the individuals that are most influential in reaching the companies and executives you most want to reach? Lawyers, bankers, accountants, and trade association leaders are all in the category of influentials, for one another and to one degree or another.

o What do you have to offer these influentials in return for their recommending you to prospective clients?

• *Identifying the access to the influentials.* The individuals who are influential to the people you want to meet are found in . . .

o Your family and personal friends

o Your current clients

o Banks

o Brokerage firms and investment banks

o Attorneys

o Organizations you belong to or can join

o Trade association meetings and conferences

o The person sitting next to you on the plane

o Seminars you give

Don't forget to mine your current lists of contacts—particularly the ones you never followed up on. Bring them back into the network.

And don't forget to involve all of your partners. Pick their brains—and their lists. Make them part of the process.

In other words, the sources are many, and need only be organized for access.

• *Having an objective.* Random networking may be fun, particularly if you're naturally sociable, but if you perceive of networking as a business tool, then you have to be businesslike about it. Why are you doing it? What do you hope to accomplish?

• *Organize.* Be systematic. Make lists and schedules. Recognize that networking takes time, and although you should allocate that time to the process, it should be a considered, planned, and limited amount of time.

• *Do it.* When you've committed to the process in an orderly way, make your lists of people to call and organizations to join, and make the calls and join the organizations. With some thought, it's easier than you think.

THE PROCESS

The process goes in defined steps . . .

- Once you've identified the individuals with whom you plan to establish relationships, you have to call them, or arrange to meet them through mutual contacts, or through organizations in which you're mutually active. It helps to try to find out as much as possible about them, as a basis for understanding how to converse with them. Seminars, which we discuss further on, are really the first step in networking.
- You have to have the first meeting. Whether it's lunch or breakfast or just an office visit doesn't really matter. It's the meeting that matters.
- You have to establish the mutual benefits, in terms of the prospective client. "I have clients who need better banking relationships; you have clients (or customers) who can benefit from better financial or accounting or legal services."
- You have to establish your own credentials. "This is what we do and this is who we do it for."
- You have to be prepared to follow up—to keep in touch, to keep the relationship nurtured and alive, to keep your name and capabilities in the forefront, and highly visible.

WHO DO YOU CALL?

- Start with the people—or the organizations—that are most likely to help you meet your objectives.

If it's bankers, make a list of the bankers you know, or the bankers you don't know but who have the clientele you want. The important thing to know about banks, in this context, is that they're after business as much as you are. They want your clients as much as you want theirs. The people involved with new business at banks are lending officers with new business responsibility. It's amazingly simple to find out who, at any bank you want to do business with, is responsible for new business. He or she will be delighted to hear from you.

If it's organizations, choose those to join that have the greatest number of people who can help you reach a prospective clientele, or whose members may be potential clients, and then choose the activities within those organizations that will give you the greatest visibility. (A caveat here. To join an organization whose cause is inimical to you but will give you valuable contacts, or to not join an organization you want to support because there's no business potential, is cynical.)

If you're an accountant, you want lawyers who serve the kinds of clients you serve—companies that need the service you have to offer. If you do valuations for divorces, you want matrimonial lawyers, for example. If you're an immigration lawyer, you want law firms that do business overseas. If you're a tax attorney doing IRS work, you want tax accountants. These people can be easily identified. And they, too, can be as glad to hear from you, as you would be to hear from them.

- *Contact.* Yes, you can call some people cold. Remember, good networking is for mutual advantage. If you have—or will have—prospective clients for them, they'll be delighted to talk to you. Other than cold calls, you can...

  o Meet people at seminars. That's the secret of so many seminars—it's not the subject matter, it's the networking. Choose them carefully, and go prepared to meet people.

  o Organize joint ventures. Do joint seminars to selected target audiences. Invite your influentials to speak to your staff. Offer to speak to their staffs.

  o When you join organizations that have prospective clients or influentials as members, take an active role in those committees or positions that display your talents, and your skills. Find ways to help the organization solve its problems, or sponsor appropriate programs, and every member will cherish your skills.

WHAT DO YOU SAY?

It would be foolish to deny that there's an element of interpersonal skills involved in networking. But if you're not totally comfortable in social situations with strangers, there's still a process you can follow that can relieve some of the anxiety and still accomplish the objective. It's a mistake to pretend that you're establishing a relationship for purely social reasons. All parties involved know that business is business. All you're doing is putting an aspect of business into a social context, to make it more enjoyable.

But there's another aspect of the social context. People want to do business with people they know and trust. The social context helps establish that platform of trust and comfort.

Still, it shouldn't breed self-consciousness, or anxiety. It's just a pleasant overlay to a business discussion—and the business discussion comes first.

The process begins with the phone call or first contact. After some very brief pleasantries—very brief, until you know one another better—you simply say, "I'm calling you because I think we have some areas of business that can be mutually beneficial. I'd like to get together to talk about it." The object is to establish the meeting, so don't get trapped into a phone discussion, or you'll preclude the meeting. If he or she presses, you should say something like, "I'd prefer to talk about it in person, but I think we each have clients who can benefit from our mutual services. Are you free for lunch next Thursday?" Your only objective, remember, is to get that meeting.

MAKING YOUR POINTS

• At lunch (or breakfast or in the office), your objective is to be sure that your points are made, clearly and quickly. "The reason I wanted to talk to you is that we have clients who can benefit from your services, and you have clients who can benefit from ours. Let me tell you what we do, and for whom." Then do it, and ask for the same information. Don't be coy. You're both there to establish a basis for business referrals.

You don't have to be brutally cold about it, but don't get mired down in telling one another personal troubles, and complaining about business, or putting down competitors. It's a soft selling situation, and it will be done with advantages and disadvantages of doing business together, not raucous jokes.

No one can teach you much about social skills. Everyone has a different way, and you're going to have to find your own style. In a networking situation, if you're naturally charming and outgoing, you've got a leg up. If you're not, stick to pleasantries and business, and you'll do fine. Eventually, by the third meeting, the barriers will be down, and you'll both be enjoying each other's company.

THE FOLLOW-UP

Follow-up is the most crucial part of networking—yet it's the part that gets the least attention. And it's the part that requires the communications skills.

After the initial contact—no matter what the source—comes a schedule of follow-up. It's important, even if you think your first meeting didn't go well.

It consists of . . .

- A follow-up note, saying, "Thanks for your time. I enjoyed meeting you." And a brief summary of what was discussed.
- A plan for the next meeting, which, if you're comfortable with the person, becomes a little more social.
- Adding the person to a mailing list of contacts. That list is used for periodic— and fairly frequent—notes, articles illustrating points made at the meetings, clippings on issues that concern you both, material you've written—anything relevant to your budding business relationship.
- And of course, referrals of your own clients to him or her.

Networking is a process that matures contacts. Rarely does it produce clients overnight. It takes time. But eventually, it pays off. Vast firms have been built on it.

Successful networking can indeed be as simple as this. It can be more involved, as well, if you want it to be, and if you feel that you like one another enough to turn it into a real friendship.

You can build a network of social/business contacts that can be as large—and as productive—as you can sustain.

After all, that's how Mr. Price and Mr. Waterhouse and Mr. Skadden...

THE SEMINAR—NETWORKING STARTS HERE

Too often, seminars are perceived simply as a way to tell people what you know and what you think they should know. Those are the seminars that waste everybody's time and your money. The key to a successful seminar is not what you want to say, but what your target audience wants to learn. Failure to understand this point is a guarantee of a failed seminar.

What a seminar really is—and should be—is a magnet for attracting prospects.

While seminars are ostensibly for the purpose of educating clients, which in fact they do, they serve an even more important purpose in practice development. They afford the opportunity to reach out to the business community to project expertise, and to engender their perception of that expertise and enhance your reputation as a leader in your field—in a context that can result in turning nonclients into clients. They afford an opportunity to develop and cement relationships, and to establish contacts, with nonclients who might become prospective clients and with those who influence their decisions in changing professionals. They can be a focal point for both press coverage and reprintable material. Seminars, with all their advantages, can be done as easily by sole practitioners as by larger firms.

But a seminar's greatest and most sustaining value is that it affords a face-to-face contact with a prospective client, or with somebody who can recommend one. How you use that contact is your choice—but there, in a seminar, is your target.

You will find, too, that seminar attendees also come to network, which is a major reason why seminars are so popular.

Seminars have been a practice development tool for many years—well before *Bates*—and so professionals are experienced in running them. But it should be remembered that no two seminars—even on the same topic with the same panel—are alike in terms of timing, place, depth of subject material, mixture of clients and nonclients, and so forth. No matter how many seminars you've done, the next one is different. Some simple planning makes a difference.

FORMULATING OBJECTIVES

Organizing a successful seminar begins with a defined objective and ends with a carefully structured follow-up. Planning a seminar should begin with asking and answering these crucial questions...

- What is the purpose of the seminar? Merely to impart new information? To cement relations to clients? To expose clients to a broader base of your firm's people? To develop relationships with nonclients and influentials as prospective clients?
- Who is the target audience?
- What is it you want people to know, think, or feel as a result of the seminar?
- How will the seminar be followed up for best marketing advantage?

For an attendee at a seminar there is an investment of time, and the return on that investment is information. Even though a seminar may not be comprehensive on a subject, it should still include sufficient material to make the attendee feel that his or her valuable time has been well spent. *If the seminar is to be successful, it must ultimately be cast in terms of what the audience wants and needs, and not simply what you want to impart.* The subject matter for a seminar should be clearly defined, well focused, and not too diverse. Don't attempt to cover too broad a spectrum of a topic in a seminar that will last only half a day or a full day, and don't confuse a seminar with a course. *The narrower and more urgent the topic, the greater the likelihood of success.*

A consideration is whether the seminar is to be free to invited guests or one in which admission is to be charged. A seminar to which you charge admission becomes a separate marketing problem.

THE PANELISTS

In a seminar that's shorter than a full day, rarely is there time for more than four speakers, each covering an aspect of the subject, plus one person to act as mediator to introduce the program, introduce the speakers, and handle questions. And obviously, the panelists' expertise and credentials should be sufficiently strong to serve as an attraction.

In a seminar that goes through lunch, a luncheon speaker may be appropriate, and preferably should not be one of the panelists. It could be a distinguished individual from outside the firm, or a ranking nonparticipant, such as the firm's managing partner or national director. The luncheon speech ideally should be an overview— broader in its perspective than any of the presentations by the panel.

Each panelist's material should be prepared in much the same way as for a speech. And questions should be anticipated to the fullest degree possible, with answers prepared beforehand. This is to avoid surprises from tough questions.

TARGET AUDIENCE

Assuming that you know who you want to come to the seminar (clients, prospective clients, accountants, lawyers, bankers, etc.), you've got two major primary tasks— specifically identifying the targets, and finding the lists. It's assumed you've got those lists. Each of your partners may have lists of the particular clients they want to invite, as well as lists of prospects, lawyers, bankers, accountants, and so forth. Beyond that, you may have to go to secondary sources, such as mailing list houses.

Getting lists together early is important, because they define your audience, and also tell you how many invitations to print, which then tells you about both cost, timing, and how large a room you'll need.

CONTROLLING COSTS AND MECHANICS

The mechanics of a seminar are beset with details that can easily go awry. The details can also be a focal point for breaking the budget. Stratospheric postage charges.

Unanticipated rush charges from the printer. Unexpected expense charges from guest speakers. They can all add up to more than you budgeted for.

How can these budget busters be avoided? The obvious answer, of course, is planning. Assigning an individual to coordinate the project can be the largest step toward cost cutting and a successful seminar you can make, because the greatest waste comes from late charges—rushes, overtime, lack of options in site selection, and so forth—that result from inattention to details and timing.

Assuming that you have a clear understanding of the objectives of the seminar, you must cover at least the following general categories in the planning flow chart...

- *Target audience.* The more precisely you define the audience, the easier it is to determine and focus the material. The less diverse the audience, the more technical and intensive the material can be.

- *Site selection.* Site selection depends on geographic convenience, budget, size of audience, available services (catering, audiovisuals, etc.), appearances, and postseminar plans (cocktail party, dinner, etc.). All of these bring their own cost factors, and each can affect costs. For example, the closer you get to the chosen date, the fewer available sites there are. If you're working with a new site, it should be very carefully checked beforehand for all amenities, including audiovisual capabilities (slides, films, etc.).

- *Panel.* If your panel is to consist of only your own partners, then you've got less to worry about than if you import an expert or a name. Transportation, out-of-pocket, and food go with the outside expert, as sometimes does an honorarium. Each panelist must be invited early enough for a confirmation, which must arrive early enough to include in the printed material promoting the event, or to find a replacement if the invitee can't make it. The response must include biographical material and a summary of his or her presentation. For publicity or follow-up purposes you may want more—a photo, a copy of the speech, for example.

- *The seminar itself.*
  - *Date.* As a general rule, you should allow at least six to eight weeks prior to the seminar for the first invitations to go out. Add to that any preparation time that's needed for the seminar itself and for clearing schedules of panelists and participants.
  - *Invitations.* First invitations should go out six to eight weeks prior to the seminar and should be carefully written in terms of the advantages to the attendees. It should be remembered that even free seminars are competitive

with other seminars on the same subject and, even more significantly, for the attention and time of very busy executives. And as with all direct mail, it can't be assumed that every piece of mail you send out will be read and digested by the recipient.

An invitation letter should, where possible, be individually addressed and personalized. Great care and emphasis should be placed in the first paragraph to state the problem clearly and urgently, as a context for which the seminar offers a solution. *The invitation to the seminar doesn't come in the first paragraph—it comes after the problem has been stated.*

Invitations should have a response mechanism, such as a phone number or post card, and arrangements should be made to deal with responses in an organized manner. Not everyone who accepts on the first invitation will actually attend, and so follow-up becomes necessary. This may be done by mail or by phone call, usually three weeks prior to the seminar, depending upon the response of the first invitation. If response to the first invitation is not satisfactory, a second letter should go out. If attendance and response require it, a follow-up phone call two or three days before the seminar to those who indicated that they would attend can be a helpful reminder.

○ *Brochures* used to promote the event should emphasize the problem to be addressed and the expertise to be brought to bear to address the problem. It should clearly define who specifically would benefit from attending.

○ *Mailing lists.* Mailing lists of existing clients are relatively easy. Mailing lists of nonclients can be considerably more difficult. Presumably every firm has a list of prospects, as well as contacts with those who influence prospects. Beyond that, there are many sources of mailing lists that can be used. The best, of course, is a mailing list developed out of your own marketing program, in which you've identified and targeted specific companies as prospective clients, and specific influentials. Mailing lists can also be purchased from reliable mailing list brokers.

○ *Site preparation.* In selecting and preparing a site for a seminar, you might consider the following points...

• Room size should be smaller (slightly), rather than larger. Fifty people in a room for 200 looks like a small group. Eighty people in a room for 75 looks like an enthusiastic crowd.

• Some rooms, even with sound systems, have poor acoustics, making it difficult for people in parts of the room to hear the speaker. The sound system should be checked to see that it's adequate for the size for the room.

• Check the walls. You don't want to share your meeting with the meeting next door, nor for them to share yours.

- Decide whether you want tables or not, and how they should be set up. Classroom-style? U-shape?
- Check the chairs and make sure they're comfortable. If you're not using tables, chairs should preferably be set up in semicircles rather than straight rows.
- Lobby signs and signs outside the room are necessary to help people locate the seminar.
- Amenities should be attended to, such as water pitchers and glasses for both speakers and the audience, plenty of ashtrays (you should consider smoking and no-smoking sections), and microphones for questions from the floor.
- Be sure that the site supplies adequate audiovisual equipment to meet your needs, including maintenance and spare bulbs for projectors. If possible, check their equipment beforehand.
- If meals are to be served, check menus beforehand, and if possible, try to see (or even eat) a sample meal. Know precisely what you're getting.
- Tell the site managers that you expect 20 percent fewer people than you really do, and then get the real capacity of the room after the price has been quoted. Check penalty arrangements and deposits required.
- If there is to be a cocktail hour, be sure to understand beforehand exactly how beverages are to be served.
- Arrange for a sufficient number of registration tables at the entrance to the seminar room, preferably just outside. Determine beforehand how many people you're going to need to man those tables to help you register attendees, the form of registration you're going to use, and the number and kind of badges you're going to need.
- If press is attending, arrange for press facilities, such as seating, phones, computers, faxes, a press room, and so forth. If broadcast media is expected, be sure to have setups for them, including room in the aisles for cameras.

- Not only should the site be inspected before you sign the contract, it should also be inspected on the date of the seminar, in time to make any corrections if arrangements have not been properly made.
- In negotiating for a site, it's useful to remember that prices aren't fixed in stone. They are frequently negotiable, particularly if the hotel or meeting room isn't busy. You should always make a counteroffer. A meeting room is a perishable commodity; sites can't inventory yesterday's empty room, which is why most sites will negotiate unless there's really competition for the space.

- Regardless of the subject matter of a seminar, there should always be a kit of materials for each participant. This might include...

  ○ A seminar program

  ○ Appropriate brochures

  ○ Biographies of the panelists

  ○ Descriptive material about the firm

  ○ Useful background material on the subject, including a position paper if pertinent

  ○ Reprints of articles by the participants

  ○ Blank pads and pencils

- It may be useful to hold something back from these packages that can be sent out on a follow-up. However, given a choice between inadequate materials and the need for follow-up, the option should include the materials in the seminar packet. There are other techniques to use in following up.

If the preparations for a seminar have been made adequately, then the seminar itself should be an anticlimax except for the presentations.

Preparing and rehearsing for the seminar cannot be a casual event. While it's assumed that each panelist who participates is an expert in his field, and even that he or she is extensively experienced, a seminar is still an ensemble function.

In planning a seminar, a segment of the topic is assigned to each participant. However, it should be the responsibility of each participant to make clear to the others on the panel precisely what areas he or she is going to cover. Written copies of speeches are useful in several additional ways—they may be reprinted, they may be adopted as articles, they may serve as a background piece to help the press develop interviews. Individual rehearsal, as well as group rehearsal, is extremely important. It will improve the presentation of each individual performance and sharpen and help with the timing of the ensemble performance. It also gives you the opportunity to test and time your presentation with any audiovisual material.

THE PANEL CHAIR

The meeting leader or chair has four major responsibilities...

- To introduce the seminar and each of the speakers. While the chair may not be one of the panelists, it's his or her opening remarks that set the context of the seminar. They should consist of a brief welcome and introduction of each of the panelists, including background (with focus on the expertise on the subject) and a very brief summary of the context of the material for the panel.

- To chair the question period and direct the questions to the appropriate panelists. During the question-and-answer period, the chair selects the questions from the audience, and if they are not addressed to a specific panelist, he or she directs them. In this context, it's also the chair's role to be alert and evenhanded in choosing questioners from across the room, to keep the questions focused, and to keep the answers relevant. During the question-and-answer period, the chair should not be passive, but active in directing the questions and answers.

- To keep the seminar moving, well paced, and focused.

- To sum up at the end. At the end of the seminar, the chair should sum up the points made as briefly and succinctly as possible, thank those who attended, and make other announcements about follow-up or mechanics.

PRESS COVERAGE

Seminars frequently offer an exceptional opportunity for media coverage.

Certainly, a news release should be distributed to announce the seminar, particularly if it's open to the broader business community. A decision should be made as to whether the press should be invited.

Media should not be invited unless there's a clear feeling that material will be discussed that's newsworthy or of interest to the press.

For media coverage, the following steps should be taken . . .

- A media kit should be prepared that includes:
  - A basic press release and background sheet about the seminar and its topic
  - Biographical material on the speakers
  - Individual press releases and background sheets, if appropriate, on each of the speaker's topics
  - Any pertinent material about your firm

- About a week prior to the seminar, a basic news alert should be sent to the appropriate segment of the press including an invitation to attend. For broadcast media, include a description of available radio and TV facilities.

- The day before the seminar, the media should be called, not to see whether they got the alert, but to reaffirm the invitation.

- If the subject warrants it, an attempt should be made to arrange for an interview of participants.

- Should any members of the press attend, they should be recognized at the door, greeted by a responsible person from your firm, and given a press kit as well as other seminar material. Interviews following the seminar should be arranged as expeditiously as possible.

If the press is not interested in attending, a copy of the press kit and the seminar material should be sent to the appropriate media immediately following the seminar. Appropriate material should also be sent to the media by e-mail.

SEMINAR COSTS

The basic costs of a seminar include these elements . . .

- Mailing and production costs for invitations, press, and other materials
- Room rental and subsidiary costs
- Food and beverages, snacks and cocktail party
- Transportation and housing for guests and out-of-town panelists
- Production of slides, PowerPoint presentations, and other audiovisual material
- Tips
- Brochure and advertising (if appropriate)
- Promotional material for seminar to which admission is charged

THE MEETING PLANNER

The myriad details of seminars and other forms of meetings have given rise to the full-time role of the meeting planner. Many larger firms have them on staff, but a number of excellent independent planners and planning firms are available.

The advantages to using meeting planners are that they arrange for and manage all the details and costs, and they do it from a base of extensive experience. Theirs is a full-time role. For the nonprofessional, it's a part-time role, which means that many crucial elements are not attended to. This way lies failure and budget busting.

In making a seminar successful, and keeping within budgets, a meeting planner pays for him- or herself, more often than not, in cost savings and meeting effectiveness.

THE FOLLOW-UP

In any seminar, especially those attended by nonclients, the effort is totally wasted if there isn't immediate and appropriate follow-up.

Attendance at a seminar of itself implies an interest in the subject. Certainly, each person who attends should be registered, even if it's simply signing a log. This facilitates postseminar mailings and letters and phone follow-up.

The details of follow-up should be planned, including press follow-up, distributing attendance lists to partners, determining the follow-up process, what's done by mail and what by phone and who does it, and so forth. If this is not planned at the very beginning of the process, it can cost more to set up at the last minute. These elements should be included in a flow chart.

Because the most important part of any seminar may be the cocktail party afterward—that's where the networking is done—details must be as carefully structured as for the seminar itself. This is the occasion in which the expertise that's been projected by the seminar is turned into contact. If your firm is large enough, nonparticipating partners and others should be invited, with each assigned to cultivate prospective clients individually. The seminar may attract nonclients, but they don't really become prospects until the contact is made.

A thank-you letter should be sent to every nonclient who attended, including an invitation to meet for lunch or to discuss a specific question that may have been raised during the informalities of the cocktail hour.

Everyone who attends the seminar should be placed on an appropriate mailing list to regularly receive material issued by your firm. This might include reprints of the presentations of the seminar. This same material, incidentally, can be sent to invitees who did not attend.

NEWSLETTERS

Newsletters are an effective marketing device because when they're well done, they can accomplish a great deal. They can...

- Target a specific and defined audience
- Inform both clients and prospects
- Demonstrate your knowledge, concern, and interest in the reader's industry and company
- Enhance both name recognition and reputation
- Generate inquiries regarding specific subjects covered in the newsletter
- Establish your franchise in a particular industry, or with a specific expertise

Why, then, do they often not work? Why do they so often go directly into the wastebasket? What does work?

The concept may be wrong. You're trying to tell the wrong things to the wrong audience. Or you don't understand that people get a lot of newsletters and junk mail, and nobody is waiting with bated breath for your newsletter. If your concept and content aren't designed to make a difference, or to be practically informative, don't bother.

What does work . . .

- The content is based on what the readers need to know, not on what you want to tell because it's what you want to offer.

- Supply meaningful content, particularly information not available elsewhere. Although you know it as a marketing tool, the readers don't care about your marketing. If they don't see it as uniquely informative, they won't read it. If you can't supply meaningful content, don't waste your time and money.

- Your mailing list is crucial. The value of direct mail of any kind, including newsletters, is the ability to get directly to the individual target you want to reach. If your mailing list can't do that, you're wasting your time and money.

- The design should be vivid and inviting. If it's dull and uninviting, or so dedicated to win the designer kudos that nobody takes the content seriously, nobody will read it. In newsletters, design should support content, not the other way around. The designer should work for the editor, not the other way around.

- The design should be consistent, both from issue to issue, and with other newsletters you publish. If your newsletter is useful, you want it to be quickly recognizable in a mailbag full of competitive newsletters. Design a simple but attractive format that identifies your firm and all the newsletters from your firm.

- The design should be a standard format that allows your own staff to enter copy for each issue, without making each issue a major project. With today's computer programs, you should be able to do this in-house, after a designer has developed a template.

- The frequency should be set based on content and availability of staff to write the content. If there isn't that much to write about that's timely and valuable, don't make the newsletter a monthly. But whatever schedule you set, stick to it. Keep the schedule on target.

- While you need not write your entire newsletter, buy a service that supplies content to supplement what you do write. But except in rare instances not a newsletter service that supplies a generic newsletter. They're usually too general and contain information that everybody has read in *The Wall Street Journal* or *Business Week*. Not particularly valuable for you or your clientele. Unless you find one that's exceptionally good, keep it your newsletter, not that of an outside supplier.

- Give one person editorial responsibility, and spread the content around. Use bylines, because that's how you demonstrate your expertise, and give a sense of originality and dedication to your firm.
- Use feedback devices. Not simply asking people if they like your newsletter, but specific questions that give readers the opportunity to help choose the content they will find most useful. Keep surveys short and simple, and no more than once or twice a year.

Ultimately, you have to realize that you're competing for attention against every other piece of mail, every other publication, every other newsletter that your target gets. There are a lot of publications out there, and you've got to be equal to—or better than—all of them. Not as difficult as it seems, if you plan carefully and run your newsletter thoughtfully. After all, you have the expertise. Business journalists simply *know about* the expertise.

THE WEB SITE

It's now difficult to think of a marketing program without a web site. It has become as standard in marketing as brochures and other descriptive literature. More so, in fact, because the information in printed material is finite and cast in stone, until the next revision and expensive printing. A web site, however, is dynamic. It can be changed virtually moment by moment, it can be interactive with the reader, and it can be colorful without the added expense of four-color printing.

While it doesn't fully replace brochures, which can be read any time and anywhere, it adds a new dimension to marketing.

Moreover, web sites have now reached a point at which they're routinely expected by the business community, for whom they're an instant reference tool, a source of judgment about a firm, a recruiting tool, and a measure of a firm's standing and status in the business community. A firm without a web site is like a firm without a fax machine (which, by the way, is now rarely used, as e-mail replaces most faxes).

From the invention of the printing press and movable type, to the telephone, radio, and television, and now to the Internet, every medium has imposed its own dimensions and process for communicating ideas. And the same message is conveyed differently in each medium. The medium, in other words, is not simply the conveyor of the message. The medium, as Marshall McCluhan said, is indeed the message. Those who've started working with the Internet and web sites are learning this, expensively and painfully.

Put the same message into print, or over a telephone, or in radio or television, and it becomes a different message, at least in the way it's heard and perceived, and in the way it moves the reader or viewer to action. A site is not simply another form of conduit. It's a medium with its own distinctive characteristics. It conveys information in unique ways, and has a different quality of impact.

The proliferation of authoring programs, such as *Dreamweaver* and *Front Page*, and of easy graphic design applications, make producing and getting a site online a relative cinch. Anybody can do it. Add to that the growing body of web design professionals, e-commerce specialists, and enthusiastic marketing consultants, and the elevator to the web site design tower is beginning to get a little crowded. But unfortunately, not every site contributes much more than static and noise for the eye and mind.

There are some great sites online. Sites that understand why they are there, and what they are meant to accomplish. What are the differences? What are the pitfalls, and what are the ways to best take advantage of the new medium? New ideas emerge every day, as do new technological advances.

The differences between a web site and other media in the way that messages are conveyed are distinctive and important to realize.

- Just the look of the word or image on a page is different on a computer screen. You can control the look of the printed page, but you can't always control the look of that same information on a computer screen. Different web browsers show the same images differently. The viewers' screen sizes differ, as do their skills in using a computer. You must review your site using several different browsers to see and correct the differences.

- Because of the size of the screen, the need to sit in front of it to read the material, and the dynamic of time, text works better when it's brief and gets to the point quickly. For the most part, and unlike printed material, it's a quick read. Writing for the web is a different art form.

- The clarity of the image is not always the same as it is on the printed page. Allowances must be made for these differences in designing a site. Some typefaces are more readable than others, for example.

- Color is used more freely on the computer, and doesn't add to cost. Add color to the printed page and your costs go up dramatically.

- Dynamic motion—images that move—are useful on a web site, and obviously, not on the printed page. These devices are relatively easy to put on sites, and if used tastefully, add to the interest and attractiveness. (But they can also slow down loading time.)

- Dynamic content includes the unique link, in which any word or image in the text can be linked to any word or image or content anywhere else on the Internet. In a sense, this expands any web page or site to a realm almost beyond imagination.

- The content, look, design, and colors of a site can be changed at will. Obviously not so in other media. (This is both an opportunity to be creative, and a prospective pitfall that can subvert the message by overwhelming it.)

- It's true that many of the elements of a web site can be found in other media. Film and television have color and motion, but at greater cost. Newspapers change content daily, but a web site can change content in real time. The amount of text and illustration is limited by the format of other media, but the only limit in a web site is the ability to sustain attention and interest.

Perhaps the most important difference, and the one that should most affect the site's design, is that a web site is dynamic, and the printed page is not. Just the ability to link to other pages makes a site a significantly different medium. The printed document may describe a firm and its practice, but it's a static description. Pages are generally turned sequentially, like a book. A good web site allows a reader to jump to the information that's most immediate—most valuable—and back again to a home page. This is an extraordinary power in managing and conveying information.

These qualities suggest that the site should be designed by someone who really understands the medium, and not just the graphics or content. Designing a web site is a special skill, requiring a greater sense of communication in several dimensions. In fact, it often takes two different professionals, with two different skill sets, to do it right—the communicator, who knows how to get the best out of the medium, and the technician, who knows how to make it happen. A web site, it must be remembered, is ultimately a communications medium—not merely a technical device.

What, then, are some of the major considerations in producing a successful and valuable web site?

- There's an easy tendency to misunderstand objectives. Or more accurately, *expectations*. What do you want the site to do? What can you reasonably expect from it? Name recognition? A display of your firm's skills and capabilities? Access to individual specialists within your firm? A demonstration of your firm's breadth and scope? *What do you want people to know, think, or feel after they've looked at the site?* Without a clear view of objectives for your site, it's impossible to design a site that can accomplish those objectives.

- Today's news gets stale very quickly on a web site. Change content as often as possible. Give the viewers a reason to keep coming back, and to stay on your site for as long as possible. *This is why a firm's web site shouldn't be simply a download of its brochure.*

- Given the relative ease with which web site images can be produced, it's easy to allow the design to overwhelm the message. No matter how elaborate the design, including color and graphics, it should let the message do its work. Design should *support* the message and the site, not *dominate* them. Here, artfulness counts. Complex graphics may look great, but may take so long to load that viewers quickly move on to other sites.

- You may have the most attractive site on the Internet, but if there's no reason for people to revisit your site frequently, your objectives for it will rarely be achieved. Repetition is impact, as every marketing professional knows. The competition for attention to any one site is overwhelming. Fight competition for the viewer's attention with a combination of technical skill and artistry (but don't confuse one with the other—they're two different things).

- Think of the difference between sitting straight in a chair in front of a computer screen, and relaxing in an easy chair, reading a brochure. If you want your viewer to get your message onscreen, it has to be easily readable, and worth reading. If you can't sustain interest in large blocks of text, with a message that's interesting and important, then stick to short messages.

- Everybody knows how to read printed text, but not everybody is computer literate. Make sure your site is usable and navigable by the least sophisticated person you want to reach.

- Check your mechanics and links. Make sure your site is accessible to all major browsers (different browsers see code differently) and to major search engines. Keep an eye on loading time. Double-check links.

- A tip. A site called www.netmechanics.com is loaded with good advice and lots of help in designing and running a site, no matter what your level of experience. Try it.

That it's so easy to get online with a web site is a double-edged sword. On one edge is the fact that even a computer beginner can do it. With programs like *FrontPage* and *Dreamweaver*, you can be up and running in no time, on a shallow learning curve.

On the other edge is the reality that its ease is deceptive. A good site is an art form, not only in its graphics, but also in the professionalism of it's ability to convey a message in ways that meet your objective. That's why what makes doing a web site so hard is that it's so easy.

DIRECT MAIL

Direct mail is a powerful tool in marketing a professional firm. It works, but not in the same way as it does for product marketing. The differences are profound—and quite significant.

If you send out 20,000 letters offering a desk clock, and the list is carefully chosen to include people who can afford to buy clocks, and who've bought desk items in that price category before, and the selling material is good, then you can count on getting back about 1,000 orders with checks. Five percent.

Easy. There's nothing personal between you and the individuals who buy your clock. They don't expect to see you again. They like the clock and want it. When it comes, they have the clock and you go away.

Now, why shouldn't that work the same way in professional services? If you send out 20,000 letters to a carefully selected list of small business owners, people who use or need the services of a lawyer or an accountant, and offer your services, why can't you, too, anticipate that you'd get 1,000 new clients? Or even 1,000 opportunities to discuss ways in which you can serve them?

Because people don't buy professional services the way they buy products. And that's why you'd be wasting your money using direct mail with the same matrix you'd use for selling a product.

With rare exceptions, the object of a direct mail campaign is not to sell your service. It rarely will. The objective is *to get an appointment to sell your service.* Why? Because...

- The detachment in selling a product, in which the product stays and the seller goes, doesn't exist in professional services marketing. The professional who sells a professional service *does* stay after the sale is made.

- Not every company, or individual, regardless of the numbers or the profile on paper, is the right client. No matter how hungry you are for clients, there are still those prospective clients you want to screen—be it for financial reasons, or personalities, or the nature of the business, or the kinds of problems.

  This is a problem with mass marketing—no choice of who buys your product. But with products, it doesn't matter. With services, it does. *Controlling the nature of your clientele is extremely important in successful practice. And so it's important in professional services marketing.*

- Direct mail may sell a product—even to someone who doesn't really need it—by virtue of appeal or impulse. Everybody who needs an accountant probably has one, and except for those with attorneys on retainer, anybody who might need a lawyer at one time or another may not need one at the time you send your letter. That means that your description of what you have to offer must be sufficiently focused and intriguing, to inspire confidence in you and your firm.

This does not constitute a sale, however, which can come only through further discussion and personal contact.

- There are more broad general categories of those who buy products than there are of those who buy professional services. The category of people who buy cat books is very large and homogeneous. They may, as individuals, differ in many different ways—but in their affinity for cats they're the same. The people who use professional services almost always include much smaller groups with much more specific needs for aspects of those services.

  For example, all Americans and all companies with income must pay taxes. But within those very large categories, specific tax problems, or compliance needs, or tax planning objectives, tend to be more distinctive, and of concern to smaller groups of companies or individuals.

  This focus is a crucial factor in marketing. It means that the target market for a very specific service is relatively narrow. It also means that the opportunity to sell to that smaller group improves the ability to sell successfully.

  Now, you can call this niche marketing, or just plain intelligent marketing analysis and response. It doesn't matter, because it's simply rational.

  Approach number one, then, is to identify the most cohesive group possible (cohesive in the sense of commonality of the problem), and address that group in terms of a specific problem—and your ability to help its members solve it.

  That narrows each mailing list, then, to a very manageable group. And it's a group to which you can make a highly focused appeal.

THE DIRECT MAIL LETTER

Unfortunately, writing a direct mail letter is a combination of art, experience, skill, and luck—probably in that order. There are no hard and fast rules, but we do know some things that work and don't work for most campaigns.

- Letters that start off with "we," and then go on to describe your firm, tend not to work. Who you are and what you have to offer is your concern—not the potential buyer's. Potential buyers are intrigued only by their perception that you understand and can help them serve their needs.
- Self-serving descriptions, and adjectives that try to tell the readers how they should perceive you, are turn-offs. "We give better service," for example, is a road sign to the wastebasket. What's the obverse—"We give lousy service?" As the old saying goes, what you are speaks so loud that I can't hear what you say you are.
- Letters that start off with a question can be a trap. "Do you have a problem with...?" means that if the reader doesn't know that he or she has that prob-

lem, there's no reason to read beyond that point. (However, "Do you know that you may be paying taxes you don't have to pay?" can work. You have to be careful about hard and fast rules.)

- Letters that deal with more than one problem tend to be ignored.

- Letters that include brochures or other literature in the first mailing tend not to work for a simple reason—they tell your whole story to readers, who then feel that there's no reason to meet with you. They know what you have to sell. That deprives you of the important opportunity to make a strong personal presentation, predicated on an analysis of the prospect's specific problems and needs. Brochures and literature are for leaving behind after you've met with the prospect. One possible exception might be reprints of articles that support your description of the seriousness of the problem, or that enhance your reputation. And even these should rarely be used in a first mailing.

- Absolutely crucial is to understand that while you may get an occasional response that says, "I like your letter—let's start on Monday," *the objective of the exercise is solely to get an appointment to make a presentation—not to make the sale.* To expect anything other than that from direct mail in professional services is to doom yourself to expensive failure.

- What seems to get better readership is the letter written on Monarch-size letterhead. It looks more like a personal letter, or one from a CEO to a CEO.

- One approach that almost invariably works is to open with a strong—and startling, if possible—statement of a specific problem. It should be stated in a way to get to the very heart of what your research says really bothers your target. For example, a tremendously successful letter for a consulting firm selling maintenance system services began, "Do you know what portion of the more than one billion dollars in wasted maintenance dollars is yours?" Another sentence expanded the theme, bringing the terror of it even closer to home.

- The second paragraph simply said, "We can help you, as we've helped dozens of other companies like yours, in your industry."

- The third paragraph described the firm, and why it was qualified to help. No self-serving adjectives. Just the facts.

- The fourth and last paragraph requested an appointment to discuss ways in which "we can help you."

That letter, in a proper context, resulted in a better than 5 percent return—and that percentage continues to improve. That is, 5 percent of the companies that received the letter agreed to meet with a representative of the firm.

THE TELEPHONE AND DIRECT MAIL

In direct mail for products, you send out the letter and wait for the checks. In direct mail for professional services, you're after an appointment. This means that direct mail rarely should be trusted to work on its own. You can test it, to see how many people call you back. Some will, but most won't.

That's why you have to follow up each letter with a phone call. "I wrote you last week about accounting or legal or business problems you may be facing. When can we get together to discuss ways in which we might be able to help? Is next Tuesday at 10 good for you?" In some cases, a well-prepared and skilled telemarketer, who can arrange appointments for you or somebody in your firm, can do the phone follow-up. But the phone follow-up is crucial, even if you say, in your letter, "call me for details." In the phone follow-up, it's extremely important that you (or whoever is on the phone) not get sucked into a potential selling situation. That must be done in person. The objective of the phone follow-up is solely and simply to arrange an appointment. Any questions should be deferred with a statement such as, *"Well, that's what I want to discuss with you. I think I can give you a better answer after we've taken a few minutes for me to better understand your needs. Is Tuesday at 10 good for you?"*

Because the letter is a precursor to an appointment, you have another reason why mass mailings don't work. *You can't send out more letters than you can follow up on within a week after the mailing.*

STRATEGY

Merely sending out letters, even with a phone follow-up, doesn't constitute a direct mail campaign—and certainly not one that gives the greatest potential for success and return on investment.

Ideally, the direct mail campaign is part of a larger marketing program. Imagine, for example, the effect of a letter on a prospective client who's seen your name (or your firm's name) on articles or in interviews. Imagine the impact on the prospective client who's gotten your letter, and who is ultimately invited to a seminar you're giving, or is on the mailing list for your newsletter.

Then, too, even if you don't have such a sustaining campaign, direct mail as described here has proven its effectiveness. But still, the missing ingredient is the selling skill of the individual who follows up. You can get 100 appointments, but if you can't sell, you don't get any of those prospects as clients. That means taking considerable time to plan what you're going to do when you get to the meeting. Training in selling skills is valuable. Even if you're a natural at selling, you still have to plan ahead.

The real strategy comes in . . .

- *Choosing the target list.* Pick a small segment of companies, in one or several industries, that seem susceptible to a common problem.
- *Testing.* If the strategy you choose works on the smaller list, you can expand it. If it doesn't, you can change it for the next group, with very little lost. If, however, your strategy is wrong in mass mailing, you've spent a lot of money for no good reason.
- *Choosing the problem you're going to address.* Here, less is more. You may be capable of solving 100 problems of many companies of many sizes in a broad range of industries, but don't bite off too much in each mailing.
- Now we get tricky. In some cases, you've got to sell more than one person in a company. In one of the most successful marketing programs ever done in professional services, research determined that three individuals were involved in making a buy decision—the CEO because it was a big-ticket purchase; the CFO because it involved spending money to save money; and the project director, who was responsible for the project performance. The campaign that worked was a letter to each of the three, with each apprised of the fact that letters were written to all three. Each letter couched the same message in terms of the individual concerns. It sold millions of dollars in accounting and consulting fees, and continues to do so.

MULTIPLE LETTERS

Sometimes, letters must be sent to more than one person in each company. If that's what's called for, do it. It works.

- A direct mail campaign is just that—a campaign. It's not just shooting some letters in the mail. It may mean individual letters to two or three officers of the same firm. But it also may mean three letters to the same people. The first is the subtle one, merely attacking the problem. The second, to those in the original mailing on whom there was no impact, is stronger. The third, to those in the original mailing who seem untouched, is relatively hard sell.
- In a strategic campaign, every element must be considered, and thought of in relation to the others. This includes . . .
  - The target list
  - The letter
  - The timing—how many letters go out, at what intervals, and how soon each mailing is followed up by phone

- ○ The phone follow-up (who does it, and who says what)
- ○ The appointment (who goes, what's said)
- ○ Collateral material (brochures, etc., and how they're used)
- ○ Other aspects of marketing, and how they relate to direct mail
- ○ Telemarketing and its relationship to direct mail

All of these elements must be measured and balanced against one another.

Is this the only way to go? Of course not. This is one way that's proven to work. We know what doesn't work, but we only know some of what does work.

Now...

If you choose a single target segment, predicated on a specific problem (not necessarily a single industry, although the problem and the industry are often contiguous)...

And if you write a letter that addresses the specific problem... And if you follow up with a good phone call... then you're likely to see the best of direct mail at work.

Is it more trouble than the mass mailing? Of course it is. But in the long run, it's a lot cheaper, because it works better. It gets you more appointments and more opportunities to sell your services. It's more personal, and therefore more professional and dignified.

Direct mail in professional services marketing, it turns out, is not a spectator sport. You have to play, too.

PART V

MANAGING THE CLIENT-CENTRIC FIRM

·

10

TURNING RECIPES INTO CAKES

Managing for Results

If there is one word that separates the successful from the unsuccessful firm, it's execution—execution of the firm's vision and strategy.

—August J. Aquila

The best recipe in the book is merely words on paper until the ingredients are mixed and cooked. It's the execution that counts. The quarterback may have memorized all the plays from the game book, but the outcome of the game depends not on how good the plays are but on how well he executes them.

The same elements apply to successfully managing the marketing function in accounting and law firms. The managing partner of Firm A lays out a brilliant marketing strategy, only to find out that the firm cannot execute it. In Firm B, partners and other professionals consistently fail to meet client expectations; they have no performance strategy. Firm C has an average client acquisition strategy but executes it brilliantly, and thrives. Executing an average strategy effectively always wins over having a brilliant strategy but no execution.

STRATEGY EXECUTION AS A CORE COMPETENCY

While every firm has a different set of core competencies—those things it excels in—most firms fail to achieve the benefits of their overall strategic plan because execution is not one of their core competencies.

To excel in client service or anything, say Larry Bossidy and Ram Charan in *Execution—The Discipline of Getting Things Done*, "you don't need a lot of complex theory," you simply need to change your people's behavior so they produce results that are linked to achieving your goals and strategies.

They outline three basic steps in this process:

- Each person in the firm needs to know the results you're looking for.
- Management or firm leaders must discuss with each person what they need to do in order to achieve the results. This is an ongoing coaching process and not a one-time event.
- Those individuals who have achieved their results must be rewarded. Because not everyone will achieve 100 percent of their chosen goals, you'll need to provide some people with additional coaching. If that doesn't work, there are several steps you can take—such as providing them with other responsibilities, reducing their compensation, or ultimately removing them from the firm.

Ultimately, if good execution begins with a good vision, then a sound strategy begins with an effective system to measure and monitor a firm's performance. There are several such systems, but perhaps the most interesting and comprehensive one is the *Balanced Scorecard*, which has become increasingly popular with accounting and law firm managing partners.

THE BALANCED SCORECARD APPROACH

Harvard Business School professor Robert S. Kaplan and consultant David P. Norton, president of Renaissance Solutions, Inc., created the Balanced Scorecard in the early 1990s. And while the Balanced Scorecard was originally developed to measure performance for corporations, especially manufacturing firms, it is now being used in accounting and law firms to implement strategy and monitor objectives.

The Balanced Scorecard measures the results of management efforts and the effectiveness of the their strategies. It shows how well management is executing strategies, and how well people in the firm are achieving their objectives. It's an effective tool that can be used to measure a firm's progress in reaching its overall goals, an entire marketing program, or each of its parts.

When applied to professional services firms, the Balanced Scorecard creates an organized process that...

- Defines specific objectives, for both the entire firm and for each aspect of its practice
- Shows how different objectives interrelate
- Builds consensus on what should be measured at the firm, department, or niche, and individual level

- Identifies targets or successes at each stage of the process (milestones)
- Defines the process for successfully meeting the objectives
- Improves internal communications
- Emphasizes both financial and nonfinancial measures
- Produces greater partner and staff accountability
- Generates superior financial results

USING THE BALANCED SCORECARD IN A PROFESSIONAL SERVICES FIRM

For the scorecard to work in your firm, partners must first agree upon the firm's overall goals and strategy. It's important for a firm to gain consensus on its strategy—how will it realize its goals. Without this agreement, the firm can never move ahead in a unified fashion. Gaining strategic consensus, then, is the first step in building accountability in a firm.

Once that consensus has been reached, partners and other key personnel must then address and develop objectives, measures, targets, and initiatives in each of five primary areas—*financial, client, marketing, internal business process and employee growth and learning.* (See Exhibit 10.1.)

Exhibit 10.1   Professional Services Firms Five Key Areas

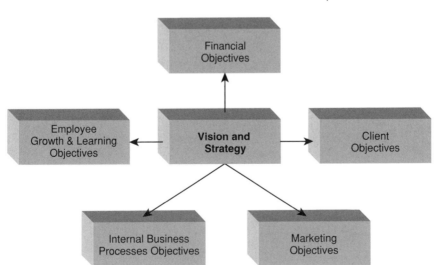

INTERRELATED OBJECTIVES

It's not enough to just determine a list of objectives. The scorecard approach requires you to determine how the various objectives *interrelate*. How does one affect the other? For example, you can't expect to enter a new market unless your people develop knowledge about it. They won't spend quality time with clients unless they know what quality time is. They won't deliver timely services until you have processes that reduce redundancies and other inefficient activities. (Exhibit A.1 in Appendix A presents a linkage diagram showing how objectives may interrelate.)

DESIGNING THE SCORECARD

A typical Balanced Scorecard begins with a specific primary goal. Assume, as an example, that you perceive a growing biotech industry in your geographic marketing area. Assume that you are willing to take prudent measures and allocate resources to capture a reasonable share of that market. Assume as well that this goal fits with the overall strategy of the firm.

The next step is for the practice unit or department to develop a set of *objectives*; *measurements*—what it plans to measure; *targets* for success; and specific *action steps* or *initiatives* in each of the five areas. Exhibit 10.2 is a scorecard template to use. (Exhibit A.2 is an example of a completed scorecard.)

Exhibit 10.3 is a completed sample format of a growth and learning objective. The *objective* is to develop staff/partner marketing skills. The *measurement* will be the percent of staff/partners who have acquired those skills. Our example has two *targets* to measure success. The first is having 80 percent of the staff/partners trained by 2006 and the second is having 100 percent trained by 2009.

While the scorecard process focuses on the key measures and targets necessary to achieve stated objectives, the process is really more about strategy *implementation* than strategy *formulation*. It's only by focusing on measures and targets that a firm can determine how well its strategy is working, how effective its marketing is, and how well it's producing quality and value-added services. These are all necessary to retain and serve clients, and to maintain a sustained competitive edge.

A WORD OF CAUTION

A strategy is predicated on a set of assumptions about what might happen if we do certain things. Unless you capture, analyze, and monitor these assumptions, you won't know how well the strategy is working. If you were concerned about only the

Exhibit 10.2   Scorecard Template

Area	Objective	Leading Measure	Lagging Measure	Target	Initiative(s)
Financial					
Client					
Marketing					
Business Process					
Growth/ Learning (Employees)					
(For additional areas)					

169

Exhibit 10.3 Sample Completed Employee Objective Template

Objective	Measurement	Target	Initiatives
Develop staff/ partner marketing skills	The percentage of staff who have acquired the skills	80% staff trained by 2006 100% trained by 2009	Bring in outside sales training professionals

financial results, you would never know what's hindering or helping you achieve the objectives. And you would never know what needed to be worked on.

For example, we assume that motivated staff has an impact on client satisfaction. And we also assume that as client satisfaction rises, there will be an increase in future sales to those clients. But unless we measure and track staff motivation, we won't be able to prove it. There is another caution to be noted. Staff motivation, however, may increase because we are overpaying and underworking our staff. While the staff may be highly motivated, we doubt that with this kind of motivation, client satisfaction would improve. Or client satisfaction, however, may improve because we are lowering our fees on new work without reducing the quality of the work. You can see, therefore, that identifying the right performance measures is a crucial and sometimes difficult step in the development of your scorecard.

SELECTING THE PROPER PERFORMANCE MEASURES

There are two types of measures that firms can select—*lagging* or *leading*. A *lagging measure* tells you what happened and provides you with the results of your previous efforts. Most financial measures are lagging measures. Last month revenues were "X," expenses were "Y," and profit or loss was "Z."

A *leading measure* tells you what might happen in the future. For example, you are tracking the number of sales appointments you are getting each month. In the first month, there are five; in the second month, five more; and in the third month, eight. Your goals were four per month. Might not this tell you that revenues in the next three to six months could increase, provided that these are qualified prospects and your professionals know how to sell and close? Leading measures are hence performance drivers. Unlike lagging measures, leading measures are useful in telling you how well you will do in the future. They effectively predict future results.

Imagine that you focused only on lagging measures throughout the year. What real control or impact would you have on performance? Now imagine that in addition to the lagging measures, you also focus on leading measures, such as the number of new leads obtained, new business presentations made, number of referrals from your key clients, or number of leads and appointments from client seminars and symposiums presented. At any time you would be able to tell whether you are falling short or exceeding targets. And you would know which areas of the practice require more attention. Now that is active management.

Every firm needs to identify what performances to measure in order to achieve its objectives. This is not a boilerplate exercise. Selecting the right measures is critical in helping management make better decisions and helping staff behave in a fashion that will support the firm's objectives. Finally, choosing the right measures will also help the firm gain a competitive edge now and into the future.

The following guidelines may help you select the appropriate measures for your firm...

- Performance measures must tie into the firm's strategies. If, for example, the firm wants to be profitable the first year of its entry into the biotech market, then one of the performance measures might be profitability per new engagement. If the objective were to build market share and not worry about current year profitability, the measure would change to the number of new clients acquired.

- Measures need to tie into actual partner/staff performance. For example, a business development partner supports the department's goal of bringing in new business. A possible measure could be the number of qualified appointments he or she is able to set up. A tax preparer's measure could deal with the amount of time he or she takes to complete returns for clients. For staff accountants or new associates, it could be the number of times a project has to be redone.

- Closely aligned with the foregoing, staff and partners need to be able to understand the measure. If they don't see how it affects their activities, it becomes meaningless to them and they won't be concerned about it.

- Finally, the measure needs to be useful to management. Leading indicators cannot be faulty. For example, you attempt to measure client satisfaction based on the number of complaints that you receive from clients. However, historically your clients don't complain, they just walk away from your firm. You have selected a faulty measure.

HOW MANY MEASURES SHOULD YOU SELECT?

Considering that you may have five interrelated areas in which to develop objectives and measures, you won't want to have more than two or three measures for each area. Too many measures will cause you to lose focus on what's important in the practice. Since this is an ongoing, dynamic process, you'll always be creating new objectives and measures. (See Appendix A for a listing of commonly used measures.)

DETERMINING TARGETS

While there are industry benchmarks for the accounting and legal professions (examples are the Annual AICPA/Texas State Society Survey, Bowman's Annual Accounting Survey, Of Counsel Annual Survey, etc.), firms should determine their own targets or points of arrival (POA). Determining targets is nothing new for professional services firms. Firms annually set financial goals, set targets for days outstanding for *accounts receivable* and *work in progress*, and assign billable hour targets for their professionals and paraprofessionals.

Without targets, firm management will never know how well it's achieving its objectives or how well it's implementing its strategies. Targets, therefore, need to be specific. For example, *accounts receivable* will be reduced from 70 to 65 days by the end of the year or the percent of clients who rate the firm a 4 or 5 for on time delivery will be 90 percent by the end of the year.

While senior management can determine targets, the targets may be more effective if the practice areas or groups determine them, with final approval from senior management.

ONE LAST WORD

The Balanced Scorecard provides a firm with a system to measure how well it's implementing its strategies. It may be more effective to implement a scorecard in your firm, though, if it is developed first by a practice area or group, with a limited number of measurements. As Ron Baker so keenly told us, "The Balanced Scorecard has a tendency to 'boil the ocean' and too many measures will be ignored." Once you have some experience in managing the firm using a Balanced Scorecard, you can then expand the process to create a separate one for each market segment that the firm serves or plans to serve.

Remember, only when the firm's objectives are clear can there be a clear view of the marketing program itself. Only then can there be valid assessment of the marketing mix—those several tools of marketing that, together, move the program forward, and of the blueprint to accomplish it. And only then is the firm's strategic plan valid.

11

WHO'S AT THE HELM AND WHO'S ON THE BRIDGE?

Firm Governance and Structure

A partnership is a bunch of people trying to go through a narrow door at the same time.

—Bruce W. Marcus

If the traditional accounting and law firms face a world today that is dramatically different than it was in the twentieth century, why are they too often managed by early twentieth-century principles?

The external environment has changed dramatically since 1960. An emerging global economy, with all of its competitive pressures, is substantially altering the nature of even the smallest businesses. New regulatory structures are shifting balances in corporate management, and bringing new regulatory forces to professional firms. Technology has brought a significant new dimension to both productivity and communication, and constantly changes the products we use. Product life cycles become shorter and shorter, putting new technical and competitive pressures on companies and the economies they serve. The erosion of gender and other biases brings a new workforce into the economy, with different needs, demands, and points of view. Some surveys claim that more than 80 percent of women between the ages of 25 and 54 are employed.

New outside competitors, such as American Express Tax and Business Services, Century Business, and H&R Block, are taking away business that was once the sole domain of the CPA. Large international and national law firms, bloated by the weight of success but unburdened by sound management practices, are merging or going out of business. International and large regional CPA firms are encroaching on the domain of law firms, and despite resistance from traditionalists, the lines separating legal practice from accounting practice are beginning to blur. Despite regulatory roadblocks that separate ancillary services from core accounting practice, and opposition to multidisciplinary practice for both accounting and law firms, consulting and other services continue to proliferate. The opportunities for all professionals to dramatically increase their income from new sources have been growing at an exponential rate.

And through all of this rapidly accumulating change, accounting and law firms have been slow to change their governance structure to meet the needs of this changing environment.

Neither market forces—nor your clients—will wait while you hold a partners' meeting to make decisions relevant to your clients' needs. Consequential decisions must be more rapidly responsive than can be done with traditional firm management structures. Clearly, the contemporary and future professional firm will have to be restructured to accommodate the structures of the contemporary corporate and economic world.

In this century, professional services firms have two major choices. Either they can reshape their firms to meet the needs of the prospective clientele, or they can ignore the needs of the clientele, and simply run their practices predominantly with the needs of the firm in mind. The first is an exercise in growth. The second is an exercise in imminent disaster.

Every firm has its technical and industry skills and experience, and every lawyer, consultant, and accountant has preferences and passions for a particular kind of practice. A litigator may be completely turned off by real estate contracts, and a tax accountant may want nothing to do with auditing. A strategic planner may not care about information technology consulting. These are legitimate wishes, and the accountant or lawyer who denies those passions may be in for a very unhappy life.

But then there is the external market, and the opportunity for the professional services firm to grow by serving that market. Given a prospective market that has little need for the practice you feel passionate about, you can...

- *Move.* Go somewhere else to find the market for your particular skills and experience.
- *Adapt.* Educate yourself in the kind of practice your market needs.
- *Hire.* Bring in someone with the skills and experience your market needs.
- *Merge.* Find a firm with complementary skills and merge with or acquire it.
- *Form strategic alliances.* Few firms have the in-house expertise to quickly get into new markets by themselves. Form strategic alliances with firms that have the expertise that you are lacking.
- *Join an association.* Join one of the many accounting or law firm associations.

What you can't do, as a professional firm, is something the product people often do very well—change the needs of your market to match your skills. That's a singular disadvantage of professional firm marketing. Yet, good marketing can penetrate a market in which a competitor is entrenched. For example, for a long time, the word processing program of choice for lawyers was WordPerfect. Microsoft coveted that market, and began a campaign to win over the legal profession. Microsoft started by improving Microsoft Word in ways that would match and exceed the WordPerfect features favored by law firms. It began an intensive program to promote those features to lawyers, using advertising and a distinctive web site for law firm managers, and even wrote a booklet on how to convert from WordPerfect to Microsoft Word. It concentrated on corporate managers who used Word, and then merchandised that fact to the corporate users' law firms. What put Microsoft over the top was that it helped law firms understand the advantages of using the same word processing program that their clients used. Within a year or two, Microsoft had captured the legal market, and virtually eliminated WordPerfect from the scene. It captured the market for itself from a strong market leader.

Can you imagine a law firm that specialized in corporate law persuading a market dominated by small privately held companies to go public? Or an accounting firm specializing in construction accounting converting a market dominated by industry to go into the construction business?

THE PARTNERSHIP STRUCTURE

The traditional professional firm is run for its partners, not its staff. But to attract more and better staff to serve a growing clientele, there had to be a partnership path and the promise of partnership. To accommodate new and better people as partners, there had to be more business than could be derived from traditional practices. How many new audit clients can a Big Four firm get from the Fortune 500 group? How many new clients can a law firm get from that same Fortune 500 list? Once a firm gained most new clients by displacing their former firms. Now with so many new services, clients come in pursuit of new kinds of help and many different specialties, and may even have one firm for the audit, and another for tax planning, and another for designing new inventory controls. Clients can have one firm for real estate practices, another for intellectual property, another for labor law, and so on. The need for new business skills proliferates.

The firm that resides in the expertise of its partners alone now finds itself inflexible, unable to summon up the diverse skills needed to serve clients as a full-scale business management lawyer. It must now draw on the skills of personnel who may not be CPAs or even lawyers, or who may not be partner material for reasons beyond skill. Successful firms have begun to recognize that the tradition of running a firm only for and with partners is no longer sufficient. Many firms today have eliminated the ancient rite of partnership-path-or-out, and now give welcome to specialists whom they accept as contributors to their business, and not as potential partners. Smaller firms are addressing the problem by banding together in regional groupings, or by joining new kinds of organizations that serve as umbrella companies to group their services.

ACCESS TO CAPITAL

All of this leads to another, more crucial problem with the existing partnership structure. Capital. Growing firms in a growing economy need capital. Even accounting and law firms. Now, accounting firms and law firms are facing the need to expand both geographically and in an inventory of practice skills. Historically, the need for vast amounts of capital for manufacturing companies was for machinery, production facilities, labor, and distribution channels.

Professional firms needed little capital for such factors as rent, furniture, stationary, and readily disposable support staff. This is perhaps one reason for the perpetuation of the partnership structure—the partners kept the surplus and very little of it had to be reinvested.

All that has changed. Now, firms seeking to compete by offering more services to their clientele need vast amounts of capital for the overwhelming costs of technology, for personnel, for training, for outreach to new markets, for acquiring new skills, for gaining access to—or serving—the growing international market, for developing or buying new capabilities, for the growing costs of competing effectively in a competitive marketing economy. All these require more capital than has ever before been invested by accountants or lawyers.

One viable definition of a corporation is that it's an organization to convert capital to profit for the owners of the capital. A professional partnership is a structure to convert capital to the profits of the *partners*. And while the sources of capital for a corporation are drawn from the public, the sources of capital for the partnership are limited to the partners.

But in today's—and tomorrow's—environment, this is clearly not enough. For tomorrow's needs, no partnership has sufficient capital. Certainly not enough when a retiring partner takes his capital with him, or takes her unfunded retirement account. Nor is it enough when decisions are made not by the younger partners, to whom the future is important, but by the older partners, near retirement, who have the voting power. They tend not to vote for the future. The older partners—the ones with the greatest number of votes—manage their firms to preserve, not invest, capital for themselves. The younger partners manage for growth—their own and the firm's. Preserving capital rather than investing it in the firm makes firm longevity considerably more tenuous.

Where, then, is this capital to come from? The partners? Only in the very smallest firms. Banks? Not enough capital available for the partnership structures. Joint ventures? Obviously, to some degree, which is why we now see more and more joint ventures with financial services organizations and nonaccounting firms. There will be a proliferation of these joint ventures, as firms recognize the potential.

The only other source of capital is the public, an idea once considered so radical that it was mentioned only as an ironic joke. But then, so, too, was the idea of nonaccountant ownership of CPA firms. That was before American Express, which now has acquired more than 130 firms and is one of the 10 largest CPA firms in the United States, or H&R Block began acquiring accounting practices.

In the early 1960s, when Wall Street financial firms were all partnerships, some firms, such as Donaldson, Lufkin & Jenrette, realized that the industry was going to need more capital than partners could supply. Despite existing regulations against it at the time, they pressed the issue with both the New York Stock Exchange and the Securities and Exchange Commission. It was recognized that the need for capital was so strong that rules had to change. And change they did, with results we readily see today.

Clearly, this is going to happen to the professions. The need for change, both managerial and in capitalization, will impel professionals to find new structures that still address the need for independence, objectivity, responsibility, and probity that are at the heart of the audit profession. What kind of structure will be responsive to these needs? Probably nothing that exists today. But as economic history tells us, inventing new forms of organization is neither as difficult nor unlikely as one might expect. It's been done before, and as the need intensifies, bright members of the profession will find ways to do it again.

REMAKING THE FIRM

Within the context of each profession, can a firm remake itself in ways that enhance its ability to serve the needs of its particular market? In many ways. For example, a firm can...

- *Restructure itself into practice groups.* The practice group structure, in which all of the professionals in a firm serving clients in the same industry, or offering a specific practice, function as a separate entity, is fast becoming the firm structure of choice in both accounting and law. Each group is, essentially, a minifirm, dealing with the same problems and opportunities. It has proven successful as both a communications structure and as a marketing platform. (See *First Among Equals,* by Patrick McKenna and David Maister.)

- *Reexamine its fee structure.* This may mean doing more fixed fees, contingency fees, or value billings. The options are legion.

- *Joint venture with other firms or other professions.* Many CPA firms and law firms are joining national and international associations that share marketing and technical information.

- *Adapt its culture to* match that of the market it serves.

- *Build a market research function* that supplies valuable data to clients in a particular industry.

- *Learn how to meet client requirements effectively* and cost effectively. Firms can focus on their internal processes and strive to become the lowest-cost producer while maintaining the highest quality.

- *Restructure its governance matrix.*

The reality is that its market shapes a professional firm—not the other way around. To understand your firm, and to shape it, you must first understand the market you serve. Otherwise, there is a vast gap in your firm's connection to your market—one that your competitors will quickly exploit.

But as important as understanding your market is to better serving your clientele, it may not be enough. You need to structure the firm so that it can quickly respond to changing market needs.

PARTNERSHIP VERSUS CORPORATE STRUCTURE

If you were to invent the accounting or legal profession today, and you had to design an organization that could best deliver the services that address today's business needs, what form would your firm take?

Would it be the partnership? Probably not, which is why the partnership—collegial, comfortable, and profitable as it's been all these years—is eroding. As many firms are uneasily discovering, the partnership structure, even for smaller firms, simply isn't responsive to the needs of the emerging marketplace for today's professional services.

Firms must evolve, then, into a new kind of organization. They have no choice. They must devise a governance model that will deal with the exigencies of contemporary and future business and market needs, but still retain the foundation for probity, objectivity, and professionalism required of the professions by both government and business. The limited liability structure is a small step forward, but doesn't actually affect governance. The ultimate guiding factor will hinge on two things— what best serves the client, and what form of governance is best able to make real-time decisions that serve both the client and the firm.

SHAPING THE NEW STRUCTURE

Part of the problem is that, unlike the corporate world, the professional world does not allow for training managers. In the corporate world, young people going up the ranks learn management skills. By the time the corporate manager reaches the top, that executive has been subjected to training in finance, personnel management, marketing, production, and so forth.

The professional has no tradition for learning those skills, nor the structure in which to learn them, nor the opportunity to be subjected to them except in the abstract. Corporate executives are most often trained professional managers. Accountants, consultants, or lawyers, no matter how bright or intuitive, are not.

When the accounting profession consisted essentially of audit, tax, and a small measure of consulting services, and the requests for legal services were carefully and traditionally defined, the structure needed to manage the practice was relatively simple. Those were the days before the need to compete was part of the practice— when professional practice consisted entirely of performing those services required by law, or demanded by the clients' traditional exigencies of running a company, and the clients came in over the transom.

But as the needs of the clientele changed, fanned by the promise of more complex and useful services by the entrepreneurial professional firms, so too did the response of the progressive firms become more complex. More services. More outreach. Better attempts to understand the market, and to build structures to relate to the changes in the market.

Those firms that learned to hear and respond to the new rhythms of the marketplace have thrived. Those that didn't hear well, or didn't respond more readily, either went out of business or merged, which is one reason that the long-lived Big Eight became the Big Five (prior to the demise of Arthur Andersen), and now the Big Four, and why so many major law firms suddenly ceased to exist.

That new economic configurations are affecting the firms may be seen in the burgeoning disarray in some fairly well established organizations. In 2003 the prestigious law firm of Altheimer & Gray suddenly closed its doors. It went bankrupt. Partners now question how the firm was managed. Unfortunately, they came too late. Two other recent examples are BDO Seidman, which has replaced its managing partner, the fourth one in about 6 years, and American Express Tax and Business Services, which has also had four CEOs in less than 10 years. Many other firms have replaced their managing partners recently in an effort to make their firms more relevant to market needs.

Further evidence of change can be seen in the accounting firm of Clark Nuber, located in Bellevue, Washington, which is now managed by David Katri, Clark Nuber's president and CEO. While Katri is a CPA, he was brought in from the corporate section. He spent the last 23 years with the Fluke Corp., a $450 million publicly traded company, as president and COO. As the leader of Clark Nuber, he is responsible for achieving the firm's vision and implementing its strategic plan.

The accounting profession has moved from the accounting and tax business to the business business. As clients were offered more services, they demanded even more, until the most successful firms were those that went beyond the supplier's role to become part of their clients' businesses. These are the firms that today participate in their clients' planning and strategy, offering a range of capabilities that scarcely existed just a decade or so ago. Where once accounting, auditing, and tax services were the heart and soul of the profession, these traditional services are now a smaller part of a larger practice.

And while the recent passage of the Sarbanes-Oxley Act has changed much of this service structure for the international firms, today's local and regional accounting firms offer a complex configuration of technical and business guidance skills, working in a broader spectrum of specialization than ever before. Increasingly, the range of services includes guidance in business skills and strategies, technical services, personal financial planning, assistance in globalization for even the smallest companies, estate planning, and legal services in designated areas.

A growing number of accounting firms have large staffs of lawyers and accountants in such areas as estates, trusts, and taxes, which puts a competitive burden on law firms. Technology, combined with the need to learn to solve other business problems, has turned the contemporary accounting firm from auditors and accountants to business and financial advisors and the traditional law firm from lawyers to consultants. It is common in print ads by accounting firms not to even find the word *accounting*.

Corporate legal staffs are growing, changing the relationship of the corporation to its law firm, and demanding a different menu of services. Larry Smith, in his book *Inside/Outside*, describes this process in chilling detail.

Technology has also driven the traditional accounting skills—the audit and tax compliance—closer to the commodity column. The firms that understand this have been rewarded for farsightedness. The smaller firms, unable to supply some of the more sophisticated services demanded by their clients, are banding together in groups and associations. Technology is changing the legal profession, as well, at least in automating jobs once the province of lawyers alone, such as Shepardizing. Technology has changed the labor formula at law firms. But more significantly, it has given new status and values to the former underclass of paralegals and associates.

What is emerging is exactly the same thing that happens to a manufacturer that expands a product line, or a geographic distribution system. Greater depth, range, and professionalism in management are urgently required.

Unfortunately, the skills of the accounting or legal process that once made senior partners so valuable to their firms come up seriously lacking in management skills. Where, in even the largest partnerships, is the training in finding, qualifying, and managing people of diverse skills and talents? In setting performance management systems? In creating fast-track development programs? In managing skills not traditional to the accounting or legal profession? In understanding the nuances of the marketplace? In using new technology wisely and effectively as a management tool? In dealing on a global scale for even the smallest clients, and managing those who do know how to do it? In raising and managing capital for growth and expansion? These are the skills needed by the managers of every enterprise, and particularly those firms that must succeed in a highly competitive environment.

Not unnoticed is the paradox of the nonprofessionally managed professional services firm offering its clients management skills. This is a trend that's grown rapidly, and with great success. But that success merely points up the need for professional management and solves only part of the problem. Remember, it's rarely the professional firm's management that's performing the business management service.

In this complex and fast-paced environment, with its new technology and array of services, can an elected peer, with limited management training and experience, manage a contemporary firm? In a General Electric or Honeywell, where professional management is understood, the best leaders are bred from the ranks of managers, not practitioners. This is a different path from that taken by a professional who has spent his or her entire career as a practitioner, not a manager. Does the collegial atmosphere of the traditional partnership lend itself to producing strong leaders who are trained and experienced in understanding not only the skills of management—the market outreach, the technical skills, the people skills, the capital markets—but the changing demands of the marketplace that drive the professional firm in new directions, as well? With luck, maybe. Serendipity is great, but you can't build a firm on it.

Ultimately, too much information is needed to serve the needs of the market, particularly in a competitive environment, and a partnership, unlike a corporation, is not geared to gather and distill information in ways that make it most useful. Nor can the collegial partnership structure function fast enough, nor make decisions handily enough, to change a firm to meet the needs of changing times. Time for the professions to move on.

EMBRACING THE CORPORATE MODEL

The corporate model is still rare among professional services firms, even in its virtual form. The primary reason may be that it's threatening to the professionals. There is no corporate tradition in professionalism, and the professional has always considered him- or herself as an individual—an entrepreneur. There's fear that control, implied (but not always delivered) in partnership, may be lost. Control as an element of partnership is a myth, of course, but it's the history of professional practice. Too, if professionals take on the corporate role, they usually need to give away their books of business. Traditionally, the book of business relates to one's value and security in the firm. But not embracing a corporate model inhibits a firm from a more scalable business model and higher profits.

The change to new forms of governance will not simply go from point A to point B. It will evolve, keep moving, keep changing, and keep challenging. So far, the profession's response to the new context has focused primarily on only one major factor—the liability of the individual partners in a litigious society. Thus the rush to the professional limited liability partnership structure. But this defensive response ignores the problems—and the opportunities—generated by other aspects of the accounting firm environment.

We have also seen firms that have formed alliances with investment bankers and insurance companies, and many firms that are moving into investment management. And certainly, one can't ignore such factors as the many accounting firms now owned by American Express Tax and Business Services, H&R Block, Centerprise Advisors, and Century Business (Cbiz). These have all adopted the corporate structure.

Firms that have embraced the corporate model usually follow these steps...

- Move from the managing partner concept to a CEO position. This is not a glorified administrative partner but the true leader of the firm.

- Maintain some client contact. If the CEO is a CPA, he or she should keep some supervisory role with key clients, so that he or she doesn't lose touch with the reality of the practice—serving its clients.

- Hire a chief operating officer to handle the daily operations and work closely with the CEO.

- Depending on the size of the firm, bring in a CFO.

- Have the CEO and the COO report to a board of directors, which is usually all or part of the partner group.

- Reduce the number of partner meetings held throughout the year.

- Eliminate having partners perform administrative duties.
- Keep partners focused on servicing clients.

And ultimately, for the corporate model to work, in any new or classic form, the professional will have to change his or her attitude about the meaning of professionalism. There is also the anachronism that must be overturned—that there is no hospitality in an accounting firm for a nonaccountant, or in a law firm for a nonlawyer.

THE DYNAMICS OF CHANGE

We are convinced that much of the dynamic of the change in the professional environment is driven by the relatively new right of professionals to compete overtly—a right they were slow in seizing but now pursue intensively. When the *Bates* decision was handed down in 1977, and competition became a force in the professions, it was thought that independence would be lost. In fact, of all the changes in the profession brought about by the forces of marketing, the crucial factors—independence, objectivity, and the respect for the probity of the professional—have been untouched. The doomsayers were wrong. It is this experience, and the steadfast view of professionalism, that portends for the future the foundation for even more change, without losing the patina of professionalism.

The value of the CPA and the lawyer is obviously enhanced, not lost, by the ability to reach out to the market. This change, this evolution, has not really hurt the profession nor undermined the sense of trust inspired by the professional. Giving up the partnership structure will not diminish the traditional objectivity or trust that's the foundation of a profession.

Nor have clients lost as a result of the ability of professional firms to market—a cry of the antimarketing traditionalists. In fact, clients have benefited mightily, by better service, more valuable and innovative services and products, and even, in some cases, in pricing. The louder the cry of doom, the less likely the fulfillment of the cry.

In the changing environment, is there any protection for the management of today's accounting firm? Is there something tangible that the partners of both small and large firms can do now to avoid being made obsolete in the future? Yes.

- Learn to listen to your market, and be prepared to find ways to respond to what the market is saying. Be flexible, and open to change. Recognize that clinging to old styles in the face of new demands is not heroic or valiant — it's anachronistic. Recognize the new competitive environment, and respond competitively. Seek, with the rest of the profession, to find new forms of governance that are more realistic, in the face of tomorrow's demands.

- Understand that change must be managed. The problem must be addressed. In only the rarest instances will evolution occur painlessly, and without help from objective professionals who understand and can bestride both worlds— accounting and management.

- Fight for the right to bring professional management into a firm, and train partners in the skills of management, even though that training may use non-billable hours. Run the professional firm like a business, and not like a club. Cherish and nourish the skills of management in your own firm, at any level, and reward for those skills.

Develop trust within the partner group that everyone will do what is right for the firm. Without trust, no business, no matter how it is structured, will survive.

If you do all this, you'll find change not only less painful, but more profitable.

12

HOLDING A HANDFUL OF MERCURY

Managing the Knowledge Worker for the One-Firm Firm

Once more unto the breach, dear friends, once more. Follow your spirit, and upon this charge Cry "God for Harry, England, and Saint George!"

—William Shakespeare, *Henry V*

What's the point of developing a terrific marketing program, of having a visionary business plan, if the people who have to make it a reality haven't been motivated to make your vision a reality?

In the annals of marketing professional services, particularly since *Bates* in 1977, there've been two factors inhibiting marketing success have been outstanding. One is motivating professionals to participate in the marketing effort—to become part of a marketing culture. The second is motivating professionals and professional staff to build a truly client-centric firm—one that provides the extra increment of effort and skill that makes a firm outstanding.

Peter Drucker, the dean of American management consultants, said, "We know nothing about motivation. All we can do is write books about it."

Dwight D. Eisenhower, the thirty-fourth president of the United States and the general who marshaled and motivated a vast army to win World War II, said, "Motivation is the art of getting people to do what you want them to do because they want to do it."

Motivation, then, is an arcane and elusive art, but one that is necessary to manage other people. Books and articles have been written about it, and seminars *ad nauseum* have been held on the subject, and most of it just doesn't work.

One possible reason is that most motivational material is in the abstract, like simply telling people to do good. "About what?" they ask. Another reason is that what inspires and motivates one person may not inspire and motivate another. Yet a third reason may be that too often, people are asked to be motivated to do things that haven't been made clear to them. Motivational programs imposed on people without really understanding what the motivators are looking for is wasteful and fruitless.

Is Drucker right, then? It's true that everyone is motivated by different factors. Just take a quick look around your practice. What motivates you may not motivate your partners. Is there any way to inspire people to consistently do their best work?

If there's an answer, it doesn't lie in canned motivational programs, but rather in understanding the relationship between your interests and those of your professional staff and partners.

What does work, though, is focusing on clearly defining the firm's culture and goals. On setting realistic performance goals, and then constantly weeding out those who do not perform to your performance levels. People will do what they should do because they believe in your goals. They will want to accomplish what you want to accomplish. If you have goal alignment, you will always have team motivation.

WAYS TO INCREASE EMPLOYEE MOTIVATION

While the average firm won't be getting its people ready to land on the beaches of Normandy or follow King Henry V into the breach, it still needs to instill in them a passion for the firm's vision in order to make it real. How?

- *Communication.* Make sure that those who have to make the goals a reality understand them—what they are, why they are realistic, how each individual benefits when the firm achieves them.

- *Give responsibility and authority.* The knowledge worker in today's professional services firms is looking to take on additional responsibility and the authority to make decisions. The more responsibility and authority they have, the more they feel responsible for attaining firm goals. *If I can't make a decision, how can it be my fault that the firm did not achieve its goal?* In fact, many thoughtful people point out that the better and more imaginative the knowledge worker, the lesser the ability to manage that individual.

- *Compensate fairly.* The acoustics of any profession are magnificent, and everybody knows the compensation scales of the profession. To not compensate fairly is the surest way to dampen motivation. To not compensate personal growth and contribution to the firm is to throw ice water on the otherwise motivated professional.

- *Hire motivated people.* And fire those whose personal agenda runs counter to the firm's goals. Remember, though, that not everybody is motivated by the same things or to the same degree. The question often arises, "Is the skill and capability of the unmotivated individual worth the effect of that individual on the rest of the staff?" The answer is yours.

- *Provide opportunities for advancement.* If there is no opportunity for advancement in the organization, there will be little if any motivation. And advancement can only come in a growing firm. That's why building a vibrant practice with the right kind of clients is at the core of a successful practice.

- *Create winning teams.* Employees are often motivated when they are part of a winning team. A team will more often set higher standards than an individual working by him- or herself will. Firms are more efficient as teams when team members play for the team and not for themselves. Teams carry their members through the tough times and increase motivation and commitment.

- *Understand and cherish motivated individuals.* Not every individual is a team person. The highly talented and self-motivated individual can, in fact, motivate others by example.

- *Provide challenging work.* Staff people who are underutilized or performing work below their level will usually become demotivated quickly. Being properly staffed is a critical element here. If you are not properly staffed, you wind up having partners doing manager- or associate-level work or managers in a CPA firm doing staff-level work. In either case it will demotivate both groups.

- *Offer opportunities for personal growth.* Today's knowledge worker is often motivated by opportunities for personal growth. Whether it's learning a new technical skill, understanding an industry or skill, or learning how to become a good manager of people, the amount of personal growth that all your employees obtain is critical in determining how motivated your workforce will be.

- *Use soft currency.* A pat on the back goes a long way. It costs very little to send a note of appreciation, acknowledgment, or encouragement to a staff person or partner. It costs nothing to make people in the firm feel special.

MANAGING KNOWLEDGE WORKERS

There is an inherent danger, in a professional firm, of individuals residing in the task and not motivated by the *reason* for the task. This is the mark of the unmotivated firm—of a firm in which people go through the motions without understanding why they're doing it. We see it in the firm without a marketing culture, whose people don't understand who the client is and why the firm's future resides in winning new clients.

. In an article in the *Harvard Business Review*, James Brian Quinn, Philip Anderson, and Sydney Finkelstein define a professional intellect as a body of knowledge that a professional must constantly update.

Firms today have three critical assets that need to be managed in order to keep everyone motivated toward the firm's growth.

The first is *client capital*—the value you derive from your unique relationship with your clients. Client capital drives everything else in the firm, and is at the foundation of the successful firm.

The second asset is *organization capital*, the firm's systems' capabilities. These assets include client and market databases, proprietary software, a client relationship management (CRM) system, and the firm's referral networks.

The third asset is the firm's *intellectual capital*—the skills and knowledge of your people. What you do with this asset and how you nurture and develop it has a tremendous impact on your *client capital*.

Professional firms must deal with two knowledge- and skill-oriented groups: the professional, who is a knowledge worker whose skills are based upon intellect, and the professional marketer, a relatively new factor in the professions, but one whose work is an integral part of firm management. The professional marketer brings to the firm a new set of skills, a new bank of experience, and a different kind of imagination.

Personnel management, then, involves keeping the body of knowledge that is integral to the life and work of the knowledge worker fresh and relevant. Firms that fail to accomplish this soon find that their *client capital* is on the wane. Few clients will stay with firms that are out of date in technical or market proficiencies.

Managing the knowledge worker—sustaining the firm's intellectual capital—is a function of understanding four basic facts about professionals as intellectual workers...

- The most basic level is *know what*. Professionals graduate from college with a diploma in hand and a lot of basic knowledge in their heads, but with little, if any, real-life experience. They may *know what* the most current tax code sections are. They may know the most recent technology better than anyone else in the firm, but they haven't had the opportunity to apply this knowledge. *Know what* provides no guarantee that an individual will be successful. We all know extremely intelligent people who can't seem to get things done.

- If you can't bring your people to the next level—*know how*—you haven't enhanced your firm's intellectual capital. Individuals with *know how* are able to take book learning and apply it to a real-world situation. For example, you can read about sailing all day long, know all the terms and rules, but it isn't until you actually get out on the water and begin to tack or come about that you have moved from *know what* to the *know how*.

- In the long run, *know how* is still not enough to ensure your success. Professionals need to *know why*. This requires that a professional truly understand the interrelationship of the various elements of a system. Accountants and lawyers with a deep understanding of *know why* can often tell you with uncanny accuracy what will happen when you tinker with one element of a project or system long before the final report is done.

- The last stage in the development of intellectual capital is *care why*. This consists of will, motivation, and adaptability for success. Firms that operate at this level exhibit a high degree of motivation and creativity. Without *care why,* a professional firm will often fall behind and fail to adapt to a rapidly changing marketplace.

Managing and nurturing the knowledge worker, both the legal and accounting professional and the marketing professional, may ultimately be an art, but there are still steps that can be taken to do the job effectively. An approach to managing the knowledge worker effectively includes . . .

- *Recruit and hire only the best you can find.* Recruiting has always been important, but now, in this burgeoning competitive environment, it becomes paramount for the firm of the future. Firm leaders should play an active role in the recruiting effort. Recruiting gives you the opportunity to set forth the firm's goals and guiding vision. Get the new recruit excited about what could be, not just what is.

- *Provide staff with on-the-job training immediately.* If you hire the best, you will be challenged to provide them with an outstanding professional developmental program. They expect it. Don't make the mistake of keeping new staff away from clients. With mentoring, guidance, and team assignment, young professionals will do an outstanding job for your clients.

- *Demand the best and be intolerant of the rest.* Develop a culture similar to the Marines. They look for those few individuals who are willing to stretch themselves and take the demanding initiation of Marine boot camp. Mediocre firms will not survive in the twenty-first century. Push your people to excel and go beyond their comfort levels, and you will create a more successful and profitable firm.

- *Frequent and meaningful performance feedback.* Performance feedback should be a regular part of your staff development. Feedback should be given as close to the actual performance as possible. Waiting until the end of the quarter or, worse yet, to the end of the year provides little, if any, value to the staff.

No marketing plan will work, nor will any marketing culture be developed (see Chapter 7) if the firm's leadership doesn't enthusiastically endorse and support it. But in the new competitive environment of the professions, the firm with the strongest marketing culture wins.

13

FOR LOVE OR MONEY—OR BOTH

Paying for Performance

In business, words are words; explanations are explanations, promises are promises, but only performance is reality.

—Harold S. Geneen, American industrialist, CEO, ITT

In today's complex world, traditional compensation schemes are no longer adequate. They no longer measure and reward all the areas of performance expected of today's professional.

To a large extent, marketing is to blame. The ability to compete has substantially altered the nature of both law and accounting firms, at least by adding to the performance mix the ability to generate new business. And while the traditional firm has always had the few partners who brought in clients, and compensated them appropriately, in today's environment, marketing is everybody's business. That contribution to a firm's performance is often substantial. What it's done is cause the contemporary firm to reexamine its traditional compensation methods, and frequently, to invent new methods.

WHAT IS COMPENSATION?

Traditionally, partners have equated compensation with their cash draw. Law and accounting firm compensation systems often fail to differentiate between salary and profit distribution. The majority of firms pay out most of their earnings in monthly draws to the partners. Partners don't tend to differentiate between base pay, profit allocation, pension contributions, and other benefits and perquisites.

But in the world of modern business, there's more to compensation than that. Executive compensation in the corporate world is normally presented as *total compen-*

191

sation. This consists of base pay, short-term incentives (for example, year-end, quarterly bonuses), long-term incentives (for example, options, other deferred compensation, retirement benefits), and benefits and perquisites (health, disability, life insurance, etc.).

Some firms claim that they pay according to what they consider *market compensation.* This is a dodge. If by market compensation they mean what comparably sized firms are paying, then they're ignoring a vast array of factors that make a difference. There are, in fact, no two firms so alike that they can set a norm, not even in terms of competing for personnel. Professional firm partners are not, after all, hourly workers, even though they may charge clients that way.

WHAT IS A FAIR COMPENSATION?

What makes compensation methods more complex is that valuing an owner in valuing a firm—for merging and selling a firm—is different than it is for compensating an owner for current performance and as a business practice.

For example, Nicholas J. Mastracchio writes in *Mergers and Acquisitions of CPA Firms*, that a fair compensation (salary, e.g.) for owners (if they sell their firms) is based on the following formula:

$$Owners' \ salaries = professional \ staff \ salaries \times$$
$$(owners' \ billing \ rates/professional \ staff \ billing \ rates)$$

Could this formula be used to set base salaries for law and CPA firm partners? Here's how it could work. In the *Best Service Law Firm*, associates have an average salary of $100,000 and an average billing rate of $144 per hour. Partners have an average billing rate of $225/hr. Using the above formula, partners in this firm would be paid $156,250 in salary. Partner salary = $100,000 × $225/$144 = $156,250.

Remaining income after base salaries then could be paid out in bonuses or be used for capital improvements. The strategic value of having such a compensation system is clear. Partners will now have much more of their income at risk, and therefore will not only perform at a higher level, but also will help the firm achieve its strategic objectives. The questions that firms struggle with are "How then should profits be distributed to the partners?" and "What criteria should be used to determine profit allocation?"

BUILDING THE NEAR-PERFECT COMPENSATION SYSTEM

The old school of seniority-based compensation and compensation based on ownership is no longer effective for the contemporary, client-centric and market-oriented firm. In the last 10 years, the pressure of an extremely competitive marketplace has made it even more troublesome.

If you were to reexamine the assumptions on which traditional compensation systems are based, you would have to ask, "What is the purpose of our existing compensation system?" Is it to...

- Reward longevity?
- Reward equity owners?
- Reward seniority?
- Reward teamwork?
- Reward political harmony?
- Reward production?
- Reward current performance?
- Reward client maintenance?
- Reward business development?
- Reward professional development?
- Reward leadership?

Without appropriate—and contemporary—answers to those questions, then the compensation system you use must surely be questioned. And while no one has yet developed the perfect compensation system, that doesn't mean that there aren't better ways to determine partner compensation than the traditional methods of billable time and origination often used today. Whatever system you ultimately decide on, it's critical that the performance measures be tied to the vision and strategic initiatives of the firm.

Ultimately, the purpose of your compensation plan should be to enhance performance, provide better client service, and thereby enrich employees and partners.

Those firms that set high standards of performance, in both financial (quantitative) and nonfinancial (qualitative) areas, base performance on current rather than historical levels, and hold management and employees accountable for their performance or lack thereof tend to outperform all others.

Consider, then, these key strategic points in building your compensation system...

- Compensation systems are self-funding unless the firm decides to borrow money from the bank to pay partners. Obviously, not a good idea.
- Use your compensation system to shape your firm's culture rather than have your firm's culture shape your compensation system.

- Compensation systems should be flexible. As your firm and the external environment change, so should the system.

- Ownership means putting your compensation at risk. Partners should realize that, as owners, their compensation is never guaranteed.

- Not all owners provide the same value to the firm. That is not to say that all owners are not valuable. They just make different contributions to the overall success and profitability of the firm and should be rewarded accordingly.

- Compensation should be tied to results. Efforts are important, but results count more.

- Owners need to be held accountable for their own actions.

- Compensation systems should measure multiple areas. A successful firm requires many different talents. It's like a sports team. Can you image a winning baseball team with all shortstops?

- Seniority means nothing when it comes to determining an individual's compensation. If that were the case, the oldest person in the firm would make the most money.

- The system should be easy to understand and administer.

- The system should be retrospective. You want to pay the majority of the dollars at the end of the year, not throughout the year. This keeps owners focused on a potentially large year-end distribution.

- Since compensation is a management tool, only firm leaders should set compensation, and no one else.

NINE GOALS YOUR COMPENSATION SYSTEM SHOULD ACHIEVE

Every compensation system should have a specific objective predicated on achieving business success. Results your system should aim for are . . .

- Motivate your partners to peak performance
- Modify partner behavior if necessary to improve performance
- Retain the best partners and remove nonperformers
- Attract desirable lateral hires
- Reward for results first and efforts second (i.e, the partner's total contribution)
- Drive business results and create value

- Focus partners on their own results and compensation, not on that of other partners
- Promote associates to partners based on economic, not just professional, criteria
- Create an equitable system over the long term

SOME COMMON COMPENSATION SYSTEMS

While few of the current compensation systems can achieve all of the above goals, many still offer more viable alternatives than traditional methods. Among the traditional options are...

- *Equal compensation.* Small professional services firms will often start with an equal compensation system. It often works for a short period of time. It avoids partner conflicts around compensation in the beginning, or until one of the partners realizes that he or she is worth more than the others because of the value they bring to the firm. Producers especially don't like this system since it ignores individual efforts. Since all partners share income equally, they should all be focused on making the pie larger. That is seldom the case. And what happens when a firm brings in a new partner? Does the junior partner also share equally?

- *Lockstep.* Many law firms have tried this approach, and many are still using some modified version of it. It basically states that the longer you practice at the firm, the more valuable you become. Unfortunately, there is no correlation between value and tenure. This system only encourages partners to retire early.

- *Pure formula.* Professional services firms were attracted to this system because of its so-called objectivity. It's simple and easy to administer, and it can eliminate disagreements over pay (again, at least in the short term). A major problem is determining what the right formula is. One formula doesn't work for all partners in a firm. This approach causes partners to work the system to their personal benefit and not to the benefit of the firm. A pure formula approach causes silos to be constructed, wherein each owner looks out for him- or herself rather than for the good of the firm. Under this system, it's difficult to measure a partner's intangible contributions.

- *Paper and pencil.* Partners are given the total amount that will be available for distribution for the coming year and are asked to allocate that amount among all the partners in the firm. This method gives each partner a say in the compensation of all the other partners. Firms that resist formulas may lean toward this approach. It usually works best in smaller firms where the partners really know each other. In larger partner groups, it is almost impossible for partners to know how each partner is performing.

To try to make this process less political, the firm will normally throw out the highest and the lowest recommendation.

- *One person decides.* In those firms that are controlled by a strong leader, this is the common system. The partners abdicate their input to one person in the firm. As long as this person keeps everyone happy, the system works, but no one really ever knows why or how their pay relates to performance.
- *Compensation committee.* Many large firms have moved to compensation committees to determine partner compensation. These committees use a variety of methods discussed here to get input of each partner. A major question is "Who gets on the committee and why?"
- *Shared overhead.* This is not so much a compensation system as a pure economic business model. Overhead expenses are allocated to each partner, and the partner essentially keeps what is left after he or she pays a portion of the overhead. It's certainly not conducive to creating a real firm.

If these compensation methods seem anachronistic, then the contemporary answer is ...

- A *performance-based system.* While a performance-based system can achieve the nine goals listed above, no system, in and of itself, will solve performance or people-related problems that management doesn't want to address. Management must first decide what is important for the firm to achieve, and second it must assign to each partner specific goals that moves the firm closer to reaching its strategic focus.
- While billable dollars, other forms of revenue, and collections may form the basis of every compensation system, multiple alternative criteria are being found to be particularly useful. Consider compensations systems that include measures of ...
  - ○ Client satisfaction scores
  - ○ Employee (staff and associate) satisfaction
  - ○ Reduction in accounts receivable (A/R) and work-in-process (WIP) days outstanding
  - ○ Realization (the number of hours billed divided by the hours charged)
  - ○ Hours managed or the owner's book of business

- Development of a new practice area or group
- Process improvement suggestions and implementations
- Marketing and new business development
- Pro bono work
- Client retention/attrition
- Collaboration efforts
- Firm management (achieving the firm's vision, etc.)

Add to this list whatever criteria you think will improve your partners' performance. Once you've identified the criteria for each partner, the next step is to create the *individual* partner's scorecard. The emphasis is on *individual*. Under this system partners don't compete with each other but with themselves. A win for one is not a loss for another. No matter what the individual partner's criteria are, the total possible points that any partner can achieve are always the same.

For example, Partner A has five criteria to be measured against. The total of the five will be weighted 100 percent. Partner B has three criteria; those three will be weighted 100 percent. The total possible points for each partner will be the same, let's say 500. Each criterion is rated from 1 to 5. At the beginning of the year, each partner knows what is considered a 1, 2, 3, 4, or 5 performance rating. A 3 means the partner did what was expected, while a 1 indicates total underperformance and a 5 far exceeds expectations. Management also needs to decide the weight that it will give to each criterion for each partner.

PARTNER A

Criteria	Weight (%)	Rating	Total Points
1. Billable dollars	25	2	50
2. Research	30	3	90
3. Client satisfaction	10	1	10
4. Associate training	25	4	100
5. Pro bono	10	3	30
	100		280

PARTNER B

Criteria	Weight (%)	Rating	Total Points
1. Client satisfaction	20	3	60
2. Business development	30	4	120
3. Firm management	50	5	250
	100		430

Partners A and B earned a total of 710 points (280 + 430). Partner A earned 39 percent and Partner B earned 61 percent of the total points. If the available bonus pool for these two partners were $125,000, Partner A would receive $48,750 and Partner B would get $76,250. This would be in addition to their base compensation. Since both partners' goals are set at the beginning of the year, each knows what is needed to accomplish in order to earn the bonus. If each partner achieves an outstanding rating (say, 5), there should be additional dollars to allocate since they have exceeded their goals for the year. Best of all, this approach keeps them focused on the areas that have been mutually identified at the beginning of the year—areas that are good for the firm and the partner.

GUIDING PRINCIPLES

In *Paying for Performance: A Guide to Compensation Management*, John D. Bloedorn, a partner at KPMG, outlines 10 guiding principles for equitable compensation plans . . .

- *Start with a compensation strategy.* What role should compensation play in your firm? Once the compensation strategy is determined, then the total compensation package—base, short-term incentive, and long-term incentive—can be tailored to meet the firm's needs.
- *Reinforce your firm's desired culture orientation.* Each firm has different values and strategies for success. Determine your prevalent culture orientation.
- *Get buy-in.* Partners will be affected by the new compensation program. Get buy-in before you unveil the plan.
- *Take incentive eligibility deep into the firm.* Incentive compensation is not just for partners. Eventually you will want everyone in the firm eligible for the program. This will cause all employees to focus their attention on the firm's goals.
- *Leverage incentives.* Bloedorn notes, "The relationship between performance results and pay will be strengthened if the incentive opportunity is substantial for performance excellence and minimal if performance is below standard."
- *Make shareholder value creation a top priority.*
- *Emphasize the long-term* for executives.
- *Benchmark long-term performance* through comparative measures.
- *Communicate initially and regularly thereafter.*
- *Do not reward poor performance.* There is not too much more to say about this point. When thinking about rewarding someone for poor performance, remember this—Do not reward poor performance.

Firms with incentive/performance pay programs fund them solely on the basis of meeting budgeted results. This protects the firm from borrowing dollars to pay the partners what they did not really earn.

A word of caution. You can't move your firm into a performance-based pay system unless you embrace a performance management system as well. This requires that firm's goals and strategies be communicated throughout the organization and that the individual's performance criteria be tied to those goals. Employees must understand how results are measured and how they have an impact on those results.

The firms that compete successfully in a client-centric environment will be those that move toward a performance-based compensation system—one that rewards all firm members who meet or exceed their goals.

14

DIDN'T WE TELL YOU WHAT WE'RE DOING?

Internal Communications— Let Me Count the Ways

I wrote the memo, so you must know it.

—The Managing Partner

A terrific definition of chaos is when a client asks two different people in your firm the same question—and gets two different and conflicting answers.

Another form of it is when there's a crisis, and the press calls and gets somebody on the phone who hasn't been briefed—but who answers the questions anyway. There's real terror for you.

A managing partner bemoans the fact that his clear and well-defined vision of his firm has gotten so diluted by the time it gets transmitted down the line to staff that he wonders if everybody is working for the same firm.

The Arthur Andersen, Enron, and other corporate fiascos certainly suggest a failure in internal controls and communication, and its high cost.

Internal communications—getting the right information to the right people at the right time—is a process that has never seemed more primitive at the very time when it's most needed. It rarely works to the satisfaction of the communicator and the communicated to. This, at a time when we now have access to more data, in virtually every area of human endeavor, than we have ever had before. The tragedy of failures in internal communications is the cost to a business of valuable information that can supply the competitive edge—whether in production, marketing, or managing a company or professional firm.

But despite its dismal history of frequent failure, internal communications can work. We now know a great deal more, in this so-called knowledge economy, about managing knowledge and internal communications as a process. Knowledge, we know, can be managed to serve the needs of the organization.

Keeping people informed, and allowing them to be heard—internal communication must work both ways—is crucial to making a firm of any size function as a single phalanx to the marketplace. The many compelling reasons to sustain a high level of internal communications, in even the smallest firm, go beyond mere random distribution of information to give a company a real competitive edge...

- If everybody who shows up for work every morning has a different view of why he or she is there, then there's no cohesive motivation or function. It is profoundly counterproductive.

- If there's no basic but clearly defined internal communication plan, the most urgent instruction, no matter how clear or simple at the outset, gets garbled and distorted as it goes down the management line to the people who have to act on it.

- The best and most effective business promise you make to clients or customers is useless if the people who have to make the promise a reality don't understand and accept it.

- The nature of business today requires that a great many people within a firm are in touch with a great many people outside the company. It's crucial, then, that as many people as appropriate be informed and knowledgeable.

- Most firms function on several levels—the management, the professional staff, the administrative staff, the production staff, the maintenance staff, and so forth. A great deal of information must be imparted to people on different levels, each of whom has a different measure of responsibility, education, and access to the company's practices and performance, and each of whom must use the information differently. A firm's marketing or quality control programs mean different things to each individual in a firm. But they mean *something* to each individual in the firm. They could mean things that conflict—in which case there's chaos—or they could be made to mean the same things to everybody—in which case there's productivity.

- Most firms today, regardless of size, are dynamic. People move around. They go to clients, to the offices of other firms, to other cities. An effective system puts all the firm's people in a position to participate in—or be responsive to—the firm's activities.

- In even the best-run firms today, turnover can be high, with people leaving or changing job responsibilities or transferring from other offices. New people must be educated constantly. Training without planning or system is expensive.

- A management with no access to what its firm's people are thinking about the firm and firm matters, or that has no access to ideas that come from the bottom up, is a firm that's, in effect, not managed at all.

- And of course, there's always the double-edged sword of e-mail, which communicates faster—but also spreads rumors and misinformation faster. With today's technology, misinformation flies around the world at a very rapid pace.

Most people in a company or professional firm are turned off by most internal communications systems—even in this age in which we know that information is the competitive edge. Why?

- Management assumes that telling is hearing.

- People are inundated with more data—under the rubric of information—than they can thoroughly understand or use.

- There is no information discretion—information they can use is obscured by information they can't use.

- There is no training in how to use information.

- Reliance is on information vehicles instead of managed content.

Ubiquitous computer systems and the Internet have been a blessing and a curse. They've given us a new dimension of knowledge, and the ability to accumulate and retrieve vast amounts of data.

But we now find ourselves inundated with data from many sources, without the consistent ability to use it all to our advantage. These raw data are the ore that contains the nuggets of knowledge that can really help us. Today we know how to find and refine the ore—the raw data. We know how to turn the ore into precious metal—information. But we don't always know what to make with the metal, or how to value it. We don't always know how to get the metal—the knowledge inherent in the information—to market.

We live, we're constantly told, in a knowledge-based economy and society. But not knowing how to use and manage that knowledge, and how to integrate it into our businesses and lives, is costing us immeasurable sums of money in lost opportunity and in lost competitive advantage. Not knowing how to get useful knowledge to the people who must know can cause serious economic, health, and social problems.

It is frustrating to have such easy access to so much data, and to be unable to turn so much of it into information that can be effectively applied to enhance and serve business. It's frustrating to want a firm's staff to know what it needs to know to compete, to improve sales, to increase productivity—and yet not be able to effectively communicate to those who can use that knowledge best. The price we pay is to lose an incremental competitive and managerial edge. And the difference between one professional firm's or company's success and another's is rarely more than incremental.

That we fall so far short in managing knowledge in more useful ways is not surprising. We are still somewhat overwhelmed by the wonders of the sheer technical skills that have built and made available our knowledge base. But increasingly, we wonder why access to so grand a trove of data has not better served us. The answer may lie in understanding the nature of knowledge itself, a complex and multifarious subject.

WHAT IS INFORMATION?

First, we know that *data* is not *information*n, and information is not *knowledge*. *Data*, we know, is basic facts—unalloyed, with little or no value outside their own existence. To say, for example, that a tree is a tree, merely defines that object. It says nothing of its structure, its purpose, and its value. It tells us nothing about forests or forestry, or uses of its leaves or trunk. That a tree is a tree is *data*, not *information*. *Information* is when we integrate the existence of a tree with the existence of, say, furniture. Then the fact of a tree takes on a new meaning.

Knowledge is when we take the information about the tree and the furniture and use it to inform either forestry or furniture manufacture. *Knowledge management* is when we codify knowledge and convert it to useful information.

WHAT IS KNOWLEDGE?

Theoretically, knowledge may be defined as information that is now, or may in the future, be useful in a specific context. Knowledge may also be abstract, with no immediate use or application, in which case it may serve as a foundation for an ultimate use. For example, when the laser was discovered in the AT&T labs a few decades ago, it was merely a scientific phenomenon, with no apparent practical use. The uses emerged and were developed much later.

In a business context, knowledge is information that can be applied for a specific and useful purpose. For example, the demographics of a particular market area are raw *data*. Analyzing that data in terms of the ability to make decisions about serving that area provides *information*. Knowing how to apply that information to make those decisions is *knowledge*. Knowing how to deliver knowledge to those who can use it most effectively to meet a specific objective is *knowledge management.*

Knowledge is dynamic. Its value and quality change constantly. An illustration of dynamic information is an *address in space*.

For example, if someone asks where you live, the answer can be defined as a fixed position, say the corner of X and Y. That is a constant static point that was there yesterday, is here today, and is most likely to be here tomorrow.

But if you ask for the address of a body in outer space, the answer is, *in relation to what?* Objects in space are in constant motion, and are located in relation to other objects in motion. This is dynamic motion. Knowledge is, in the same way, dynamic.

Even with the common language needed for communication, we know that this dynamic must be recognized if knowledge is to be useful. Knowledge is subject to…

- Changing sources of input
- Changing input from the same sources
- Changes precipitated by the use of knowledge
- Changing needs for the same information

Knowledge is cumulative. Nothing is often known by any one person—nor is it ever known in an entirety. For example, what bits of knowledge did the Wright brothers bring together to make an airplane? Or Edison, Bell, or Morse, for their inventions?

The same knowledge can serve different purposes. For example, an area's demographics may help the marketing department define the nature of a product. That same demographic information may help the finance department determine the cost of serving that market for.

Moreover, people process information differently. Each person receives information through a screen of personal experience and knowledge. Give two people the same information about a company and its investment potential, for example, and one will choose to buy the stock and the other to sell it.

Another form of knowledge is *tacit knowledge*—what we know only intuitively, but what can't always be tested pragmatically. For example, Freud's view of infant perception and psychology could only be surmised, but not tested. But if we build a system predicated on that intuition, and the system works, then we may assume that the intuition may be valid.

Merely accessing knowledge can change the nature and value of that knowledge. For example, accessing information about a company's stock can change the value of that information, both in the way it's perceived and in the way it's acted upon. Another example is in the botanical *Rauwolfia Serpentina*, whose medicinal properties were well known by researchers in India and reported in Indian scientific journals, but unknown abroad. When drug companies in the United States discovered it, *Rauwolfia* became the foundation for the pharmaceutical reserpine.

Cognition for cognition's sake is a fine abstraction and academic exercise, like any pure science. Cognition to serve a process is a different science, although the two need not be mutually exclusive. But the danger of analyzing and philosophizing beyond usefulness can dilute the currency of the information.

MANAGING CONTENT FOR VALUE

And why is managing content more important than managing communications vehicles? Because as data proliferate, they become more difficult to manage. Consider...

- Data comes from multiple sources. It is too often transmitted raw, without analysis. There's often indiscriminate overload.
- Information is dynamic—it takes on different meanings in relation to other information.
- Information changes as it's used.
- People process the same information differently.
- It's not always clear how information can be used to advantage.
- There is too little understanding of what the recipient of information must know in order to make it useful (e.g., all the data about a company's financial condition may be known, but it's useless to someone who can't read a balance sheet or cash flow statement).

The contemporary science of knowledge management has long been a function of the computer scientist, who quite naturally focused on the devices for accumulating and retrieving data. But now, the need to use information for competitive advantage and profit dictate that the focus shift to managing content. This process begins by...

- Analyzing and classifying information by need and value
- Determining internal distribution patterns by...
  - Company goals
  - Function of content
  - Competitive needs

THE STRATEGY

What do we want people to know, think, or feel as a result of our internal communications efforts, and why? The answers to these questions are the foundation for any communications activity, internal or external, and for an internal communications strategy. These answers define the dynamic of the program, its focus, and its program goals. They make possible a foundation for defining and shaping the communications strategy.

We define the knowledge base by asking...

• What do we know as an organization?
• How can we create more value from it?
• How can we learn faster than competitors?
• What do we need to know that we don't know now?

What we know as an organization defines the information that must be imparted, and to whom. It is the information that must be categorized and evaluated. It is the substance of the communication process.

How we create more value from what we know is to define what pieces of information go to which internal audience that best enhances the skill, knowledge, and experience of each individual in the firm. Value is a result of people focusing on the right things—the information most relevant to their needs. Understanding what a firm knows, in an organized fashion, creates value by understanding how that information can be used to the best interests of the firm, and how it will be used to serve the firm and its clients and customers.

We can learn faster than competitors by applying knowledge to the firm and its business. When knowledge, unfettered by extraneous information, is focused and directed to the individuals who can make the best use of it, information becomes streamlined and powerful.

What we need to know is defined by the business plan, and may include market data, technical and professional information, competitive information, and economic information. The sources are usually clearly defined, once the needs are known and defined. What we need to know relates directly to what we do know now.

PROCESS

An effective internal communications system is a dynamic process. The mechanics of internal communication are finite and relatively simple. But the efficacy of internal communications depends upon content, not mechanics. It is a process that includes...

• *Defining information.* What are the kinds of information that must be imparted to each appropriate group? What is the firm's information, as seen in terms of the following groups (there may be other categories in other firms)...

- o *Firm or practice related.* Pertaining to managing a company's practice
- o *Skill related.* Pertaining to a company or firm's professional, business, and trade skills
- o *Customer or client retention and practice development*
- o *Administrative*
  - • Professional
  - • Managers
  - • Support staff

The information needed by each group is then organized and codified. For example, all professionals or executives responsible for business development should be aware of all aspects of the marketing program, but only managers or partners may need to know long-term strategic plans. The entire firm has to know about changes in certain firm procedures, but only secretaries may have to know about nuances in word processing or rotating work schedules. In each department or professional practice group there are some things that every member of the group should know. There are some things that professionals and managers in other groups should know. Social events should be accessible to everybody, and clearly defined as such, but shouldn't clog sensitive business communications lines. In anticipating a crisis, it is prudent to keep everybody in the firm aware of the crisis, but the core details and crisis management strategy need only be known to those who must deal with it. By defining and classifying information, people will get only the information that's meaningful to them, unencumbered by irrelevancies. This should lead to pertinent information being more readily accessed, appreciated, and useful.

- • *Defining audiences.* By defining the audience, using any appropriate designation within an organization, you begin to see how different messages must be tailored to fulfill the overall communications objective. Obviously, not every bit of information is for everybody on the payroll. What is to be communicated to each audience is a function of a policy predicated on clearly defined objectives. With a well-delineated policy, and clear objectives, the how is relatively easy.
- • *Kinds of information.* There are several kinds of information, some of which is urgent and crucial, some of it important but not urgent, some of it interesting and useful on some level. Examples of information characteristics that might help classify information are . . .
  - o *Creative.* Original ideas, new uses of old ideas.
  - o *Proprietary.* Information that gives a firm competitive advantages, or that might be harmful in the wrong hands. Company plans and strategies, for example.

○ *Opportunistic*. Information that can lead to improvement in the practice or business, or to competitive advantage.

○ *Anticipatory*. Information that anticipates either opportunity or crisis.

○ *Competitive*. Important for understanding trends, ideas, competitive strategy.

• *Acquiring information*. The better techniques for gathering information internally will emerge only when the people involved understand what kind of information the firm is looking for, and the benefits that individuals get in return for supplying it. If you do a good job of categorizing information, and it results in a demand for less (if more pertinent) information from each person, then the process has a greater chance of functioning well. Feedback mechanisms are crucial. Two factors are important—*be specific in defining the kind of information you expect each person to contribute. Use devices to streamline the process, such as forms that can be filled in simply.* Motivating and educating secretaries to gather important information can help.

• *Feedback*. Internal communications are a two-way street. The feedback function is a push-pull process, requiring mutual understanding and motivation. There must also be a process for gathering information internally. This encompasses . . .

○ *Training*. What should people know that has to be shared?

○ *Cross selling*, which is a process of both morale and information

○ *Mechanics* for communicating and customer and client feedback

○ *Motivation*

• *Spreading responsibility*. Unless you want to build a staff of professional internal communicators, the process must be simplified so that it can be done internally by staff, with the least effort and time. For example, the marketing professionals have the responsibility to keep the firm appropriately informed of marketing activities and techniques, as well as to structure the internal communication devices and channels.

• *Manage the operation*. Internal communications programs don't work by wishing it so. They must be organized and managed, with written agendas, plans, schedules, and attention to the details of defining, sorting, and classifying information. Appropriate systems and mechanisms must be established. Relying on chance is rarely an acceptable information process. It seems logical that it's a task that should be in the hands of a dedicated information specialist—a marketing director, a librarian, or an information technology director. The choice depends on the structure of the firm. It's important to realize, though, that it is not a low-level job.

CATEGORIES OF INFORMATION

While the types of information vary, of course, from firm to firm, there are some general categories to consider...

- *The firm's goals* within the profession (e.g., share of market, quality leadership, shareholder value, increased productivity, and so forth).
- *The firm's business plan and strategy.* Firm policies and strategic information, much of which may be confidential. New practices, new products and services, new marketing strategies, new territories, new opportunities. Keeping people on all levels informed and involved in marketing initiatives, for example, adds a new dimension to marketing. When people can anticipate an ad, and understand the rationale and the program behind it, that ad has as much value internally as externally. And if you have a clearly defined marketing position, you'd better explain it to the people who have to make that position a reality, and breathe life into it. *Not everybody has to know everything, but everybody has to know something.*
- *Daily firm business.* Matters concerning firm day-by-day operations, such as medical plans, secretarial scheduling, and so forth. Pension and health benefits, holiday schedules, expense rules, and other housekeeping information. Included may be rules of confidentiality, software piracy regulations, and payroll deduction information.
- *Technical information.* Continuing professional education may be mandated, but the degree to which it becomes a truly useful professional tool is a function of carefully devised internal communication. To remain competitive, key people have to know the latest rules, regulations, laws, findings, results, and techniques. This includes productivity instructions, such as making the new intranet system work, company rules and why they're important, dealing with client complaints, and so forth.
- *Morale factors.* Social information, softball scores, weddings and births, company's progress and what everybody has contributed to it, addressing adverse rumors, and so forth. Specific opportunities at every level, such as sales incentives, rewards for increased productivity, and so forth.
- *Crisis control.* The mechanics of dealing with a crisis, how to handle inquiries from the press, how to handle rumors, and so forth. A prime consideration here is the concept of *no surprises.* People who might have to deal with others outside the firm (such as the press) should be aware of crisis information and the process for dealing with it. Crisis management is a function of anticipation and

planning before the crisis occurs. Internal information and planning are an integral part of it.

- *Client and customer information.* Information about clients and customers that should be shared by others in the firm, such as new clients and new client matters, cross-practice needs and opportunities, and so forth. Who the clients and customers are, who the key people are, who does what for each client, matters pertaining to best serving the client. Some of this may be sensitive; some may be housekeeping. The housekeeping information goes to everybody administratively responsible; the sensitive information only to those who must perform for the client.

- *Firm performance.* New clients, new business from old clients, cases won, projects completed, feedback on the effectiveness of the firm's activities and practices, and so forth.

- *Marketing.* Firm, practice group, company, and individual marketing plans and activities, techniques, opportunities, and results. Media releases, new firm literature, new ideas. When people are well informed about marketing activities, there is invariably a greater sense of pride and support, and a reinforced marketing effort. Marketing works only when the people who must make the marketing promise a reality are fully aware of that promise. A firm's marketing position is everybody's business.

- *Competitive intelligence.* What other firms are doing in every aspect that you can discover. Not as benchmarks (which can be retrogressive), but for market trends, ideas, and opportunities.

- *Practice groups.* In professional firms, the practice group concept is becoming increasingly popular. Practice groups, formed by a firm's professionals with the same practice areas, skills, or markets, are distinctive units within a firm that serve a number of important needs. Properly managed, and integrated within a firm, they address best practices, strategic plans, marketing to target audiences, and both external and internal communications. A well-run practice group can enhance all aspects of a professional firm's practice.

TARGET AUDIENCES

Target audiences must be defined. Obviously, not every bit of information is for everybody on the payroll.

By defining the audience, using any appropriate designation, you begin to see how different messages must be tailored to fulfill the overall communications objective. What is to be communicated is a function of a policy predicated on clearly defined objectives, defined for specific audiences. The end should be known before the means are determined. With a well-delineated policy, and clear objectives, the *how* is relatively easy.

Every professional firm has myriad segments that require different information in order to function effectively. In a professional firm, this might include...

- Managing partners
- Executive committee
- All other partners
- Nonpartner professional staff
- Administrative and office staff
- Outside consultants
- Joint venture partners

PROFILES OF A SUCCESSFUL PROGRAM

While each firm is different, and each internal communications program is different, there are common elements that redound to an effective program. Among these elements are...

- *Motivation.* We can do the most effective job of structuring a communication mechanism, but we can't force people to use it. We can, however, perhaps do a better job of making people understand the necessity of communication—of why it's essential to the growth and success of the firm, and that it's not just a great theory, but a realistic need and a practical idea. Without adequate motivation, and the enthusiastic support of management, no internal communication program can succeed.

- *Time.* As the flow of information increases, the amount of time available to communicate internally diminishes. Only by making people recognize the investment aspect of internal communications can we get them to allocate time to it. At the same time, formalized structure can control and manage the time needed for it.

- *Priorities.* A professional's or manager's day demands attention to more matters than even the most competent professional or manager can address. It's virtually a given that in any professional's day—or week—there are more things to do than can get done. Too often, then, matters of internal communication are relegated to the bottom of the pile. This can be changed only by clearly delineating priorities.

- *Better use of communications vehicles.* We have the vehicles. We can use them better.

- *Overcoming personal reluctance to share information.* This is a real behavioral problem. It may in some cases be dealt with by enhancing motivation, education, and affirmative leadership to remove the threat so often inherent or implied by sharing information. This is a major obstacle to successful cross-selling—which is at best a function of internal communications, as well as education.

- *Defining what must be communicated, and to whom.* Uncategorized information means information overload. When people are inundated with information irrelevant to their needs, they stop hearing things they should hear. This kind of information overkill is in some ways the greatest cause of communication failure.

- *Keeping the objectives in sight.* It's easy to get caught up on the details of a program such as this, and to lose sight of the objectives. Doing so can be disastrous.

- *Flexibility.* There is a dynamic in information flow that can be destroyed if the program becomes too rigid. Here, too, the objective is more important than a rigid structure. The medium, remember, is not the message here. The message governs the medium. Keep it as simple as possible.

- *Accept imperfection.* It's people, not systems, that drive the communication process. People are not perfect, and therefore no system devised by people is likely to be perfect. Accept it, but keep your eyes on the program's objectives, and keep trying.

MECHANICS

The possible vehicles for internal communications are easy to determine. Each vehicle has its purpose, and each its advantages and disadvantages. None is generally better than others, but value depends on how each is used. There are not many options, although imagination may breed innovation. But given clearly defined objectives, each vehicle functions differently, serves a different purpose, has a wide range of alternative uses, and frequently functions better in conjunction with others.

- *Face-to-face meetings.* They are the ultimate form of targeting information, because they allow interpersonal relationships to be enhanced, and offer the opportunity to ask and answer questions, using graphics and audiovisual material to explain and clarify. Whether on a one-to-one basis, or in a group, meetings guarantee that the information is imparted and heard, and with questioning, that it's understood. Unfortunately, the larger the firm, the more difficult it is to rely on this method as a primary source of general information. And too frequent meetings of large groups can be counterproductive.

- *Internal newsletters.* Properly done, a great deal of general information can be conveyed. Firm newsletters that are well written are usually read, and can be a friendlier way to discuss general firm policy than are memos and booklets. A question-and-answer type of article on employee benefits in a firm newsletter is more likely to be read and understood than might be a legalistic brochure. Internal newsletters are increasingly being replaced by intranets—web sites accessible only internally.

- *Electronics.* E-mail is increasingly popular in larger firms, but with its popularity has come e-mail pollution—a glut of dubious information in which, like some electronic Parkinson's Law, the message expands to fill the available space online. Wireless PDAs expand the reach of e-mail. More firms today are beginning to understand the power and value of intranets—internal computer networks that allow members of the firm to work on projects as a group. Closed circuit television is also growing in popularity as a means of reaching a lot of people in several places at once. Video is used in some firms to impart information, or to build morale, or to teach an important technical point. Teleconferencing, when several cities are involved, can be very effective, and a new process—the extranet—allows firms to integrate their own intranets with the clients'. It's internal communication with the client participating, which opens a new realm of possibilities.

- *Bulletins.* Distributing advance copies of an ad campaign, for example, makes people feel part of the campaign, and privy to something positive before the public sees it. Distributing copies of press releases informs and energizes people internally.

- *Policy manuals.* Sometimes policies and procedures are too complex not to put in a manual. Still, manuals are not a prime communications document—they're a reference tool. Newsletters, bulletins, and meetings should communicate any policy that's active. Company policies are not secret battle plans, nor are general marketing strategies ever so sensitive competitively that their general outlines can't be imparted internally. There's more to gain than to lose.

- *Memos.* As terse and succinct as possible, to the point and focused, memos impart specific and cogent information. Memo writing may border on art (or, as Lord Chesterfield is supposed to have said in a long letter to his son, "Had I but the wit to be brief..."), but people can learn to write better memos, sans platitudes and clichés. They can learn to make points clearly, inspiring understanding and appropriate action. When you can't tell everybody, and you can't tell it to the right people face-to-face, a good memo may serve. Fortunately, more and more memos are now being done by e-mail, which means they are terser. They are also distributed faster, too, particularly in a large firm.

* *Practice group meetings.* A well-run practice group is a laboratory for internal communication. The members of the group share the group's purpose in common, and each member is generally aware of the information he or she and others in the group need. The group is also a vehicle for exchanging information with other groups within the firm.

* *Training programs.* A training program is its own form of communication, assuring that within the subject of the program, every participant is learning the same thing.

* *Word of mouth and rumors.* This is the form of communication that prevails when there is no other communications structure. Suffice it to say that its main purpose is to breed discontent. It can destroy the best of firms.

These are the key methods of communicating internally. There are, of course, myriad other devices. The bulletin board and the water fountain and coffee machine. Faxes. Computer-to-computer transmissions of data and text. With today's technology, there's no shortage of internal communications devices.

The trick is not in the mechanics, though. It's in the policy and the planning. It's in the effective use of each vehicle. Without clear objectives, without a plan, without managing the plan to meet the objectives, internal communication becomes simply messages written in chalk on the sidewalk on a rainy day.

USING KNOWLEDGE

If knowledge is indeed dynamic, then it must be recognized that people must often be taught how to use information. It's not always a natural skill. Those who work with knowledge must be educated in the process of turning data into information, and information into knowledge. Training programs need not be elaborate, but they must address the techniques of acquiring, assessing, and integrating knowledge into their own activities.

At the same time, feedback systems must be developed as an integral part of knowledge management. Here, too, the concept of dynamic information—information that changes as it's used—dictates that the flow of information throughout a company is essential. Results of the activities using information must be monitored and adjusted regularly.

PULLING IT ALL TOGETHER

The contemporary science, art, and practice of knowledge management as a philosophy of internal communication is relatively new, although people have been managing information in an elementary way since the beginning of time. It is the development of the computer and other media that have made a more scientific approach to knowledge management and internal communication techniques necessary.

If we are indeed in a knowledge-based society, then the science of managing that knowledge becomes increasingly important. Internal communications, which is the process in which we use information to better serve a company's objectives, makes it necessary that we better understand the nature of all firm information, the value of each kind of information to each segment of the firm, and the structure to categorize it. It's the information that matters, not the vehicles to convey it. Information well used is the competitive edge. And the beneficiary, of course, is the client.

Ultimately, the basis of successful internal communication evolves into three areas—content, motivation, and knowledge management. It is here, not with the mechanics, that the process should begin, if there is any progress to be made in successful internal communication.

PART VI

ECONOMICS IN THE CLIENT-CENTRIC FIRM

15

A FARTHING FOR YOUR GOAT

Pricing in a Client-centric Firm

Everything you want in life has a price connected to it. There's a price to pay if you want to make things better, a price to pay just for leaving things as they are, a price for everything.

—Harry Browne, American financial advisor, writer

Script became scripture when a simple accommodation to clients became the revered rule of the profession. Thus was born hourly billing. It took on a life of its own, and thus began an extraordinary and complex narrative.

Some years ago—decades, it was—lawyers and accountants sent clients bills that said, simply, "For services rendered," followed by a dollar sign and a number. It was tacitly understood by both clients and professional firms that this vaguely determined figure was arrived at as a mystical mix of both time spent and value of services.

Then some cost accountants got wise to it, and demanded a better breakdown of the mystical number. The response was hourly billing. It served to convince clients that they could now understand what they were paying for. And in those pre-*Bates* days, when there was no competition to raise the issue, it was tacitly assumed that each dollar billed had a dollar's worth of value. The clients were pleased. Or at least, appeased.

The professionals, annoyed at first by the bother of logging hours, came to be pleased as well. They came to believe that an hour of their work has a set value in the eyes of their clients. *My hour is worth $250, while my manager's hour is only worth $180 no matter what we do.*

How did that calculate? For example, the aforesaid manager is paid $124,800 yearly. Most firms would take that salary, divide by 2,080 hours (the normal working year), and come up with a cost of $60.00 per hour. In order to cover direct and indirect costs and have something left for a profit, the firm would write up the cost

219

by a multiple (anywhere from three to five times). In this case, it's three times, or $180.00 per hour.

The view that an hour of my time is worth $X.00, unfortunately, is a false assumption, and ultimately deludes the client. With this view, the lawyer's and accountant's total vision and focus is inward—*how much time am I spending on this work, rather than being outward—what is the client getting for the time I spend?* The fact is, the lawyer's or accountant's time may or may not be worth what their hourly billing rate is. For example, is the work done by one accountant or lawyer who bills at that rate of the same quality as another professional who bills at the same rate? Or, a professional who spends time drafting a covering letter to a client and that same professional working on a complex matter? Should the client be charged the same amount for an equal amount of time spent on each? Of course not. In some cases it's worth more, in some cases worth less. In fact, the hourly billing rate is nothing more than a cost writeup factor, an internal piece of information.

The problem is that the clients are beginning to catch on. Competition has done that by allowing price to become a competitive and marketing factor, as it is in other areas of commerce. Competition is teaching clients to comparison shop, and that has begun to teach them that too often, the hourly billing rate has nothing to do with value received. Competition is also eroding the mystique of the professional. Witness, for example, the fact that fewer and fewer corporations are loyal to only one firm for all their legal or accounting needs, which at least brings greater transparency to pricing. The mystery is unraveling and the turmoil beginning. The clients are demanding a pricing system based upon value, because that's what the firm down the street is offering.

At the same time, the professional firms are entrenched in hourly billing, precisely because of its mystique and the potential profitability it brings. Something has to give.

BREAKING THE PARADIGM

Professional service providers—accountants, lawyers, and consultants—must first break the existing paradigm that time spent equals value. Focusing on production (i.e., the amount of billable time an individual has) can have several negative consequences for a professional services firm. From a marketing and client-centric view, hourly billing usually has these negative effects on your professional practice...

- By emphasizing volume, owners in accounting, legal, and consulting firms use internal measures to price and evaluate their services and the contributions of their staff. It's clear that there is no relationship to what the market thinks the service is worth. By emphasizing volume (i.e., revenue), firms fail to pay attention to profitability. Professional service providers need to consider the value of the service to the client and then determine if they can produce the service so that there is sufficient profit for their labor. When professional service providers take this point of view, they will then pay more attention to getting the work done in the most efficient manner and focus more on a value-based approach to their services.

- Spend more time, make more money! Isn't that what the existing paradigm tells professionals to do? This mind-set creates several barriers to becoming a client-centric firm.

  o By emphasizing billable hours, professionals follow a natural instinct to bill more hours, rather than to perform the service in the most economical fashion.

  o The professional may not even be aware that he or she is giving a silent—or not so silent—message to the client that the time spent is more important than the value provided.

  o Because the focus is on time, the professional's mind and energy is on the hours and not on the client.

  o A focus on billable hours encourages individual rather than team performance. We have nothing against individual professionals keeping score as to where they stand throughout the year. But as any coach knows, teamwork and cooperation are just as important as having great players if the team wants to go all the way to the championship.

  o Hourly billing diminishes time allocated to other important aspects of firm management, and certainly, marketing. Any hour spent on writing a brochure, giving a speech, or any other such activity diminishes the number of billable hours.

  o Finally, if my focus is solely on billable hours, I will chase after them wherever I can find them. Every client that the firm takes in should take the firm one step closer to achieving its strategic vision. Remember that just having clients is not enough; you need the right kind of clients—the profitable ones and the ones you can really help.

- The existing paradigm also encourages professionals to stick close to the *technical* skills they were trained for—accounting, tax, legal, and consulting services. Clients want and demand more from their professionals. Just having outstanding technical skills and talents, but lacking skills in building client relationships, providing value-added services, and effectively communicating with clients, is no longer sufficient to be competitive in a client-centric environment.

- There is a marked difference between a good technician and a good client service professional. When firms emphasize the production approach—the technical aspects of the engagements—they then fail to develop and create a cadre of client service professionals. Every firm needs professionals with excellent technical abilities. The client-centric firm will not only have this type of professional but will also encourage its people to develop marketing, communication, listening, and client service skills. Client-centric firms realize that professionals with just technical skills often develop an employee mentality rather than an entrepreneurial spirit. They soon become more comfortable working for other professionals' clients rather than going out and getting clients of their own.

- Finally, no firm can serve two masters. If your master is production, then this orientation will keep you from developing a true marketing culture in the firm. This could be the most significant and most harmful consequence of using billable production to determine compensation and performance evaluation. Emphasis on production results in professionals who do not understand marketing or its importance to the livelihood of firm.

MATURE MARKET

Many believe that the accounting and legal professions are in the mature stage of the product life cycle (stage one being introduction, two is growth, three is maturity, and four is decline). There are certain characteristics that will apply to this stage, no matter what business you are in.

Two main things start to happen as professions and industries start to move into the mature stage. First, there are many competitors in the market space. With the exception of the Big Four and some of the second-tier accounting firm and some of the very large international law firms, this is abundantly the case for most professional services firms. The barriers to entry are low. A lawyer or accountant unhappy at his or her current firm need only to hang a shingle across the street and is now in business. Second, sales and corresponding profits begin to level off as industries enter into the mature stage. This only makes sense, because competition increases and firms lower prices in an attempt to stay competitive and capture a larger market share. This begins a downward spiral that places even further pressure on profits.

There are identifiable factors that prove professional services firms are indeed in the mature stage of their life cycle:

- *Consolidation.* Mature industries often see a rash of consolidations. There are simply too many players in a given market for all of them to be profitable. As prices and profits decline, it is natural that only the strongest will survive. The Big Eight have already become the Big Four. The broader legal and accounting consolidation movements of the 1990s are other examples of industries in the mature stage. Major consolidators such as American Express Tax and Business Services, H&R Block, Century Business Services, and Centerprise Advisors have acquired many of the top 100 CPA firms. Regional accounting firms are acquiring smaller practices to gain more market share. New CPA and law firm mergers are announced almost on a monthly basis. More than 40 of 1990's top 100 accounting firms have since been acquired or no longer exist.

- *Name recognition.* Firms such as H&R Block, American Express, Deloitte, and Ernst & Young all enjoy certain name recognition and reputation. Name recognition becomes a powerful marketing tool in a mature market. Clients will tend to select a better-known firm over a "no-name" firm in mature markets. Clients want to make sure that they are working with winners.

- *Competition from the outside.* Competition is one of the most important marketing factors affecting a firm's pricing policies. In mature markets, competition comes from many traditional and nontraditional service providers. Today, banks, financial advisors, lawyers, and other non-CPA firms all offer many of the same services that Certified Public Accountants offer, with the exception of attest work. Even foreign companies have acquired U.S. tax preparation firms. The French firm Fiducial acquired Triple Check Tax Preparation in the late 1990s and continues to acquire accounting firms today. While lawyers are not facing the same issues today, business clients often take advantage of the myriad of service providers by working with more than one law firm at a time. The firm that becomes client-centric has a better chance of becoming the provider of choice.

- *Price competition.* Price competition in professional services started more than 20 years ago, when the Big Eight began responding to requests for proposals for audits in order to obtain more profitable consulting work. Intensive price competition has become a way of life for most national and international services firms. Price competition is no longer limited to just the big firms; even sole practitioners are dealing with it on a regular basis. In the legal arena, firms are being asked to provide fixed fees and compete in beauty contests. The changes brought about by technology and a more sophisticated client base have certainly changed the environment in which the professional service provider lives.

- *Sophisticated buyers.* As we have said before, clients today want to feel that their professional services provider is offering them real value—that they are providing them services that will have a positive impact on their personal and business lives. As much as the personal relationship is important, it's the services that ultimately count. If your services are not satisfying the needs of your clients, no relationship is worth the fee. The more you satisfy client needs, the more valuable your services become. A client who is willing to pay for your services feels that the price paid is certainly equal to the value he or she has received.

PRICING IN THIS NEW ENVIRONMENT

It may be true that most professional service providers find themselves in a mature market. But that does not mean there is no hope, or that clients won't pay for valuable service. The secret is *increase value and you increase price.* Of course, this is much easier said than done, but it's the point of arrival that every client-centric firm should be heading toward. And only firms that put clients at the core will be able to accomplish this. These are the firms that understand their clients the best and are constantly trying to gain an even deeper understanding.

There are several things that you can do to increase the value of your services in your clients' eyes. Our experience has been that different types of clients have different perceptions about value. In some cases you may not materially change what you are doing for your clients. What will change is the way you communicate value to your clients. In other cases, you will drastically change the way the service is provided or charged.

Both the American Bar Association and the American Institute of Certified Public Accountants publish subjective guidelines for pricing legal and accounting services. The ABA's *Model Rules of Professional Conduct* lists several pricing factors to consider and the *Management of an Accounting Practice Handbook* (MAP) lists those that apply to the accounting profession. Only one of the pricing factors relates to the time and labor required.

The most important thing is that clients understand the value you bring to them. Here are various things to consider when trying to determine your fee...

- Responsibility assumed. The more responsibility that you assume for an engagement or matter, the more you should be able to charge. That's why contingency fee lawyers can get 30 percent or more of the settlement, no matter what the time element is.

- Your firm provides the service in the manner that the clients needs and wants it. For example, your client wants to be able to file an electronic tax return. If your firm does not offer that service, your tax preparation service will be perceived as having a lesser value than a competitor that offers electronic filing. A law firm client might want to be able to track the progress on his matter on line. If the firm allows the client access to its systems, this can be a value add to this particular client.

- Multinational or regional clients will perceive that firms with more than one office provide them with greater value than single-office firms. By having your offices closer to the client's facilities, you are providing the client with place utility. Remember that we said it is critical for the firm to have the right kinds of clients. If you service regional clients, but if you don't have regional offices, you probably are not providing clients with the value that they expect. So unless you plan to become a regional firm, and do so quickly, you may be at great risk of losing such clients.

- Clients often perceive professional services to have more value if they are provided by experienced professionals who have a reputation in the field.

- There is a certain value to the client when the firm meets all promised delivery dates and is highly responsive to client calls. Clients like to feel important; in fact, they like to feel that they are the most important client to the firm. When they call, this is your opportunity to make them feel like the most important client in the world. If you are going to make the client feel important, make sure that you first do it for your most profitable clients.

- A difficult issue is always worth more to a client than something that the client perceives to be just a commodity service. A Form 1040 tax return is surely considered a commodity by clients. If that same tax accountant is working on a complex merger and acquisition matter, the client will perceive the latter work to be more valuable.

- Clients will especially perceive as valuable those services that create a change in their physical, emotional, and financial well-being, such as an estate plan that puts their concerns at rest and assures them that they have minimized estate taxes.

- Certain working conditions or time-sensitive matters will be considered more valuable to the client.

- Clients also feel there is value if your services add something to what they already have—for example, you are able to save the client from paying additional income taxes or you protect the client from a frivolous lawsuit.

- There is also real value if your service saves a client from an unpleasant experience. You protect a client from having to undergo a full IRS audit. You help a two-person partnership settle their legal differences and keep the partnership intact.

- Clients always consider services that provide them with additional profits and efficiency-generating ideas valuable. If you don't understand the client's business or the client's goals for the year, you won't be able to provide these types of value-added services.

- Finally, specialized skills, such as valuation expertise, negotiation experience, turn-around talent, and so forth, are always considered more valuable than non-specialized services. They are usually harder to find in the marketplace.

PRICE-VALUE EXCHANGE

Under the new paradigm, the fee that a professional services provider charges a client is ultimately tied to the value and the outcome of the service provided. Pricing, as we have said, is truly a marketing function. Ronald Baker, in *The Professional's Guide to Value Pricing,* defines value pricing as "the maximum amount a given customer is willing to pay for a particular service, before the work begins."

Moving from a traditional hourly based pricing system to a value-based system is both an evolutionary and an educational process. To move into this new environment, professional service providers will need to have more discussions with clients regarding the fees before the service begins. This requires that the service provider find out up front what the client is willing to pay for the service. Remember, this is an exchange that must have some equilibrium. But there are strong indications that clients not only look at the change favorably, but also may ultimately demand it.

Then you provide clients with a service that they need and value, and in return the clients pay you something. How do you determine what the fee should be?

Some things are clear.

- It's the client who determines the true value of your service and hence what he or she is willing to pay for the service.

- The exchange has nothing to do with the amount of time that you spend. It's totally dependent on the value that you bring to the client. *The harsh reality is that clients really don't care how much time you spend, if they feel they're getting value for their money.*

- The price you charge is also determined by the number of competitors you have in the marketplace. If you are a tax preparer, there are a lot of competitors who are willing to do the same "tax preparation" at a lower fee than you may be able to do it. H&R Block does an average tax return for less than $150, but does more than 15 million of them. A small accounting firm with full-time tax professionals can't afford to compete with H&R Block if all it does are individual tax returns and nothing else. If you are a residential real estate lawyer, you, too, have a lot of competitors. If you are a divorce lawyer who only handles high-profile divorces, there will be significantly fewer competitors.
- Pricing also depends on the types of services your firm offers. For example, firms that have developed specialized knowledge or are known as the *go to* firm for a particular service usually have fewer competitors and are doing work that's more valued by clients. Because of lack of competition and the nature of the work of such firms, clients perceive a higher value and are willing to pay more for the services. Certain firms offer unique services, similar to those of a stem cell researcher or a brain surgeon. These services, when the client requires them, are usually related to a life-or-death situation. The business is about to file for bankruptcy; a hostile takeover is in the wings; the owner/CEO suddenly dies with no heir apparent. When these events happen, the clients will seek the firm that they feel will best meet their needs with little concern for the price of the service. While these service opportunities are rare, they do offer those firms that specialize opportunities to price their services aggressively.

The best way to determine what the client will pay is to know the following figures...

- Your actual cost to conduct the engagement, to which...
- Add your desired profit margin.
- Add some contingency because engagements never run totally smoothly.
- Determine if a risk premium is necessary.

Now you have a figure in your mind of what you could charge. You can now start the discussion with the client. For example, if you know that your cost, plus profit, plus a contingency factor is $25,000, that's the price you want to put out as a trial balloon to the client. Remember, a number one rule of pricing is you can never raise the price once a number is given, but you can always go down. The client may surprise you and say fine, or may come back with, "Gee, I thought it would be more like $20,000." Now you know what figure the client had in mind. Your task is to show added benefits, the positive outcome, the return, and so forth, that the client might get. Just because the client says $20,000, it does not mean that is the price he or she will pay.

Many times a client has a budget for the service needed. Just ask.

Once the fee is agreed on, then your engagement letter needs to clearly outline what would cause the fee to increase. This will give you some protection if the client wants additional services under the original agreement.

You have now engaged the client in the pricing of the service. The client has agreed up front, and when the invoice is sent for services rendered, there will be no surprises.

Pricing based on the value you provide a client will continue to become important in a client-centric environment. The shift from a method based on cost to a method based on value will take time. The truly client-centric firm will embrace this change well before it becomes widely accepted. How you decide to make this change is up to you. The important thing is that you decide.

16

WHAT DID I GET FOR MY MONEY?

Measuring the Marketing ROI

Half the money I spend on advertising is wasted, the trouble is I don't know which half.

—George Roy Hill, American Tobacco Company

Of the many reasons that professionals and marketers always seemed to pass one another like ships in the night, one significant reason is the difficulty in measuring the results of the marketing effort.

It's easy to understand. If you run an ad offering lollipops for sale, you measure the results by counting the number of lollipops you sell. It doesn't work that way in professional services, where the objective is not to sell your services to someone who doesn't need them, but rather to persuade someone to choose you over your competitors when he or she does need your services. A vast difference in the same thing.

If the objective of professional firm marketing, then, is not to produce clients with each ad or press release, then it is at least to build name recognition and a reputation for skills, competence, and integrity. That reputation can be measured, other than anecdotally, by professional surveying. But beyond demonstrating that the respondent has heard of the firm and understands and trusts its capabilities, the logical next question might be, "If the need arises, would you retain this firm?" Again, a measure of the effectiveness of the marketing program, but not of the return on marketing investment.

In the early days of marketing for professionals, much was taken on faith. But there was little faith, and the average tenure of professional firm marketers was about 12 months. Now the average tenure is up to 30 months, which means that there is a growing accommodation to marketing by professionals—which, considering the mind-set of professionals, means that obviously some methods have evolved for determining the return on investment (ROI) in marketing. Not only is marketing becoming an integral part of a firm's management, it is also moving closer to the firm's finance area.

Other than quantifying results, which can be difficult and complicated if increasingly necessary, the traditional measurement of the efficacy of a program is not—and possibly could not be—measured accurately by the number of clients each ad, each press release, each brochure produced. Rather, it was considered sufficient to measure marketing activity against the detailed objectives of a marketing program. This is still a rational approach, but it doesn't address the problem of results against the cost of achieving those results—the return on marketing investment—the ROMI.

MEASURING THE ROMI

In their constant effort to justify marketing as an investment and not an expense, marketing directors have been taking the lead in tracking and measuring what their efforts are doing for the firm.

Leisa Gill, marketing director at Lattimore, Black, Morgan & Cain, CPAs (Brentwood, Tennessee), sums it up for the marketing professional, saying "If it is worth doing...it is worth doing right. If it is worth doing right...it is worth measuring."

Yes, we know now that a great deal can be measured. At least enough to gauge how the marketing dollar is being spent, and what is being delivered for it.

WHAT ARE FIRMS MEASURING?

There are several categories that can be measured, the ultimate one being those factors that record the growth of the business. These include...

- Number of new clients
- Market share
- Number of clients by target market segment
- Number of profitable clients
- Share of client's wallet
- Number of new products or service segments developed during the last year
- Number of new geographic markets entered
- Number of cross-selling opportunities created

- Cost of new client acquisition
- Number of proposals written
- Number of pending proposals
- Number of presentations made

Then there are results-to-efforts ratios, including ...

- Ratio of proposals won to total proposals
- Seminar-to-leads; seminars-to-client
- Networking-to-leads; networking-to-client
- Sponsorships-to-leads; sponsorships-to-clients
- Mailings-to-leads; mailings-to-clients
- Newsletters-to-leads; newsletters-to-clients
- Percent of sales from new services
- Revenue growth rate by service
- Total marketing cost as a percentage of total revenue
- Average fees per client
- Average fees per new client
- Profitability by client

Then there are the business measures ...

- Client profitability
- Accounts receivable adjustments
- Client retention rates
- Client service guarantees implemented
- Number of new services developed
- Percentage of a direct mail campaign that produces invitations to present

There are the elements produced by research ...

- Personal interviews with clients
- Client satisfaction surveys
- Name recognition and awareness

And finally, there are the measurable marketing activities, such as . . .

- Number of seminars presented
- Number of ads placed
- Number of interviews
- Number of articles written
- Number of press releases placed
- Number of times firm/partners are quoted or mentioned in publications
- Number of trade shows attended
- Number of trade shows exhibited at

While measuring these elements will reveal a great deal, there is still more that can't be measured except by survey. For example, you can measure seminar attendance, but not the degree to which it contributes to turning an attendee into a prospect and a prospect into a client. You can measure the efficacy of an ad only by survey.

At the same time, it should be remembered that in professional services marketing, rarely does a single marketing element function by itself. Name recognition, reputation for skill and integrity—these are a function of a total program, never of a single ad or press release.

Still, compared to what we knew just a few years ago about measuring ROMI, this is a giant step forward. There is still a distance to go to match the ability of a product marketer to measure ROMI.

17

CASH IS KING

What's the Lifetime Value of Your Clients and the Financial Health of Your Firm?

Revenue is vanity, margin is sanity, and cash is king.

—Anonymous

Indeed, cash is king, and any business, no matter its size or industry, is as healthy as its ability to generate cash. Client-centric firms know that it's not sales or marketing that ultimately drives profit and cash. It's clients. And if you don't have enough profitable clients, they eventually may go out of business.

In July 2003, Altheimer & Gray, a major Chicago law firm, informed its partners that the firm was bankrupt and would be closing the next day. Staff and associates were let go without any severance. Retired partners were left in the cold without their retirement pay. Current partners were in shock.

Brobeck, Phleger & Harrison was the epitome of a large successful law firm. It was one of the most powerful firms in San Francisco and an innovative national leader. The firm was selected by *Fortune* magazine, at the end of 2000, as one of the "100 Best Companies to Work For." It advertised on national television, it created a brand identity. Ed Wesemann, a principal with Edge International, wrote in a monologue entitled "When Good Law Firms Go Bad," "From 1998 to 2000, the firm skyrocketed to over 900 lawyers and $476 million in revenue, then, in 2003, plummeted to dissolution."

How could this happen to such successful firms? Easy. According to Wesemann, "The proverbial wolf was not at the door of any of the . . . firms that went under. None of them were insolvent. What happened is th.t profits declined. Owners weren't putting as much cash in their pockets. According to the *American Lawyer*, in 2002 Altheimer & Gray saw a 12.9 percent decrease in profits coming off of a

233

record year in 2001. In fairness, Brobeck was down 38.6 percent but it ended up paying $26 million in income to the bank instead of to partners. Still Brobeck's profit per partner for 2002 was a not too shabby $420,000. What happened was the firm simply didn't generate enough cash to compensate the owners at the level to which they had become accustomed."

Many professionals and businesspeople confuse cash with net income or, worse yet, with revenue. Net income is merely an accounting definition. It doesn't tell a firm where it's making money or where the cash is coming from. Remember that cash is king, not revenue or margin.

FORGET ABOUT REVENUE

Gerald Riskin, one of the founders of Edge International, outlined the most common reasons firm leaders focus on revenue...

- Various publications rank firms by revenues. Firm leaders are therefore motivated to try to achieve as high a ranking as they can, for both wholesome and unwholesome reasons—wholesome, including positioning to obtain marketing advantages, and unwholesome being ego.

- The partners themselves understand the simplistic measure *percentage increase*, and it is appealing if you don't know any better.

- *Percentage increase* includes inflation, without highlighting it, so even if there are margin squeezes, revenue enhancement still sounds good.

- Revenue is simpler to calculate than profit, at least firmwide.

FOCUS ON PROFITS

Too many firms today still measure performance by measuring the amount of billable hours that are entered on the time sheet. At the end of the year, Partner A has more hours than Partner B, and everyone in the firm assumes that A is producing more than B and that A is perhaps more valuable to the firm than B. Unfortunately, neither assumption can be proven by the facts at hand.

Other firms tie billings to cash receipts at the end of the year. This is one step better than just measuring billable time, but it still doesn't provide any indication of the profitability of a partner's book of business, or the profitability of any individual client.

There's only one way to measure the true profitability of a practice: Specific costs need to be allocated to the revenue source. For example, Partner A has a

$750,000 book of business. Time sheets will give a close approximation of the actual time spent during the year (provided that the partner is capturing most of the time spent). Knowing how much time was actually billed provides what is commonly called realization.

Total cash collections divided by the total number of billable hours will give you a net realized rate per hour. This is all valuable information, but it still does not provide you a profit figure since we still do not know the costs associated with the revenue generation.

Profit is typically deduced by subtracting expenses incurred to generate the revenue (Profits = Revenue less expenses). Only then can you determine the net contribution of that book of business. This seems so easy, and it's something all accountants encourage their business clients to measure. But like the shoemaker's children, accountants, attorneys, and other consultants fail to do it for themselves.

Why, then, are so many accounting, law and consulting firms reluctant to allocate costs? Riskin provides us with several reasons in his article "Forget About Revenue":

- It's not simple to allocate costs. What do you count and what don't you count? It may be easy to allocate staff if there is a 100 percent allocation to a group or team, but in the real world it usually gets a lot messier than that. And then there are issues like this: Is the new office in Timbuktu, which specializes in Practice Area X, a cost of that practice area, or is it the beginning of a presence that benefits and adds international credibility to the entire firm and therefore a cost of all practice areas? Having discretion as to allocation creates dilemmas.

- The computer systems may not allow the flexibility to do the combinations and permutations of calculations, or the people who operate those systems may be ill-equipped or just plain reluctant to handle the changes.

- Change means some uncertainty, and therefore discomfort. It won't be done the way we have always done it so successfully. It's not broken, is it?

- Politics. Individuals with significant personal power are not about to allow any new measurement process that they have not already analyzed to the nth power to determine exactly how it might affect them personally. Partners are as sensitive about cost allocation as they are about compensation.

- The ramifications of doing the analysis may be dangerous. If practitioners in Practice Group A were to learn how much more profitable they really are compared with Practice Group B, they may begin putting tremendous pressure on decision makers as to compensation and other important issues. There might even be a drive to expel Practice Group B from the firm. Worse, the entire Practice Group A may shop for another host firm where they will be more appreciated, or break away to become a boutique. Either way, the firm's fabric is torn.

While we agree that allocating costs in a professional services firm is not the easiest thing, firms need to start doing it sooner rather than later. All firms currently calculate their profit on a firmwide basis. This is not sufficient when you're operating under the *clients at the core* concept.

Firm-wide profit doesn't indicate which client is profitable or not; it does not let the firm compare, from a profitability index, one partner's book of business to another; it does not tell you which segment or industry group is more profitable; and it makes it impossible to make strategic decisions about which clients to keep or fire.

DETERMINING THE CLIENT LIFETIME VALUE

How can you determine the value of your current clients? The client lifetime value (CLV) model is a methodology used by businesses that determines the worth of the client—not only of the initial work, but also of the work throughout the entire relationship.

Most professionals agree that the profitability of a new client is less in the first year or two than over the lifetime of the client. In fact, this may be true for many businesses that offer incentives for new clients. How else could a business spend money to acquire clients if there were no payback down the road? *Amazon.com* may be a perfect example. It started out selling books at deep discounts, even losing money on each sale. But once customers got used to buying books and other items over the Internet, they began to purchase more from *Amazon.com*. It's similar to the record clubs of old, or the DVD clubs of today. You can purchase six DVDs for the low price of 99 cents plus shipping and handling. And you only have to purchase six more over the next two years. Well, most people who join such clubs purchase several hundreds of dollars in DVD over the life of their membership.

American Airlines was the first airline to introduce the frequent flyer program. Can you imagine the CEO's reaction to the person who suggested that the airline start giving away free tickets? This is where determining the client lifetime value comes in. Yes, you may lose some money with the first engagement, but what will you gain over the lifetime of the client?

We're not suggesting that you give away your services. But we are proposing that you determine the customer lifetime value for your own practice overall, and for your various practice groups or service groups. *Client lifetime value is the total financial and intangible benefit that the client provides to your firm throughout the life of the relationship.*

When it comes to determining the lifetime value of a client and lifetime client profitability, firms need to look at more than just a single client transaction. Most firms can tell you who their top 20 clients are by revenue for any given year. Few, today, can tell you who their top 20 clients by profits are over the lifetime of the client.

For example, which client is more valuable to your firm? Client A, who pays you $5,000 for a project done during the current year and then never uses the firm again, or Client B, who paid $1,000 in fees last year? Client B is a recurring individual tax client who has been with the firm for 5 years. Client B will probably continue to pay you at least this much for the foreseeable future (5 to 10 years). If you're just paying attention to annual fees generated, you're probably not serving some of your more important clients. A $10,000 client with one engagement every 10 years is not as valuable as the $3,000 a year client over the course of 10 years.

By analyzing your client's average annual fees and multiplying by the total number of years of a relationship, you can determine the CLV. And by calculating a typical client's future cash flow, you can determine a new client's lifetime values.

There are several reasons why you should start tracking the client lifetime value. For example...

- How else will you know how much to pay to acquire a client? Focusing on top-line revenue, as we have said, doesn't help you. There is an old joke about a retail store that was losing $1 dollar on every shirt that it sold and the manager told the sales force not to worry about it. The store would make it up on volume.

- Once you know the lifetime value of the client, you can determine how much effort you are willing to invest in order to retain that client.

- From an intangible perspective, you should know which clients are providing you valuable referrals for new business.

- Knowing the lifetime value may encourage your partners to be better at cross-selling. They will see that from a pure cost perspective, it will be cheaper to cross-sell than to go out and get new clients.

DETERMINING CLIENT LIFETIME PROFIT

While lifetime value is important, more important is the lifetime profit that a particular client may generate for your firm. Most time and billing systems will provide the necessary information. If your system won't give you the information, then find one that will. Your first step is to enter the fully loaded cost per hour for every person in the firm. Second, for indirect cost, you may want to apply a firm-wide standard percentage.

Next, begin to analyze what's happening in your practice. Where is profitability being enhanced, and where is it less than desirable? What's causing the problems?

- Is it as simple as a rate issue? Perhaps you haven't raised or don't raise rates annually.

- Is there too much emphasis on chargeable hours and not enough on what can actually be billed and collected?

- Have you ever culled your client list? Are those at the bottom of the list really profitable for the firm?

- Are you measuring for return on your marketing investment (ROMI)?

- Do you have underperforming partners or staff?

- Are you operating under a performance-based compensation system?

Next...

- Compute your average profit per engagement or matter for the particular client (total net revenue minus direct and indirect expenses).

- Determine how many times the client will use your services, say over a life-time period.

- Determine the lifetime period.

- Calculate the amount of profit you make from that client over the lifetime (multiply your average net profit for your client by the number of years you will retain your clients).

The calculation may not be 100 percent accurate, but it gives you a good idea of what the client is really worth to your firm. Remember that your existing clients will also generate new clients from their referrals. This value is not included in the above calculation.

WHAT DOES CLIENT LIFETIME PROFIT TELL YOU?

Obviously, it tells you what each client will bring to your firm in terms of profit over its lifetime. More important, it tells you how much time, effort, and dollars you should be spending to get that client in the first place. Unless you have this knowl-edge, you can't have an intelligent marketing campaign. It provides you with the guidance necessary to take a short-term loss in order to obtain a long-term gain. It also provides you with a fresh way to look at existing clients and prospects.

PART VII

WHAT WILL WE DO TOMORROW?

18

THE FUTURE FOR PROFESSIONAL SERVICES

Are We There Yet?

A mind at rest tends to remain at rest. A mind in motion tends to remain in motion.

—Bruce W. Marcus

Predicting the future is, as the British say, a mug's game. A fool's errand. While some logical progressions of existing conditions might seem to foretell what is to be, there are still too many random events to derail the wisest of prognostications.

At the same time, there are indeed values in anticipating the shape of the future, to better adapt to it, and to help shape it.

What do we know now?

- Growing doubts about the infallibility and integrity of the professions have been crystallized, if not entirely in reality, then certainly in the perceptions of the business and investment community, as well as in the minds of the general public.

- Legislators on both sides of the aisle have long coveted the opportunity to tamper with the professions (thereby gaining greater visibility and notoriety for themselves). Unfortunately, with few exceptions, the eagerness to regulate the professions is supported by the flimsiest misconceptions. The public statements of legislators, following the recent scandals, indicated a lack of any understanding of the role of professionals in auditing and consulting, and of the appropriate relationships between lawyers and accountants and their clients.

- Trends of change in the professions have been abruptly halted. The growth and value to accounting firms of the consulting practice have shriveled. The multidisciplinary practice, which seemed to portend a new paradigm of not just practice, but service to clients, is now shunted aside. The losers, of course, are not just the professionals, but also the clients.

- The traditional structure of governance for the professions—the partnership—has now produced tangible evidence of its weakness. Witness that Enron, for all it did wrong, still survives as an entity. Arthur Andersen, its accounting firm, is completely destroyed.

- The impact of the Sarbanes-Oxley Act on corporate governance has caused dramatic changes in how public companies select and work with their auditors. The cost of compliance for most firms will surely continue to rise over the next few years.

- Consolidation of accounting firms—the once Big Eight is now the Big Four—is now posing a new dilemma in major corporations. A report by the American Assembly entitled "The Future of the Accounting Profession" notes that a company that uses one Big Four firm for the audit and another for consulting now has little choice if it chooses to change auditors.

- The traditional practice of hourly billing structure is no longer sacrosanct. As comfortable as it is for the professional firm to use, it's increasingly impractical as a marketing tool. The change will come not from the professionals, who profit most from it, but from the clients, who have begun to under-stand that the relationship between the hourly charge and real value is tenuous at best.

- Outsourcing of white-collar and professional positions will continue in the future and cause additional pressure on professional services firms.

- Consolidation in the legal and accounting professions will continue as firms attempt to gain economies of scale. This consolidation is taking place with professional firms of all sizes.

- There will be tremendous pressure on human productivity in firms. How many more billable hours can law firms expect from their new associates before they decide to leave the profession?

In all this, in the rush to regulate and to diminish the regard for the traditions of the professions, there is a missing ingredient. The client.

While there is no doubt that much of the new regulation does indeed eliminate many of the ills—or perhaps, the symptoms of the ills—too much is written for re-action and not protection. The SEC proposal to have lawyers resign, with "noisy" public explanation, from clients spotted in wrongdoing, simply ignores the role of lawyers and how that role is played. It does more harm than good, which is why it was quickly rescinded. Debates about such accounting practices as how to deal with stock options are being fought in the political arena, and not in the business and economic realm where they belong.

What, then, is likely to work for the professional firm in the future?

First, to radically separate the audit function from the consulting function without carefully and thoughtfully defining the services can cause serious problems in serving both clients and the public. Despite the rush to divest consulting arms, the professions will not easily allow themselves to be driven back to the dark ages of pre-*Bates*. Nor will clients, desperately in need of the very kinds of services they are getting now, allow it to happen. Many consulting services are relevant to improving the audit. Better systems to improve the flow of financial information, new technology to speed the audit—all are relevant to the needs of the audit, and can be performed without subverting the integrity, the objectivity, and the independence of the audit. This new consulting relationship can be monitored effectively by an independent outside body, but only with clearly defined rules that can cut away the consulting practices that flagrantly taint the attest function.

Nor will clients long tolerate losing the input of lawyers in a broad spectrum of expertise ancillary to traditional legal practice. The lawyer with financial or organizational skills, with a lawyer's grasp of investor needs or accounting, will always find appropriate ways to bring this expertise to clients, no matter what the strictures of professional ethics.

Second, systems of internal communications, based not on process or technology alone, but on content and the new paradigms of content management, must be mandated in all professional firms. Today's business entities generate too much information to allow for unmanaged communications within the professional firms that serve them. The proliferation of information that can contribute to the firm's functioning and to the clients' business must be harnessed. Techniques to assure control of a firm's business by keeping the right people informed of the right things are crucial.

Third, the partnership structure of professional firms, which has too long obscured the inner workings of those firms, must be reconsidered. Transparency is needed. This can be accomplished by reworking the governance structures for better management and to allow the outside world and regulators to see more clearly how each firm is serving the clients and protecting their shareholders. How is it possible that the structures of business, of the economic world, of the capital markets, can change, and the structures of the professions that are so integral a part of this economic world can remain unchanged?

Fourth, the professions, and those who regulate them, should remember that the professions are not so exalted that they function in isolation from the markets they serve. The time has come for all professionals to recognize that they exist only in their ability to meet the needs of their clients and the public—and not themselves. Eliminate the practices that so readily breed the kind of hubris that leads to the Enron-type scandals, such as hourly-based fee structures and opaque client relations. Institute structures for internal oversight of each audit. Develop oversight structures for quality control.

Fifth, the hourly fee structure may be sacrosanct, and at least useful in filling the coffers of lawyers and accountants, but its obsolescence will be proven not by debate, but by the demands of clients. "We buy your services," they are beginning to say, "not for your time, nor for your own concepts of your own wisdom, but for the value of the solutions you bring us."

Let's look, for the moment, at the rash of lawyer jokes and accountant jokes, bristle though we may at them. They hurt because they have roots in truth. When the accountant brings accounting solutions that are decades old to twenty-first century problems that grow out of new paradigms of business, jesting may be the only way to cope. When the public feels used by lawyers who wallow in outrageous fees, jokes are the relief of pain.

At the same time, what is really happening is that the professional practice of the past, in which clients accept what their professionals tell them because they don't really understand what professionals do, is fading quickly. Why? At least because competition sheds light on dark places. Because people today—executives as well as private citizens—are better educated and no longer accept the paternalism that's been inherent in professional practices since the nineteenth century.

The professional firm of the future will recognize that there is a difference between client relations and client service. When the client is unsophisticated and comes to you in pain, client relations helps the medicine go down. But when the client is sophisticated, then client service becomes paramount. And as any experienced practitioner knows, client service is not only more satisfying to perform, but it lasts longer. Client service, well performed, is in fact the best form of client relations.

What seems to have been lost in recent years is a measure of the independence of the professional that was so powerful in building the professions in at least the first half of the twentieth century. As recent events have shown, it's been supplanted by accommodation to the clients' wishes. The culmination of those same practices has been the scandals of the past decade. The firm of the future cannot be built on this foundation—it will not survive. Independence, one way or another, must come back in full force and with integrity, or else chaos will.

In the years since *Bates*, despite the residual professional structures of the past, many things have indeed changed in the professions. The new regulatory environment will bring about more changes. The first post-*Bates* marketing efforts were very different from much of the sophisticated work being done now. Acceptance of many sound marketing techniques brings us a long way from the early days. (Unfortunately, acceptance of some useless marketing fads also deter us.)

But for the professional firm of the future, for the firm that means to thrive by being relevant to the dynamic market it serves, there is still a long way to go. As we hope you will have seen from the preceding pages, there are ways to get there.

In all measures of professional firm marketing, as well as in professional firm management, success resides in an understanding that it's the client who is at the core of the professional practice, at the root of professional firm success.

APPENDIX A
THE BALANCED SCORECARD

THE BALANCED SCORECARD—FINANCIAL MEASURES

In the Balanced Scorecard world, financial goals are the results of achieving objectives in the other key areas. But according to Kaplan and Norton, "Financial measures are inadequate for guiding and evaluating organizations' trajectories through competitive environments." The reason is that they are lagging measures—they tell you what happened, not what will happen. And worse yet, they don't tell you why it happened. You can't manage a firm until you know why things are happening. Explaining financial variances each month at owners' meetings changes nothing in the firm nor helps the firm achieve its stated objectives.

The proof is in the pudding. The financial perspective tells a firm if its strategies are really working. If the firm is hitting or exceeding its growth and profitability goals, then it's effectively implementing its strategic plan. If the plan is not working or not working as well as expected, the firm needs to examine the underperforming areas and tweak them to get better results. While most firms are good at setting financial objectives, it's what's behind the numbers that often gets them into trouble.

The most common measures in the financial area include:

- Staff cost as a percent of net revenue
- Revenue from new services introduced
- Revenue growth
- Net income per partner (NIPP)
- Return on investment (ROI)
- Return on marketing investment (ROMI)

(Text continues on page 251)

Exhibit A.1   The Balanced Scorecard—Linkage Diagram

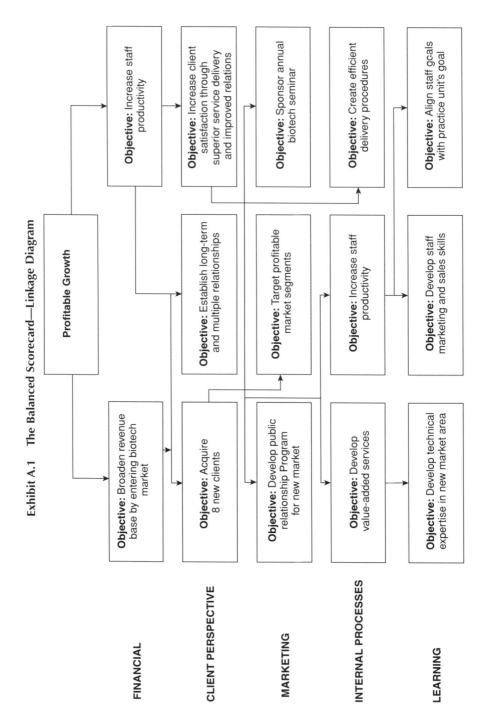

FINANCIAL			**Profitable Growth**

FINANCIAL
- **Objective:** Broaden revenue base by entering biotech market
- **Objective:** Increase staff productivity

CLIENT PERSPECTIVE
- **Objective:** Acquire 8 new clients
- **Objective:** Establish long-term and multiple relationships
- **Objective:** Increase client satisfaction through superior service delivery and improved relations

MARKETING
- **Objective:** Develop public relationship Program for new market
- **Objective:** Target profitable market segments
- **Objective:** Sponsor annual biotech seminar

INTERNAL PROCESSES
- **Objective:** Develop value-added services
- **Objective:** Increase staff productivity
- **Objective:** Create efficient delivery procedures

LEARNING
- **Objective:** Develop technical expertise in new market area
- **Objective:** Develop staff marketing and sales skills
- **Objective:** Align staff goals with practice unit's goal

248

Exhibit A.2   Scorecard Template

Area	Objective	Leading Measure	Lagging Measure	Target	Initiative(s)
Financial	F.1 Broaden revenue base by entering biotech market		F.1 Service mix	F.1 40% of new revenuea from biotech area	
	F.2 Increase staff productivity		F.2 Utilization	F.2 70% of staff's spent in biotech area	
Client	C.1 Acquire X new biotech clients	C.1 Pending opportunities	C.1 Sales	C.1 5 pending opportunities per month C.1 $250,000 in new biotech clients	
	C.2 Establish long-term relationship with clients	C.2 Quality time staff spends with clients	C.2 Retention rates	C.2 95% retention rate	
	C.3 Increase client satisfaction		C.3 Annual client satisfactioin survey	C.3 90% of clients rate us 4 or 5	
Market	M.1 Develop PR program for new market		M.1 Number of placements obtained	M.1 3 major placements minimal performance, 5–7 superior	
	M.2 Sponsor annual biotech seminar	M.2 Number of leads from each seminar	M.2 Number of seminars held	M.2 4 seminars held in first year with 20 prospects in total	
	M.3 Develop 2 new services offerings	M.3 Number of new services developed	M.3 Number of new services implemented		

Exhibit A.2 (Continued)

Area	Objective	Leading Measure	Lagging Measure	Target	Initiative(s)
Business Process	B.1 Create efficient delivery procedures		B.1 Delivery time	B.1 90% of projects completed and delivery on time	
Growth & Learning (Employee)	E.1 Develop technical expertise	E.1 specialized knowledge Niche expertise Employee motivation Employee satisfaction		E.1 80% of staff go through levels 1,2,3 or biotech training program	
	E.2 Develop marketing and sales skills			E.2 100% of biotech trained in marketing and sales skills	
	E.3 Align staff goals with practice unit's goals			E.3 85% of staff have aligned goals by 12/31. 100% the next year	
(For additional areas)					

250

- Operating margin
- Market share
- Return on equity (ROE—earnings available to shareholders/shareholders' equity)
- Profits per professional
- Profits per full-time equivalent (FTE)
- Revenue by service mix
- Cash flow from operations
- Receivables as a percent of working capital
- Days outstanding in accounts receivable (A/R) and work in process (WIP)

THE BALANCED SCORECARD—CLIENT MEASURES

Client objectives tell you how well you're servicing the market segments in which you have chosen to compete. As discussed in Chapters 2 through 4, firms need to first identify the clients they want to service, determine what client needs must be met to be successful in the market, and develop the firm's value proposition to the different market segments.

To determine how well they are achieving the firm's client objectives, firms often select one or more measures from the following list:

- Number of personal interviews with clients
- Client service guarantees implemented
- Profitability by client
- Number of clients inside the target market segment
- Number of profitable clients
- Share of client's wallet
- Accounts receivable (A/R) adjustments
- Work in process (WIP) adjustments
- Client retention rates
- Satisfaction scores in problem areas
- Service attributes
- Percent of clients rating firm 4 and 5 (on a scale from 1 to 5)
- Retention rates/percentage of clients who are repeat
- Number of client complaints

- Number of redos in work products (error rate)
- Number of clients exercising service guarantee
- Number of new services sold to existing clients
- Service quality
- Turnaround time
- Percent of delivery deadlines met
- Percentage of total revenue that comes from repeat clients
- Percentage of lost clients
- Net clients gained
- Percent of clients providing referrals

THE BALANCED SCORECARD—
INTERNAL BUSINESS PROCESS MEASURES

While some accounting firms, and many consulting firms, provide processing reengineering for their clients, few do it for their own firms. Simply stated, a process is a series of steps that change input into an output. The ultimate objective in every business process is to help the firm achieve its goals. Most firms have a goal of efficiently servicing their clients. But if their work review (quality control) process is redundant and ineffective, the process does not help the firm achieve the goal. While there are many processes in a firm, the most important ones are those that have an impact on the client's experience with the firm and on the financial results.

Process improvement requires the professional services firm to identify, document, and ultimately refine a process in order to better meet firm goals. It's an ongoing endeavor. But once you begin to capture the way your firm does things, you can start to get more consistency in the way you service clients.

We encourage firms to review their existing processes by flowcharting the activities and decision points that take place in converting the input into an output. The flowchart will tell you how the system is currently working. Since many processes involve many different functions in a firm, you will want the flowchart to show all the cross-departmental/functional responsibilities.

When setting process improvement objectives that impact customers, think about the following broad questions...

- How does the firm need to be structured to meet client needs?
- How does the firm ensure a quality product that eliminates redos?
- How does the firm ensure a timely turnaround?

- What does the firm need to do from a process perspective to achieve its client and financial objectives?
- What processes does the firm need to develop or improve in the service innovation, operations and post sale stages?

Here are some examples of key firm business processes that you will want to examine...

- Marketing and sales
- Client acquisition
- Service delivery
- New service development (R&D)
- Postsales follow-up
- Client service (handling complaints, billing issues)
- Pricing
- Client billing and collection
- Improving utilization
- Turnaround time for projects
- Rework time
- Number of tax returns completed per day
- Number of new services developed
- Time to bring new services to market

THE BALANCED SCORECARD—MARKETING MEASURES

It should be recognized that while an entire firm can sometimes—but not often—be marketed as a firm (for example, *The Firm of Smith and Dale Does Nice Work*), the most effective professional services marketing is for the parts of a firm. The same holds true for the Balanced Scorecard. For a law or accounting firm, a scorecard should be developed for each practice group. For any professional firm, it could be based on an industry specialization (for example, real estate, construction, health care, executive search, etc.). It could be a legal or financial skill (for example, expatriate taxation, litigation, SEC, etc.). It could be a geographic capability (for example, international, regional, multicity, etc.). The important thing to remember is that each of the areas needs to be considered. The objectives and measures of every practice group or service team all need to support the firm's overall strategies.

There are several ways to measure whether your marketing efforts are supporting your firm's overall growth and financial objectives. For example, you can measure...

- Number of new products or niches developed during the last year
- Number of new geographic markets entered
- Number of cross-selling opportunities created
- Cost of new client acquisition
- Number of personal interviews with clients
- Results of client satisfaction surveys
- Number of client service guarantees implemented
- Client profitability
- Number of clients inside the target market segment
- Share of client's wallet
- Client retention rates
- Total marketing cost as a percentage of total revenue
- Number of seminars presented
- Number of ads placed
- Number of interviews
- Number of articles placed
- Number of press releases placed
- Number of times firm/partners are quoted or mentioned in publications
- Number of presentations made
- Ratio of proposals won/total proposals
- Number of pending proposals
- Number of trade shows attended
- Number of trade shows exhibited at
- Market share
- Number of new clients
- Brand name awareness
- Average fees per existing client
- Average fees per new client

- Percent of sales from new services
- Revenue growth rate by service

THE BALANCED SCORECARD— EMPLOYEE GROWTH AND LEARNING MEASURES

The employee perspective in a professional services firm is perhaps the most important one, because the main differentiating factor among services firms is the people who actually deliver the service and have contact with the clients. The professional services firm mainly succeeds or fails in its marketing and client service based on the skills and talents of its workforce.

Employee measures help the firm determine how well it's doing to enhance the technical, marketing, and client service capabilities of the staff and partners; how well it's retaining key people in the firm.

Here is a list of some specific measures that will determine how well you're achieving your employee-related objectives...

- Number of professionals who are trained in more than one service
- Number of professionals trained in new technologies
- Firm's investment in technology as a percentage of net revenue
- Professional satisfaction
- Professional perception of firm leaders
- Number of staff suggestions made
- Number of staff suggestions implemented
- Employee turnover ratio
- Average length of service for professionals
- Number of employees participating in retirement and profit-sharing plans
- Revenue generated per employee

APPENDIX B

MANAGING THE KNOWLEDGE WORKER

TAKE THE PULSE OF YOUR STAFF

If you are losing too many good people to the competitors, then it's time to change what you are doing. Whatever you are doing, it's not working. You need to develop your own recruiting and retention strategy. We can't do that for you in this book. However, we can give you some ideas as to what professionals are looking for when they look at your firm. Think about their desires in three different buckets: compensation, career advancements and firm culture. The answers to the following questions will provide you with a general idea of how you are currently meeting your staff needs. How would you answer these questions?

COMPENSATION

1. Are our salaries competitive in the marketplace?   Yes _____ No_____
2. If no, when and what will it take to make them competitive?_____
3. Are our raises competitive in the marketplace?   Yes _____ No _____
4. If no, why not? _____
5. What can we do to make them competitive?

   _____
6. Do we offer year-end bonuses?   Yes _____ No _____
7. Do we offer spot bonuses (bonuses paid immediately for achieving a certain task/goal)?   Yes _____ No _____

257

8. Do we offer equity incentives for staff (phantom stock, ESOP program)?
   Yes _____ No _____

9. Do we offer profit sharing?   Yes _____ No _____

10. How competitive is our overall compensation package to others in our market?
    Not very competitive _____ Somewhat competitive _____
    Very competitive _____

CAREER ADVANCEMENT OPPORTUNITIES

There are two types of career advancement opportunities that professionals are looking for in today's environment. One, they want opportunities for professional growth. In other words, they want to be able to do more at an earlier stage in their careers. Two, they also want to accelerate career opportunities. Limiting the advancement opportunities is often cited as the number one factor in staff turnover. To see how competitive your firm is in this area, consider the following questions...

1. We create as many opportunities for professional growth as possible in our firm. Yes _____ No _____
   If no, why not? _____

2. Our partners train our professional staff so they can do more with clients sooner.   Yes _____ No _____

3. We give our professional staff the responsibility and authority to make client-related decisions.   Yes _____ No_____

4. We have a program that identifies future leaders in our firm.
   Yes _____ No _____

5. We have a fast-track program for staff to follow.   Yes _____ No _____

FIRM CULTURE

There is no doubt that the total compensation package is an important element in attracting and retaining good staff. Pay alone will not guarantee that you keep your recruits. Even good career advancement opportunities will not do the job by itself. One of the overriding factors in firm retention is your firm's environment, for example, its culture and its overriding vision. Firm culture has a significant role in staff recruiting and retention. The workforce and its environment have drastically changed over the last few years. Many professional services firms are still working under the old paradigm, "This is the way I was trained to do it." To make sure that your firm is aligned with today's workforce, ask yourself these questions...

1. Do all professional staff members develop an annual professional development plan? Yes _____ No _____

2. Does the firm encourage professional development (such as seminars, workshops, etc.) as part of its yearly professional development plans?
Yes _____ No _____

3. Does your firm culture praise and recognize performance?
Yes _____ No _____

4. Does your firm have very open lines of communication?
Yes _____ No _____

5. Do our partners really know and care about all the professional staff?
Yes _____ No _____

6. Have we created a culture that encourages creativity and idea sharing?
Yes _____ No _____

7. Have we provided our staff with a flexible work environment (work-life balance, flexible hours, telecommuting, etc.)? Yes _____ No _____

8. Do your partners "walk the talk"? Yes _____ No _____

If no, fix the problem before you do anything else.

APPENDIX C
PRICING IN A CLIENT-CENTRIC FIRM

ANALYZING PRICE SENSITIVITY[1]

Having done a little research on what the market will bear, it seems that 10 significant factors dictate the level of price sensitivity. To understand what to charge a value-based client, ask the following:

1. How well does the client know what other law firms charge for the services sought? *(Clients without a point of reference tend to be less price-sensitive.)*

2. How difficult is it for a client to compare fees among competing law firms? *(The more defined the matter and the more routine the service, the greater the fee sensitivity.)*

3. How difficult is it for a client to change law firms? *(The more less technically complex the matter, the more price sensitive the client.)*

4. How much importance does the client place on having a high-prestige, big-name firm, and are you such a firm? *(Price-sensitive clients tend not to care about prestige.)*

---

[1]"Pricing to the Market" by Edward Wesemann, Principal, Edge International. Edge International is a consultancy working with law firms around the world. Edge limits its consulting practice to strategic, governance, and growth issues. Founded in 1982 in Edmonton, Canada, about half of its practice is outside North America. Ed Wesemann is a partner in the firm's Savannah, Georgia, office.

5. In the scope of the client's legal budget, how significant is this engagement? *(Clients tend to be more price sensitive on smaller, low-profile engagements.)*

6. How important is a successful result to the client? *(Results with little impact on a client's profitability tend to be more price sensitive.)*

7. Where does this engagement fall in the corporate hierarchy? *(Engagements involving board of directors or corporate officer visibility are less price sensitive than projects reporting to people farther down the chain of command.)*

8. Who's paying the bill? *(Engagements subject to court or agency review or those where client cost is partially shared by an insurance or other company, tend to be more price sensitive.)*

9. Who initiated your first conversation about fees, the attorney or the client? *(If the client initiates fee conversations or offers a fee agreement, it is a sure sign of high price sensitivity.)*

10. What is the business purpose of the engagement? *(If the objective is to correct or remediate a problem, the client may be more price sensitive than if the result is the accomplishment of a gain.)*

The bottom line is that if a law firm is pricing to what the market will bear, it is necessary that it understand its clients' level of price sensitivity. And, logically, pricing to the market must take advantage of favorable market conditions as well as the unfavorable.

APPENDIX D

ACCOUNTING AND LAW FIRM BENCHMARKS

In addition to calculating the client lifetime profit, there are several other economic benchmarks that firms need to pay attention to. We would like to challenge you to consider how profitable is your firm now. How profitable do you think your firm could be if it implemented some of the concepts in this book?

If you focus on your clients, and if you focus on the following economic standards for running a professional services firm, there is no doubt that you'll improve your firm's profitability.

Remember that what we are about to share are guidelines. Your firm may be well above many of them. If so, congratulations! You are doing many things correctly. If you fall below them, strive to find out why and change what you are doing.

ACCOUNTING FIRM BENCHMARKS

- *Fees per owner.* Depending on the size of your accounting practice, owners should be averaging from $500,000 to over $1 million. The October 2003 issue of Bowman's Accounting Report[1] shows that revenue per partner for all firms responding to the annual survey was $875,432. The Best of the Best Firms had revenue per partner of nearly $1.3 million.

- *Partner total hours.* While we should not confuse total hours with productivity and results, most firm partners are accounting for anywhere from 2,100 to 2,500 hours per year.

- *Average partner charge hours.* Average charge hours worked per owner has been decreasing over the last several years. Today it ranges from 1,100 to

---

[1]*Bowman's Accounting Report* is published by Hudson Sawyer Professional Services Marketing Inc., Atlanta, Georgia.

1,300 on average. Consulting owners will normally have fewer chargeable hours.

- *Marketing hours per owner.* Every firm needs to have a marketing culture which encourages and measures the new work that partners bring in. Partners should spend at least 10 percent (or approximately 250 hours) of their time bringing in more business.

- *High staff-to-partner ratio.* Unlike law firms that have a very low staff-to-partner ratio, accounting firms that achieve a high staff-to-partner ratio make more money. It takes several things to achieve a high ratio (10:1 to 6:1). Partners must learn to delegate work. Be less doers and more account managers. They must also learn to maximize the human capital in the firm.

- *Revenues per full-time equivalent* (FTE).

- *Charge hours per manager.*

- *Charge hours per staff.* The truly profitable firms in the accounting profession routinely get 1,700 to 1,800 billable hours from their staff.

- *Days outstanding for A/R.* Ideally, your A/R should not extend beyond 60 days. There are, of course, exceptions, depending on the type of work that you are doing. Contingency fee work will not be collected until the matter is finalized.

- *Days outstanding for WIP.* WIP should be billed on a monthly basis. Ideally, WIP should never be more than 30 days old.

- *Managing partner's charge hours.* Managing partners should spend most of their time managing the firm. But we encourage them to have a limited book of business so that they stay in touch with clients. Hours, depending on the size of the firm, should range from 500 to 900 hours.

- *Realized rate per hour.* This varies with the size of the firm.

- *Net income per partner.* This also varies by size of firm.

- *Management.* Effective management has the greatest potential to improve profitability. The primary benchmark for management relates to all of the above. If the firm is making its budget and profitability goals, then management is doing a good job.

2003: Law Firm Fiscal Metrics

Metric	Normal Range		
	Low	Your Metrics	High
Revenues per lawyer	$375,000		$575,000
Revenues per equity partner	$700,000		$1,800,000
Overhead per lawyer	$150,000		$250,000
Occupancy costs/revenues	6.5%		8.5%
Income per lawyer/revenue per lawyer	55%		65%
Gross profit margin	35%		45%
Average equity partner income	$325,000		$600,000
Income per equity partner/revenue per lawyer	90%		115%
Distributions per equity partner/ income per equity partner	93%		98%
Net cash available for working capital	2 weeks		12 weeks
WIP over 180 days/total WIP	20%		33%
Investment in WIP (# months at year-end)	2.00		2.50
AR over 180 days/total AR	22%		36%
Invest in AR (# of months at year-end)	2.25		3.00
WIP + AR : debt	7.0		14.0
Debt per equity partner	$12,000		$90,000
Debt/net fixed assets	50%		75%
Debt/equity partner compensation	8%		13%
Total liabilities per equity partner	$40,000		$125,000
Total liabilities/WIP + AR	8.5%		14%
Total liabilities/equity partner compensation	15%		23%
Permanent capital per lawyer	$30,000		$60,000
Permanent capital per equity partner	$75,000		$160,000

2003: Law Firm Fiscal Metrics

Metric	Low	Your Metrics	High
		Normal Range	
Permanent capital/WIP + AR	12%		30%
Permanent capital/revenues	5%		10%
Permanent capital/equity partner compensation	12%		27%
Realization from standard rates	85%		90%
Leverage (all nonequity partner lawyers : equity partners)	1.2		2.2
Billable hours/partner	1,725		1,850
Billable hours/associates	1,750		1,900
Billable hours/paralegal	1,350		1,500

Source: Edge International. Reprinted with permission.
Note: Specific appropriate metric values are determined by firm size, practice focus, and other factors.

BIBLIOGRAPHY AND REFERENCES

The AccountingWEB News. www.accountingweb.com.

Accounting and Finance For Law Firms. Law Journals Seminar Newsletters, an American Lawyer Media company, Philadelphia. Periodical.

Accounting Today. Accountants' Media Group. New York. Periodical.

American Bar Association, Commission on Advertising. *Lawyer Advertising at the Crossroads.*

American Bar Association Journal. American Bar Association. Chicago, IL. Periodical.

American Institute of Certified Public Accountants. *www.cpa2biz.com.*

American Lawyer. American Lawyer Media, NY. Periodical.

American Lawyer Media. *www.law.com.*

Aquila, August J. *Breaking the Paradigm: New Approaches to Pricing Accounting Services,* New York: American Institute of Certified Public Accountants, 1995.

_____. "Partner Compensation: Creating a Performance-Boosting Scorecard" *Law Practice Management.* January/February 2003, Volume 29, Number 1.

_____. Allan D. Koltin, and Robert Pitts, Ph.D *CPAs That Sell: A Complete Guide to Promoting your Professional Services,* Chicago: Irwin Professional Publishing, 1996.

_____. Koltin, Allan D, "How to Lose Clients without Really Trying" *Journal of Accountancy,* May, 1992.

Baker, Ronald J., *The Professional's Guide to Value Pricing, 5th Edition.* New York: Aspen Publishing Inc., 2004.

_____. and Dunn, Paul. *The Firm of the Future: A Guide for Accountants, Lawyers and Other Professionals Services,* New Jersey: John Wiley & Sons, Inc., 2003.

Barker, Joel Arthur. *Paradigms: The Business of Discovering the Future*, New York: Harper Business, 1993.

Bennis, Warren. *On Becoming A Leader*, Menlo Park, California: Addison Wesley, 1994.

Bloedorn, John D. *Paying for Performance: A Guide To Compensation Management*. New York: John Wiley & Sons, 1997.

Blanchard, Ken and Bowles, Sheldon. *Raving Fans: A Revolutionary Approach to Customer Service*, New York: William Morrow and Company, Inc., 1993.

Boress, Allan S. and Cummings, Michael G, *Master the Art of Marketing Professional Services: A Step by Step Best Practices Guide*. New York: American Institute of Certified Public Accountants, 2002.

Bossidy, Larry and Charan, Ram., *Execution: The Discipline of Getting Things Done*, New York: Crown Business, 2002.

Business Week, "An Abrupt About-Face by Accountants." January 31, 2002.

Canadian Lawyer. Canada Law Book Inc. Periodical.

CPA Managing Partner Report. Aspen Publishers, NY. Periodical.

CPA Marketing Report. Aspen Publishers, NY. Periodical.

Chingos, Peter T., et. al. *Paying For Performance: A Guide to Compensation Management*, New York: John Wiley & Sons, Inc., 1997.

Connecticut Law Tribune. American Lawyer Media, Hartford, CT. Periodical.

Consultants News. Kennedy Information, LLC. Peterborough, NH. Periodical.

Coulter, Silvia, *The Woman Lawyer's Rainmaking Game*. West Legal Publishing, 2004.

Dawson, Ross: *Developing Knowledge-Based Client Relationships*. Butterworth-Heinemann, Boston, 2000.

Drucker, Peter F., *The Essential Drucker*, New York: Harper Business, 2001.

Hornsby, William E. Jr.: *Marketing and Legal Ethics -The Boundaries of Promoting Legal Services*. American Bar Association, Chicago, 2000.

Jack O'Dwyer's Newsletter, O'Dwyer Publications, NY Periodical.

Journal of Accountancy. American Institute of Certified Public Accountants, NY.

The Journal of Management Consulting, Kennedy Information LLC. Burlingame, CA. Periodical.

Kaplan, Robert S. and Norton, David P., *Translating Strategy into Action: The Balanced Scorecard*, Boston: Harvard Business School Press, 1996.

Larry Bodine Marketing, *www.larrybodine.com*

Law Firm Partnership & Benefits Report. Periodical. American Lawyer Media Company.

LawMarketing Listserv, *www.lawmarketing.biz*

Law Marketing Portal. www.lawmarketing.com.

LawMarketing Store, *www.lawmarketing.biz/Store*

Law Practice Management. American Bar Association. Chicago, IL. Periodical.

Lawyers Weekly. Lawyers Weekly Publications, NY. Periodical.

Legal Management. The Journal of the Association of Legal Administrators. Lincolnshire, IL. Periodical.

Legal Tech. American Lawyer Media, NY. Periodical.

Legal Times. American Lawyer Media, NY. Periodical.

Levick, Richard S. and Larry Smith. *The Litigation PR Desk Reference*, published 2004 by Levick Press.

Levitt, Theodore, *The Marketing Imagination.* New York: The Free Press, 1983.

Lorsch, Jay W. and Tierney, Thomas J. *Aligning The Stars: How to Succeed When Professionals Drive Results*, Boston: Harvard Business School Press, 2002.

Marketing The Law Firm. Law Journals Seminar Newsletters, an American Lawyer Media company, Philadelphia. Periodical

McKenna, Patrick J. and Maister, David. *First Among Equals.* New York: The Free Press, 2002.

_____. and Riskin, Gerald A. *Herding Cats—A Handbook for Managing Partners and Practice Group Leaders.* Canada: The Institute For Best Management Practices, 1995.

Maister, David H., *Managing The Professional Service Firm.* New York: The Free Press, 1993.

_____, with Charles H. Green and Robert M. Galford. *The Trusted Advisor.* New York: The Free Press, 2000.

_____. *True Professionalism: The Courage to Care About Your People, Your Clients and Your Career.* New York: The Free Press, 1997.

_____.*Managing the Professional Service Firm.* Free Press, 1993.

Marcus, Bruce W. *Competing for Clients.* Probus Publishing Company, 1981.

_____. *Competing for Clients in the 90s: A Dynamic Guide to Marketing Promoting & Building a Professional Services Practice.* Chicago: Probus Publishing Company, 1992.

_____.*New Dimensions in Investor Relations* (with Sherwood Wallace). John Wiley & Sons, 1997.

_____.*Competing For Capital—Investor Relations in the 21st Century.* John Wiley & Sons, 2004.

_____.*The Marcus Letter on Professional Services Marketing. www.marcusletter.com.*

Mastracchio, CPA, PhD, Nicholas J. *Mergers and Acquisitions of CPA Firms* New York: American Institute of Certified Public Accountants, 1988.

National Law Journal. New York Law Publishing Company. NY. Periodical.

New York Law Journal. New York Law Publishing Company. NY. Periodical.

Of Counsel. Aspen Publishers, NY. Periodical.

PM Forum North America, *www.PMForumNA.org*

PM Forum Eastern Europe, *WWW.pmforum-cee.net*

PR News. PR News Publications, Potomac, MD. Periodical.

PR Reports. PR Reports Publications, Exeter, NH. Periodical.

Partner Advantage Advisory. Hudson-Sawyer Professional Services Marketing, Inc. Atlanta, Georgia. Periodical.

Partner-to-Partner Advisory. Periodical. Aspen Publishers, New York, NY.

Professional Marketing. PM Forum United Kingdom. Periodical.

Professional Marketing Blog, www.larrybodine.com/blog

Professional Marketing North America. PM Forum North America. Periodical.

Public Accounting Report (PAR). Aspen Publishers. NY. Periodical.

Quinn, James Brian, Philip Anderson, and Sydney Finkelstein *"Managing Professional Intellectual: Making the Most of the Best," Harvard Business Review*, March–April 1996.

Rackham, Neil. *Spin Selling.* NY: McGraw-Hill, 1988.

Reed, Richard C., Ed. *Beyond The Billable Hour.* Chicago: American Bar Association, 1989.

_____. *Win-Win Billing Strategies: Alternatives That Satisfy Your Clients and You.* Chicago: The American Bar Association, 1992.

Ries, Al and Trout, Jack. *Positioning: The Battle for Your Mind, 20th Anniversary Edition,* New York: McGraw-Hill, 2001.

Riskin, Gerald. "Forget About Revenues". Monologue.

Roman, Ken. *How To Advertise, 2nd Ed.* New York: St. Martin's Press, 1997.

Schmidt, Sally J. *Marketing the Law Firm: Business Development Techniques.* New York: Law Journal Seminars, 1991.

SmartPros Newsletter. *www.smartpros.com.*

Smith, Larry, *Inside/Outside—How Businesses Buy Legal Services.* ALM Publishing, 2002.

Strategic Selling And Service Excellence for Lawyers. Law Journals Seminar Newsletters, American Lawyer Media company, Philadelphia. Periodical.

Tasso, Kim: *Dynamic Practice Development.* Thorogood, London. 2003.

The Future of the Accounting Profession. The American Assembly. Columbia University, N.Y. 2003.

Thomas, Tony and August J. Aquila. *The Consolidators: A Global Study of Accounting Firm Integrations.* Southwell, England: Jobtel, 2003.

Waugh, Troy: *Power Up Your Profits.* Select Press, Novato, CA. 2001.

Tools And Resources For the Electronic Accountant.ctwww.webcpa.com

Weiner, Richard; *Webster's New World Dictionary of Media Communications.* McMillan, 1996.

Wesserman, Ed. "When Good Law Firms Go Bad." Monologue.

INDEX

SERVICES AVAILABLE

August Aquila and Bruce W. Marcus speak and consult to professional services firms and organizations all over the world.

August also writes a monthly newsletter, *Partner Advantage Advisory*, which can be ordered by calling 1-800-945-6462.

The Growth Partnership is a full service consulting firm specializing in practice management, practice development, coaching and training, and mergers and acquisitions. For more information, contact August at *aaquila@thegrowthpartnership.com*.

Bruce W. Marcus is editor of The Marcus Letter (*www.marcusletter.com*), an on-line newsletter for professional services firms, and a marketing consultant to professional firms. Contact Bruce at *marcus@marcusletter.com*.

For further information on Dr. Aquila's and Bruce W. Marcus's activities and programs contact:

August J. Aquila, PhD
The Growth Partnership
4732 Chantrey Place
Minnetonka, MN 55345
952-930-1295
aaquila@thegrowthpartnership.com
www.thegrowthpartnership.com

Bruce W. Marcus
The Marcus Letter
www.marcusletter.com
marcus@marcusletter.com